HŌKŪLOA

**THE BRITISH 1874 TRANSIT OF VENUS
EXPEDITION TO HAWAI'I**

HŌKŪLOA

THE BRITISH 1874 TRANSIT OF VENUS EXPEDITION TO HAWAI'I

The expedition's observatory at 'Āpua in Honolulu, Bishop Museum Archives

MICHAEL CHAUVIN

BISHOP MUSEUM PRESS
Honolulu

ISBN 1-58178-023-0

Printed in Korea

Design by Angela Wu-Ki

Library of Congress Cataloging-in-Publication Data

Chauvin, Michael.
Hokuloa : the British 1874 transit of Venus expedition to Hawai'i /
Michael Chauvin.
        p. cm.
Includes bibliographical references.
ISBN 1-58178-023-0 (alk. paper)
1. Venus (Planet)--Transit--1874. 2.
Astronomers--Travel--Hawaii--History--19th century. I. Title.

QB512.C54 2003
523.9'2--dc22
2003018404

Contents

· · · · ·

Figures and Credits

• • • • •

1. Using the astronomical unit (AU) to measure stellar distances. Illustration by Samson W. G. Lee.

2. Maskelyne's Limits. Bishop Museum.

3. Venus Fort, Erected by the Endeavour's People to secure themselves during the Observation of the Transit of Venus at Otaheite (Tahiti). Artist: Sydney Parkinson. Engraver: Samuel Middiman. From: S Parkinson, An Account of the Voyages…in the Southern Hemisphere…in the *Dolphin, the Swallow, & the Endeavour* (London 1773), pl.IV. Bishop Museum.

4. The "black drop" as seen by James Cook and Charles Green during the 1769 transit of Venus. *Philosophical Transactions*, 1771, vol. 61.

5. Statue of Francis Bacon at his Cambridge alma mater, Trinity College. Photo by Michael Chauvin.

6. Lunar distance tables from the 1874 *Nautical Almanac*. Cambridge University Library.

7. Parts of the Earth facing the sun at the beginning of the 1874 transit. Richard A. Proctor, *Transits of Venus: A Popular Account of Past and Coming Transits from the First Observed by Horrocks A.D. 1639 to the Transit of A.D. 2012* (London: Longmans, Green, and Co., 1874).

8. Parts of the Earth facing the sun at the end of the 1874 transit. Richard A. Proctor, *Transits of Venus: A Popular Account of Past and Coming Transits from the First Observed by Horrocks A.D. 1639 to the Transit of A.D. 2012* (London: Longmans, Green, and Co., 1874).

9. Rear Admiral Benjamin F. Sands, superintendent, United States Naval Observatory. Courtesy, United States Naval Observatory.

10. Eight metal chests, now at the United States Naval Observatory in Washington, showing the names of the eight stations to which the United States eventually dispatched observing parties for the 1874 transit of Venus. Photo by Michael Chauvin.

11. George B. Airy. National Maritime Museum, London.

12. Richard Anthony Proctor. Richard A. Proctor, *Other Worlds Than Ours* (New York: P. F. Collier & Son, 1905).

13. The Cook Family Memorial. National Monuments Record, London.

14. The papers of William Gooch. Cambridge University Library.

15. Leonard Darwin. Cambridge University Library.

16. George Forbes. *Obituary Notices of Fellows of the Royal Society*, 1936–1938, vol. 2.

Acknowledgments

· · · · ·

Because a book, although it may have a single nominal author, is in truth a socially produced phenomenon, I hereby acknowledge with gratitude the assistance of the following individuals for their efforts, their expertise, and their support in bringing *Hōkūloa* into existence: Ruth Webb (Wolfson College, Cambridge); Adam Perkins, Godfrey Waller, Elisabeth Leedham-Green, Maria Wylie, and Sarah Hefford (University Library, Cambridge); Perry O'Donovan (The Darwin Project, University Library, Cambridge); Allan Chapman (Wadham College, Oxford); Maria Blyzinsky (Old Royal Observatory, Greenwich); Kevin Johnson (Science Museum, London); Guy Grannum (Public Record Office, Kew); Marion James (National Meteorological Library and Archive, Bracknell); Stephen, Olive, and John Peet (London); P. A. Wayman (Dunsink Observatory, Dublin); Cilla Jackson (University Library, St. Andrews); Ruth Freitag and Robin Rausch (Library of Congress, Washington, D.C.); Brenda Corbin, Steven Dick, and Gregory Shelton (U.S. Naval Observatory, Washington, D.C.); Virginia Ward (The Franklin Institute, Philadelphia); Walter Steiger (University of Hawai'i at Hilo); Barbara Dunn (Hawaiian Historical Society, Honolulu); Marvin Ting and Donald Oyama (Survey Division, State of Hawai'i, Honolulu); Kathleen Robertson (Institute for Astronomy, University of Hawai'i); William Brown, Guy Kaulukukui, Betty Kam, Lan Tu, and Blair Collis (Bishop Museum, Honolulu); and Lee S. Motteler (GeoMap Corp, Pāhoa).

Research for this book was funded in part by a grant from the University of Hawai'i, Center for Arts and Humanities, Joseph Stanton, Director; by dual grants from the National Aeronautics and Space Administration (NASA), administered by the American Astronomical Society; and by an RMW Astronomy Prize.

Introduction

· · · · ·

On September 9, 1874, fewer than seven months after the ascension to the throne of Hawai'i's last king, David Kalākaua, a ship from England, HMS *Scout*, arrived in Honolulu carrying an expedition of seven astronomers. These men—recruited by England's seventh Astronomer Royal George B. Airy and trained under his imperious eye at the Royal Observatory at Greenwich—came to Hawai'i as James Cook had come almost a hundred years earlier: as the beneficiaries and the instruments of a rich astronomical heritage. That heritage, raised to glory at the Greenwich Observatory, had, in 1778 and under the guiding hand of Captain Cook, literally placed Hawai'i on the map. Yet it was Cook's earlier voyage to Tahiti in 1769 that had more truly foreshadowed the display in Hawai'i, 105 years later, of a nation's astronomical prowess.

The mission of the British 1874 expedition to Hawai'i was—as was Cook's mission to Tahiti—to observe a rare transit of the planet Venus across the sun. The purpose of such observations was to better determine the value of the astronomical unit (AU)—the Earth-sun distance—and thereby the absolute scale of the solar system. For although Copernicus had, by the sixteenth century, put the planets in their correct order and had derived from his model of the solar system a set of relative distances among its members, their absolute distances remained hostage to the uncertain value of the AU. Astronomers still needed a celestial yardstick of known length to measure distances among the planets and to link the planets to the stars beyond. Earlier graspings at the AU, including those of Captain Cook and his eighteenth-century contemporaries, had left the critical number still unclinched.

Now, as the twenty-first century dawns, the length of the AU is well known and continues to form the basis of astronomical distance measurements. But the chase after it in the nineteenth century still had some very real down-to-earth applications. George Forbes, arguably the most distinguished member of the British-Hawai'i contingent, surmised that the successful prosecution of the transit observations would have implications for navigation. And W. D. Alexander, the government surveyor for Hawai'i, understood well its implications for surveying—so well, in fact, that the Hawai'i Government Survey, just begun in 1870, was intentionally tied to the work of the British team, a team that eventually erected astronomical observatories on, and made transit observations from, three separate islands: Hawai'i, O'ahu, and Kaua'i.

Of the six transits of Venus visible since the invention of the telescope (those of 1631/1639, 1761/1769, and 1874/1882), this was the first of the nineteenth-century pair and the first to be observed telescopically from Hawai'i. It occurred, moreover, at a critical time in Hawai'i's history: during the reign of its last king and when the United States, through the Reciprocity Treaty, was on the verge of weaning the Islands away from an inveterate British influence and establishing an American preeminence in the North Pacific.

The transit operations in the Hawaiian Kingdom extended over a period of six months and attracted widespread attention from all ranks of Island society. King Kalākaua's generous reception of the expedition and his regal and scientifically informed salutation to its leader at the palace in Honolulu were indicative of the high esteem in which the enterprise and the astronomers were held. But the fuller story of this nineteenth-century scientific quest is not unlike the seventeenth-century story of triumph and tragedy surrounding the name of Galileo: The pursuit of a fundamental astronomical truth is inextricably intertwined with abundant human drama. From the piano pounding of the "madman" astronomer Henry Barnacle to the heroic daring of George Forbes, from the small irritations of a tropical landscape (mosquitoes) to the larger spectacles of *ho'okupu* rituals and volcanic eruptions, and from the timely—or untimely—use of redcoats and royal prerogatives to the bathos inherent in the juxtaposition of astronomical quests set amidst gastronomical revelations—Hawai'i provided the stage upon which polite Victorian astronomy was conducted in a teetering kingdom on the verge of being swallowed up by a global power.

The full astrodrama includes several dramatis personae: Entering in British array, the names of Jeremiah Horrocks, Edmond Halley, James Cook, George Airy, British Commissioner James Wodehouse, several members of the British Navy, and the seven astronomers constituting the British-Hawai'i observing team stand out; and even Charles Darwin and his son Leonard enter the story. The principal player in Hawai'i is King Kalākaua. He is joined by Queens Emma and Kapi'olani, Princess Ruth, Bernice Pauahi Bishop, Simon Kā'ai, Archibald Cleghorn, and Surveyor General Alexander, in addition to several other figures whose names are still preserved in historical archives.

Although there was some coverage of the transit proceedings in the Honolulu newspapers of the day, Hawaiian history books of recent vintage tend to concentrate on other features of King Kalākaua's reign—the leprosy problem, the decline of the native population, the economics of sugar production, the Reciprocity Treaty, and the agitation about annexation to the United States—and make no mention of this episode in the history of Hawai'i's own rich and unique astronomical heritage.

With the recent placement of modern observatories of international repute atop Mauna Kea on the island of Hawai'i, the continued pursuit of astronomy in these Islands is further enriched by a remembrance of the historical context from which those pursuits have arisen. This account of the British 1874 transit of Venus expedition to Hawai'i extols such remembrance of things past by fleshing out the larger story of the development of astronomy in Hawai'i with a hitherto underdeveloped chapter.

M. Chauvin
Honolulu, Hawai'i

Chronology of Events

· · · · ·

1868   M. G. Fleuriais determines the longitude of Honolulu relative to Paris;
Airy writes of Hawai'i as "indispensable" to the 1874 transit effort

1870   The Hawaiian Government Survey begins

1871   Surveying instruments arrive in Hawai'i from Troughton & Simms of London;
Charles Darwin discusses in *The Descent of Man* the decline of Hawai'i's native population

1872   George Forbes is appointed professor of Natural Philosophy at Anderson's College, Glasgow;
Leonard Darwin applies for a position on the transit of Venus expedition

1873   (January) Isabella Bird arrives in Honolulu;
(April) The 547-day eruption of Mauna Loa begins;
(October) Airy's transit of Venus model is put into action at Greenwich;
(October) Charles R. Bishop receives a dispatch from Theo H. Davies informing him that it is the intention of the British government to send a transit of Venus party to Honolulu

1874   (January) Henry Glanville Barnacle commences his transit of Venus duties at Greenwich;
(January) Robert Dunn offers his services to the Astronomer Royal;
(February) David Kalākaua begins his reign as Hawai'i's last king;
(April) James H. Wodehouse writes of the need for the British flag in Hawaiian waters;
(May) Airy completes his "Instructions to Observers";
(May) Isabella Bird sends her gift list to George Forbes;
(June) The *Illimani* and the *Britannia* embark from Liverpool with the Hawai'i expedition;
(September) HMS *Scout* arrives in Honolulu carrying the transit of Venus expedition;
(November) A cumulative rainfall of 23.99 inches is recorded in Nu'uanu Valley;
(November) Auxiliary stations on Hawai'i and Kaua'i are established by Forbes and Johnson;
(November) The Cook Memorial at Kealakekua Bay is unveiled;
(November) Charles Lambert drowns in the surf off Kailua-Kona;
(November) King Kalākaua departs for Washington for Reciprocity Treaty negotiations;
(December) Transit of Venus;
(December) A memorial to Horrocks is inscribed for Westminster Abbey;
(December) Barnacle is ordered home by Tupman;

(December) An earthquake shakes the Islands;
(December) Johnson cuts "Cook's Arrow" at Waimea

1875   (January) Forbes announces his plan to visit the crater Moku'āweoweo;
(February) King Kalākaua returns to Hawai'i;
(February) Forbes and Johnson leave Honolulu, bound for San Francisco;
(March) A post-transit sale is conducted in Honolulu;
(March) A farewell dinner is given at the palace;
(March) Tupman and Noble depart for San Francisco;
(April) Leonard Darwin arrives in Hawai'i;
(September) Forbes writes to Airy from Moscow, making no mention of the Szlenkers

1876   (February) Josef Szlenker sends a note of gratitude to Forbes;
(May) A transit of Venus exhibition opens at the South Kensington Museum in London

1877   (April) Johnson submits his official journal to Airy;
(July) A report on the results of the 1874 expedition is submitted to Parliament;
(November) Airy publishes a value for the solar parallax (8".754) based upon the telescopic observations of the 1874 transit of Venus;
The site of the Cook Memorial at Kealakekua Bay is deeded to British Commissioner Wodehouse;
Henry Glanville Barnacle is ordained a deacon

1878   (November) John Walter Nichol dies prematurely

1880   (October) Tupman concludes his "Home" journal at the RGO

1881   Airy publishes his *Account of Observations of the Transit of Venus;*
While on world tour, King Kalākaua meets Richard A. Proctor aboard the *City of Sydney*

1882   (December) Transit of Venus

1883   (February) George Tupman, en route to San Francisco from New Zealand after the 1882 transit of Venus, witnesses the belated coronation of King Kalākaua in Honolulu

1884   The International Meridian Conference is held in Washington, D.C., where Hawai'i delegates W. D. Alexander and Luther Aholo vote with the majority in favor of adopting the Greenwich Meridian as the prime meridian of the world

1

· · · · ·

A Meeting at Moku'āweoweo

S tarlight spills from the sky, touching down on a tropical island in the North Pacific. After traveling more than three decades through the stark silence and the near nothingness of empty space, it abruptly ends its journey on the blackened lip of Moku'āweoweo Crater and is met by the red light of molten lava swirling upward from the firepit. British astronomer George Forbes watches silently. It is now January 1875, and he is a lingering guest in a strange place.

Forbes should have known. Perhaps he did know. This is the home of Madame Pele, legendary goddess of the volcano. Its location: 19.5° north latitude, 155.6° west longitude, on the island of Hawai'i, at the summit of Mauna Loa, the most massive mountain on Earth.

The source of the light from the heavens also has a location: thirty-seven light-years away, in the constellation the ancient Greeks knew as Bootes, the Bear Driver. The star is called Arcturus. It is the brightest star in the northern sky. Forbes surely knew this. With a declination of +19°13′, it is also Hawai'i's zenith star. In 1875, it would have passed virtually over his head as Pele hissed at his feet.

Such a fortuitous meeting under tropical skies of a British astronomer and a Hawaiian goddess could not have easily been foretold. Protracted volcanic uprisings from the floor of the Pacific were needed to create the location for this unlikely rendezvous, as was the protracted development of positional astronomy—the astronomy of location—needed to create the opportunity. But it was just the sort of astronomy with which George Forbes was familiar.

Forbes had just spent many weeks at the seaside town of Kailua-Kona where, "in the shade of the great Mowna Loa," he had used the stars to meticulously pinpoint the location of his astronomical observatory on Pele's flank. As a member of an astronomical team headquartered in Honolulu but now spread across the island chain, Forbes had realized, even before his departure from Liverpool, that the object of his team's efforts was of no mean importance: The world's most ambitious scientific countries—of which Britain was but one—had carefully positioned similar teams elsewhere in order that they too might pursue the same object. In fact, three years earlier, in 1872, Forbes—then a fledgling professor of natural philosophy at a Scottish university—had himself become so enamored of the endeavor that he had *volunteered* his services to the campaign, soon submitting himself to a protracted regimen of training at the Royal Observatory at Greenwich under the demanding eye of the Astronomer Royal. He had therefore ventured into the Pacific well prepared to make his contribution to the enterprise. But how could he have possibly readied himself for all that awaited him?

Coming in September 1874 to an island group described by a fellow Scot as salubrious and intoxicating, Forbes was spending his last leisurely moments in Pele's warming presence and would depart from the Islands within a fortnight. Looking back, the celestial science in which he had been a most enthusiastic participant had hinged upon the high-minded notion of predictability. But now, fewer than five months after his arrival in the Islands, Pele seemed to be teaching a counternotion: Terrestrial happenings were as unpredictable as any deity.

For George Forbes, life in Hawai'i had been anything but predictable. Almost immediately after his arrival, he had found himself at the palace in Honolulu in the regal presence of a man who would prove to be Hawai'i's last king. Then, after being dispatched in November to the island of Hawai'i to take command of the observing station there, he had become, much like a king himself, the object of a lavish *ho'okupu* ceremony. Lured on, as a scientist is wont, by the unfamiliar and the unknown, he had traveled down the sea-sprayed coast to Kealakekua Bay where, near the site of a newly erected monument to his "assassinated" countryman James Cook, he had been met by the haunting spectacle of a once-vibrant village in ruins. Still, before his climb to the trembling lip of Moku'āweoweo, he had been assigned an incompetent observing partner, lost another comrade to the treacherous surf, been abandoned in a remote observing location without an interpreter, and had his cigars stolen. And, most disturbing, he had had the critical observation for which he had come so far and toiled with such fortitude sullied by bad weather—all within a five-month period. Now, after ascending to the top of Mauna Loa to drink with anxious eyes Pele's bubbling brew, how could he have foreseen that, as he circuitously worked his way back to Britain and to the sedate life of his university post, a carriageful of misadventure would accompany him homeward through Siberia?

In 1875, George Forbes, mesmerized as much by the red glow of Moku'āweoweo as by the celestial mysteries overhead, may have stared into the earthy pit as into a crystal ball, trying to understand the past, straining to see the future. With fiery marvels both overhead and underfoot, blinding and uncontrollable, how often he may have speculated about Pele, or wondered at Arcturus, is not known.

2

. . . . .

Location

A rcturus has not always been Hawai'i's zenith star. But it has long been a star of legend.[1] In Homer's time, when Arcturus passed over the mid-Mediterranean, it helped to brighten the skies of the ill-fated Odysseus who used it as a navigational aid during his legendary wanders.[2]

But after Odysseus came other legends. The heavens changed. The stars themselves wandered. And by the time the British explorer James Cook embarked upon his own series of odysseys into the Pacific in the eighteenth century, the slow but inexorable precession of the Earth's rotational axis had repositioned Arcturus, making it the zenith luminary for yet another seagoing culture where navigating by the stars was similarly celebrated in legend.

The essence of the legend, as Cook himself saw in 1778, was undeniable: Although the English captain would, by using the stars, be the first to fix their location on a map,[3] the islands of Hawai'i had already been discovered. It was Hawai'i-loa, accompanied by his chief navigator Makali'i, who had accomplished the feat.

But much like Odysseus, Hawai'i-loa had long since disappeared over the horizon and into the mists of a collective memory.[4] After sailing up from the South Pacific island of Tahiti to discover the Hawaiian group, he had, alas, returned with Makali'i to Tahiti, guided it is said by the star Hōkūloa[5] but leaving behind a legend that thickened into an enigma. For unlike Arcturus, Hōkūloa was—at least by Cook's standards—not a star at all. It was, rather, the Hawaiian name for the planet Venus.[6]

But with Cook's late-eighteenth-century arrival in Hawai'i, the astronomical traditions of Hawai'i[7] and of Greece, two island cultures once separated by half the world's girth, had met at last. And if Odysseus and Hawai'i-loa had died and disappeared, their revenant had in a fashion reappeared in the Pacific, though much modified in the person of an Englishman. Henceforth, the names and exploits of the world's navigational heroes could not neglect the name of James Cook. For the plain truth was this: A simple knowledge of the zenith passage of a star such as Arcturus gave ancient seafarers at best only a knowledge of latitude. Odysseus, lost at sea for ten years, did not know his longitude—nor did Hawai'i-loa. But Captain Cook did.

Yet if no one understood longitudes very well until the eighteenth century, others—and not merely navigators—had understood latitudes very well indeed. And from a simple knowledge of latitudes, and of the comparison of latitudes, they had arrived at some far-reaching conclusions about a very watery—but indubitably spherical—planet.

These conclusions, which took the form of elegant mathematical deductions, might have been made by Hawai'i-loa, at least theoretically. They were actually made, however, by the ancient Greeks. And they were made in a way that linked Greek terrestrial with Greek celestial interests.

That link was firmly forged when the Greek astronomer Eratosthenes (ca. 276–196 B.C.E.) used simple observations of the sun to provide a remarkably accurate demonstration of how distances on the Earth could be geometrically deduced. Posidonius (ca. 135–51 B.C.E.), another Greek, soon added his own name to the enterprise by utilizing observations of the star Canopus in a similar fashion. (See appendix A.)

But the ancient Greeks did still more. Having understood that the heavens could be used to geometrically measure distances on the Earth, they went even further by using the Earth to geometrically measure distances in the heavens. For the work of an Eratosthenes or a Posidonius—as well as the labors of European investigators who followed them—not only permits a mathematical calculation of the Earth's circumference,[8] but also a determination of its radius.[9] And it was in terms of this unit—the Earth's radius—that distances to heavenly bodies such as the moon or the sun could be and were expressed.[10]

Such a knowledge of the dimensions of the Earth—its circumference and its radius—together with a related knowledge of distances between points on the Earth's surface—a knowledge of location by latitude and longitude—were the historical and intellectual prerequisites underpinning the scientific quest that came to encircle the Hawaiian Islands nearly one hundred years after Captain Cook had first appointed them a location on a map. For it was from a knowledge of one's location *on* the Earth that would come—or so it was hoped—a better understanding of the location *of* the Earth.

In a word, George Forbes' observations of Hōkūloa in 1874 would be, as they had been for the legendary Hawai'i-loa, inextricably intertwined with the concept of *location.*

4

3

· · · · ·

The Astronomical Unit

Like questions about location on the Earth, questions about the Earth's location in space are really about distances between objects; and determinations of distance, whether terrestrial or celestial, require both a method and a unit of measurement. In the mathematically inclined world of ancient Greece, distance questions could be addressed by using the method of geometry—literally, "earth measure;" and whereas the basic unit of terrestrial distances was the stade, the basic unit of celestial distances in an Earth-centered cosmos was the Earth's radius (ER), which became the astronomical unit (AU) of geocentric astronomy.[1]

The demonstrations of Eratosthenes and Posidonius presuppose a familiarity with the geometry of a circle. An Earth-centered astronomy requires, in fact, at least some geometry. At a very minimum, it requires an understanding of shapes that have centers: circles and spheres. But so too does the heliocentric astronomy that replaced it. For if the ancient AU—the Earth's radius—is conceived as the distance separating the surface of the Earth from its *physical center,* then the modern AU—the distance separating the Earth from the sun—can be similarly conceived as the distance separating the Earth from its *orbital center.*

That there are 360 degrees in a circle and that there are nearly 93 million miles in the modern astronomical unit are, surprising as it may at first seem, two related bits of knowledge. They are also examples of the kinds of rudimentary facts that are often thought to be proper parts of the intellectual repertoire of any man making even the most modest claim to scientific literacy. But many great astronomers of yesteryear—Ptolemy, Copernicus, Galileo, and Kepler among them—had no knowledge of the latter of these two facts; and right up to Newton's lifetime (1642–1727), the Earth-sun distance was known only to within about 30 percent of its true value.[2] Man's understanding of the cosmos and of his location in that cosmos was, therefore, deficient; and although astronomical observations and measurements did in time better locate man's world, they did so only by dislocating his thinking.

The beginning of this dislocation is often associated with the name of Nicholas Copernicus (1473–1543), the Polish astronomer who is perhaps best remembered in the context of a revolution in Western thought in which his magnum opus, *De Revolutionibus Orbium Celestium,* played a pivotal role. By dislodging the Earth from the center of the universe and by placing it in orbit around the sun, Copernicus disrupted the prevailing European cosmology whose geocentric and geostatic roots had been for centuries firmly implanted in the authoritative groundworks of Ptolemy and Aristotle.

After conceptually rearranging the Greek cosmos by repositioning the Earth, Copernicus reordered the remaining planets into a system that permitted him to build into that system—now centered on the sun—a unified set of relative distances among its members. But Copernicus did not know the absolute scale of his system—neither the absolute distance from one planet to another, nor the absolute distance from the sun to any planet. Some simple mathematics, however, coupled with accurate observations, permitted a computation of relative distances (see appendix B), and Copernicus was able to determine these (Table 1).

Table 1. Relative distances to the sun in astronomical units

Planet	Copernican Value	Modern Value
Mercury	0.3763	0.387 0981
Venus	0.7193	0.723 3315
Earth	1.0000	1.000 0156
Mars	1.5198	1.523 6313
Jupiter	5.2192	5.202 511
Saturn	9.1743	9.584 306

Sources: Copernican values have been taken from Albert Van Helden, *Measuring the Universe: Cosmic Dimensions from Aristarchus to Halley* (Chicago: University of Chicago Press, 1985), and are *mean* distances. Modern values have been taken from *The Astronomical Almanac* for the year 2003, where the given distances are, again, *mean* distances (in astronomical units), the distance to the Earth is actually to the Earth-moon barycenter, and the Julian date is 245 2640.5.

Still, absolute distances remained elusive. Both during his life and for a long time after, absolute distances in the solar system—and beyond—were hostage to uncertainties in the unit distance to which they were compared. And although Copernicus' model of the solar system was impressively accurate to scale, the absolute distance from Earth to sun and thus the actual length of the new astronomical unit remained an unsolved problem.[3]

Attempts to calculate the sun's distance had been made since antiquity, but the results had been grossly inaccurate. Aristarchus of Samos, the "ancient Copernicus" and a contemporary of Eratosthenes, thought the sun to be about nineteen times as far from the Earth as is the moon—or, as a multiple of the Earth's radius, about 360 ER (1,426,732 miles) distant.[4]

Ptolemy, whose geostatic astronomical system, embodied in the *Almagest*, was at last superseded by post-Copernican advances, removed the sun to a distance that was at most only about thirty-eight times greater than the moon's—still falling short by a wide margin.[5] Before the end of the seventeenth century, astronomers had pushed the sun to a distance of 55,000,000 miles or more.[6]

Not surprisingly, the methods for measuring the AU had been as various as the resulting values assigned to it. Aristarchus had endeavored to use the geometry of eclipses for that purpose. Later, Giovanni Domenico Cassini (1625–1712) had used the favorite method of his time, measurements of the parallax of Mars.[7] But the potential bonanza was obvious and apparently worth years, even generations, of frustrated effort. Once a scale model of a sun-centered system, giving relative distances among all its known members, was in place—and, by the sixteenth century, it was—acquiring a knowledge of the absolute distance between any two of those members would suffice for the deduction of all the remaining absolute distances within that system. And this could be convincingly and sweepingly done by using an established knowledge of the Earth's radius—the ER—to measure, either directly or obliquely, the parallax of and thus the distance to the sun.[8]

But further still, the value of the astronomical unit once known would itself provide a baseline for determining, by triangulation, the annual parallax of and thus the distance to the stars (Fig. 1). Now conceived as the semidiameter of the Earth's orbit—rather than, as in the older system, the semidiameter of the Earth itself—the new AU would at once endow astronomy with a celestial yardstick of known length for measuring distances among the planets *and* for linking the planets to the stars beyond. It is, then, but a small wonder that once the ground-breaking work of Copernicus and Galileo was in place, astronomer Giovanni Antonio Rocca would opine that the discovery of the sun's parallax and distance was, in

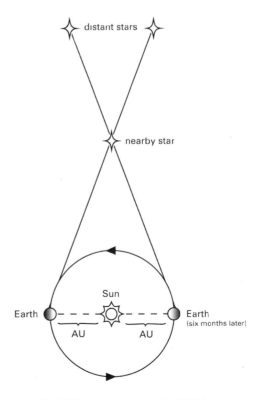

Fig. 1. Using the astronomical unit (AU) to measure stellar distances

7

the seventeenth century, already one of the most important problems in astronomy, well worth a lifetime's work.[9]

The first determination of a realistic value for the solar parallax came before the seventeenth century was out, but it required a confluence of favorable circumstances—good weather, the propitious location among the stars of a suitable planet, and the availability of a telescope. This appears not to have occurred in England until 1672–1673 when John Flamsteed (1646–1719), soon to become the nation's first Astronomer Royal, placed it (as did Cassini) in the neighborhood of 10 seconds of arc, corresponding to a distance of 21,000 ER—more than 80,000,000 miles.[10] The new value must have seemed credible because by the beginning of the eighteenth century, Isaac Newton, having emended his own earlier estimate, publicly adopted the value of Cassini and Flamsteed.[11] But even Newton's authoritative—though wavering—voice did not settle the question, in England or anywhere else.[12] Even after Newton's *Principia*, estimates for the solar parallax still ranged between 10 and 15 seconds of arc and the resulting solar distances from as small as 55,000,000 to as large as 81,000,000 miles[13]—a difference of as much as 32 percent!

Still, there had appeared to one of Newton's contemporaries at least a glimmer of hope. And when that man—one who was fated to follow John Flamsteed into glory as England's second Astronomer Royal—opined that a rare passage of Venus in front of the sun, as observed telescopically from different locations on the Earth, offered the best hope for measuring solar-planetary tethers, the forces of British imperial astronomy began to stir at Greenwich.

4

· · · · ·

From Toxteth to Tahiti

B y the middle of the nineteenth century when George Forbes was
born, Great Britain, like other great nations, had developed a formidable set of national heroes. Indeed, hero worship, if not precisely a
universal law of nature, seemed such a ubiquitous feature of human culture
that by the time Forbes' fellow Scotsman Thomas Carlyle (1795–1881) published his *On Heroes, Hero-Worship, and the Heroic in History* in 1841, the
subject was becoming a major Victorian preoccupation.[1]

Heroes—great men whose biographies constituted the essence of history—could, according to Carlyle, take many forms: god, prophet, poet,
priest, man of letters, king. Scientific men did not fit Carlyle's idealized pro-
file and did not merit a place in his six-part pantheon. But this was under-
standable. Astronomers, for example, seemed unlikely heroes. By habit and
inclination, they led lives of contemplation rather than of action. And even
Aristotle, the quintessential embodiment of Greek learning, was no match
for Hercules.

All heroes did, nevertheless, have one thing in common: Their heroic
stature, however great when living, became even greater when dead, magnified "tenfold" by time and tradition.[2] And this fact was no more evident
in the nineteenth century, when Carlyle acknowledged it, than it had been
two centuries earlier when a hero of a new type, unacknowledged by
Carlyle, was beginning to appear in Europe.

When Galileo Galilei (1564–1642) convinced himself that a spyglass[3]
aimed at the heavens could be turned into a scientific research tool, a new
kind of hero—an astronomer with a telescope—was born. Now armed with
a new weapon against an old enemy—ignorance—Galileo began to detect
a panoply of previously unseen wonders: blemishes on the face of the sun,
the jagged appearance of the lunar surface, the clocklike motion of the satellites of Jupiter, the multiplicity of stars in the Milky Way—discoveries of
such heroic proportions that they brought Galileo lasting fame.

Here, in Galileo's hands, the telescope had flung open the doors to
new and exciting areas of speculation and research, and similarly
inclined—and similarly uncommon—men would soon be needed to carry
on where he had made his beginnings. But in one particular case, where
Galileo had made only the barest of beginnings, such exacting patience and
diligence would be required that Galileo would himself not live to witness
their fruit.

9

The case in question was the planet Venus. For despite his many revolutionary discoveries, including his detection of the moonlike phases of Venus, Galileo had failed to observe a passage of Venus across the sun, even though two such events occurred during his lifetime: the first in 1631, the second in 1639.

The fault had not been Galileo's entirely: The planet itself was intractable. And the more general failure to observe Venus against the sun could rightly be blamed on the unobtrusive and infrequent nature of Venusian transits. They are as inconspicuous as sunspots, and far more rare. And however often they may have been seen in pretelescopic times,[4] only two would occur between the death of Galileo and the introduction of telescopic astronomy in Hawai'i more than a century later.

But if the infrequency of Venusian transits seemed insufferable, worse still was the even greater rarity of *transit seasons;* for the same circumstances that result in the infrequent passage of Venus across the sun also result in the second transit following closely upon the first. The overall result has been a mere six transits, in three pairs, since the birth of the telescope—those of 1631/1639, 1761/1769, and 1874/1882. (See appendix C.)

So if Galileo had missed his opportunity, so too would others. And as long as efforts to merely predict and observe a transit baffled the talents of Europe's better astronomers, the ambition to utilize the rare celestial occurrence to solve even greater puzzles would remain lofty and unrealized.

But the ambition moved one step closer to realization in 1627. In that year, a contemporary of Galileo, Johannes Kepler (1571–1630), published his *Rudolphine Tables.* Compiled from his own observations and those of his erstwhile mentor Tycho Brahe (1546–1601), the *Rudolphine Tables* constituted what has been called Kepler's "crowning achievement in practical astronomy," and astronomers, navigators, calendar makers—even horoscope casters and Jesuit missionaries in China—had long been awaiting the completed work. The *Rudolphine Tables* bore the name of Kepler's imperial patron, Rudolph II, emperor of Bohemia, and remained for more than a century an indispensable tool for the study of both the wandering planets and the fixed stars. In addition to refraction tables and logarithms put for the first time to astronomical use, the bulk of the work was comprised of tables and rules for predicting the positions of the planets, together with a network of plotted points against which those positions were measured—a catalogue of 1,005 star places.[5]

Calculating from his *Rudolphine Tables* a year before their publication, Kepler, in 1626, was the first to predict a transit of Venus—a phenomenon that some of his predecessors (Ptolemy and Copernicus, for example) apparently believed to be either nonexistent or unobservable.[6] Astronomers, alerted to the celestial rendezvous by Kepler's assistant Jacob Bartsch, awaited the spectacle, expected in 1631, the year following Kepler's death. But if 1631 came in with eager anticipation, it went out with crushing disappointment: Kepler's prediction had been unhappily imprecise. Although

10

a transit occurred as prognosticated, it transpired when the sun was below the horizon in Europe and was consequently unobservable from there.[7]

This was most unfortunate, for 130 years must pass, Kepler surmised, before the next transit. As a result, any residual interest in the likelihood that the elusive Venus might soon be observed skittering across the sun seems to have waned—at least on the Continent. This was not so, however, in England. There the quixotic chase after the apparent phantasm quickly resumed. And the story of Jeremiah Horrocks slowly unfolded.

Jeremiah Horrocks was born into obscurity at Toxteth, near Liverpool, in or about the year 1619.[8] His father's profession is uncertain; but that his family was not well-to-do is evidenced by the fact that Jeremiah matriculated at Cambridge in 1632 as a sizar[9] and left the university without taking a degree, presumably summoned home by family necessities. In 1639 he was ordained curate of Hoole, a village described as one of the most insignificant of English hamlets, where he was obliged to eke out a living on an annual stipend of £40. There the want of intellectual companionship probably encouraged his solitary study of the heavens, together with his studious perusal of Kepler. And before his sudden death in 1641 while he was yet in his twenties, he had already out-Keplered Kepler, leaving a legacy that—continued by his countrymen in 1761, 1769, and 1874—was to bring particular distinction to England.

Largely self-instructed in astronomy, Horrocks made his first recorded astronomical observation in 1635 at Toxteth, and by 1636 he was corresponding with William Crabtree (1610–1644), a clothier of Broughton, near Manchester. After his conversion to Kepler's elliptical astronomy by Crabtree in 1637, he began to compare the *Rudolphine Tables* with the tables of Philip van Lansberg, which he had purchased in 1635. Although he found Kepler's tables to be the more accurate of the two, he set for himself the task of improving the planetary parameters used by Kepler in constructing his tables, concentrating his efforts on the orbit of Venus.[10] The *Rudolphine Tables,* Horrocks noticed, were not impeccable. Small but significant errors in planetary models resulted in the prediction of planetary positions that were at odds with those positions as actually observed. And it was through his attempts to understand and eliminate such discrepancies that Horrocks was able to make a prediction missed by Kepler:[11] Venus would transit the sun on December 4, 1639 (New Style [N.S.]).[12]

By November of that year, Horrocks had already alerted his friend Crabtree of the expected event, the occurrence of which would pass otherwise unnoticed by the astronomical world.[13] Horrocks, who had come to possess a telescope adequate for astronomical observations only the previous year (1638), followed the modus operandi of Pierre Gassendi who had observed the 1631 transit of Mercury using the principle of the camera obscura. Then, improving upon Gassendi's example, he prepared the telescopic projection method for his own observations. Late in the afternoon on the predicted day, Venus entered the sun's disk less than an hour before sunset. Horrocks and Crabtree were the only ones history recounts as having observed the event.[14]

Still, after diligent and meticulous preparation, Horrocks almost missed making the observation for which he is now celebrated. His own diffidence caused him to begin looking for the transit a day early. And on the day of the transit, a Sunday, his commitment to "business of the highest importance"—business that (he tells us) he "could not with propriety neglect" for the mere "ornamental pursuits" of astronomy[15]—caused him to subordinate scientific ambition to ecclesiastical duty. But his ambition did not go unrealized. Venus paraded onto the sun as predicted, and the name of Jeremiah Horrocks paraded onto the pages of history.[16] More than two centuries after the event, readers of a Honolulu newspaper would, in 1874, still be amazed by the legend of the churchman-with-a-telescope,[17] recreated once more:

> Among the distinguished astronomers of that time was an amateur . . . a poor curate named Jeremiah Horrox, of a very poor parish, called Hoole, in the suburbs of Liverpool. . . . This poor curate divided his time between the clodhoppers of Hoole, and the beautiful stars. And faithful duty in the lowest of walks, and to the most humdrum of details, will not hinder the march of intellect; nor dull our taste for the higher range of science; but it will serve to heighten our appetite for enquiry into the wondrous arcana of nature; and its faithful performance will enoble our research, whether into the spores of a fern, or among the star dust of the universe.
>
> However let us not be understood to say that the duties of this poor preacher unto the poor were humdrum in striving to lead souls on the way to heaven; but the natures he had to deal with were humdrum and would have kept him forever dragging in the dirt of coarse duty, when he would soar in the divine empyrean. And it was so that he had to steal his chances away from the bickers and bothers of cottiers in order to hold a little converse with the constellations. And yet he was not so much a dreamer as a calculator. In fact he had the spirit of work of a true genius; and so he went over the calculation of Kepler, and discovered that the transit (of 1631) was properly set down for the day indicated; but owing to a slight error which made a difference of a few hours, the transit did not take place in respect to England and the rest of Europe in 1631, till some time *after sunset!*
>
> . . . and our amateur pursuing his favorite hobby discovers in accordance with his calculation that another transit must take place about November 24, 1639 (old style). He announces his discovery, but astronomers and the public who conceived themselves deceived by a Kepler, were not to be hoaxed by a

Horrox—and made no preparations for an observation. But this poor clergyman who had his faith fixed as the stars, prepared for an observation, and induced an intelligent friend or two to be witnesses to the truths of what he should record.

As he had not the means to construct an astronomical hut, or improvised observatory, nor any proper transit instruments to place therein, he did the best he could with such appliances as were at hand. He had an ordinary telescope, and this he placed, pointing out of an aperture in a darkened chamber, so that when it was pointed towards the sun, it threw an image of the luminary upon a sheet of white paper inside. And now he got ready and commenced his observation on the 23d, a day beforehand, as he did not feel absolutely sure about the exactitude of his calculation. This day passed without noting anything to reward his assiduous watch. On the day following, the 24th, he was faithfully at work at his astronomical post; but this was Sunday, and there was a higher post of duty for him to attend to than to watch the heavens; he had to pray for and preach to those who were dimly seeing their way to heaven.

We do not know whether he hurried that sermon or not. It may however be reasonably assumed that it was not unusually long: and when service was over, and the clodhoppers were dismissed with a blessing, we may take it for granted that our faithful pastor in returning to his home did not tarry for any village gossip by the wayside. During his absence the unerring instrument of observation had been pointed by a friendly hand, towards the sun, to challenge the great central orb of light to reveal a wondrous phenomenon of his statellitious [*sic*] system; and lo, the delighted curate when he enters his camera obscura, sees within the luminous circle on the sheet of paper a little dark spot! . . . Here was the planet of Venus crossing the disc of the sun.[18]

Within two short years, Horrocks would be dead, his work virtually unrecognized by the scientific world, and twelve long decades would pass before the next transit in 1761. In the interim, there would be ample time to ruminate about Venus and to rejuvenate an interest in transits. And as the seventeenth century went out, the torch lit by Horrocks did not: It simply passed to the other side of England and into the hands of Edmond Halley (1656–1742).

In 1677, just thirty-eight years after Horrocks' historic observations, Halley, then only twenty-one years of age, witnessed a similar phenomenon—a transit of Mercury—from St. Helena in the South Atlantic, where he had gone from Oxford for the purpose of mapping the southern sky. By this time Halley had become aware of the work of the celebrated mathematician James Gregory (1638–1675) who, in his *Optica Promota* (1663), had pointed to the utility of transit observations in the determination of parallaxes. But Halley remained unconvinced that parallactic measurements of Mercury—the only planet other than Venus that transits the sun—would yield up the astronomer's Holy Grail, the astronomical unit. Instead, Halley looked beyond his own mortal limits and into the next century—to the 1761 transit of Venus, the observation of which, he thought, could at last banish man's ignorance of the Earth-sun distance. When he disclosed in the *Philosophical Transactions* (1691) his calculations for transits of Mercury and Venus, he indicated that only the latter, as observed from different vantage points, offered any hope to those for whom the AU was the *primum desideratum*.[19] A quarter of a century later in 1716, when Halley was sixty years of age, he trumpeted in the same publication the 1761 transit, arguing that the accuracy of the parallactic measurements that would result could be unprecedented: The value of the AU could be determined, he averred, to within one-fifth of 1 percent![20]

Halley's secret lay in his proposed method of observation. Sometimes called the method of durations, it noted that the apparent path of Venus across the sun is not the same for terrestrial observers at different locations, as parallactic effects cause two observers at different latitudes to see Venus sweep across the sun along two different chords.[21] Halley pointed out that the solar parallax could be obtained by finding the difference between the lengths of the two chords and that these lengths could be obtained by precisely observing the time that the planet entered and left the sun, the length of the chords traced out by the planet being directly proportional to the duration of the transit as observed from each of two widely separated stations. Because Venus as seen from Earth moves each minute through an angle of approximately 1.5 seconds of arc, Halley saw that if the moments it entered the sun (at *ingress*) and left the sun (at *egress*) could be determined with a collective error of no more than a second of time, the solar parallax could be gotten with an error of no more than about 0.02 seconds of arc.[22]

Halley, who became England's second Astronomer Royal in 1720, died in 1742. But fame came to him as it did to Horrocks—posthumously. In 1758, his eponymous comet returned on schedule, just as he had predicted; and, in the decade following, aroused by Halley's call to arms, the transits of Venus of 1761 and 1769 enlisted observers around the globe.

Because Halley's method—including the important modification to it proposed in 1760 by Delisle[23]—required that observations be made from widely separated places on the Earth, the 1761 transit, though visible from many parts of Europe, needed observers elsewhere, and an international community of more than a hundred observers fanned out to sixty-two separate observing sites.[24] Great Britain alone sent several men abroad: The team of Charles Mason and Jeremiah Dixon—later to labor along the Maryland-Pennsylvania border in 1763–1767 and to be remembered for the line there that they defined—were dispatched to the Cape of Good Hope; and Nevil Maskelyne, soon to become Astronomer Royal, went to St. Helena.[25] But the results were doomed from the outset. Indeed, Halley, who himself contributed to the failure of the enterprise by his mistaken calculations that were themselves founded upon erroneous data,[26] seems to have had little prevision of the difficulties attending the actual observations. Two of these—the difficulty of determining by visual means the exact instant when Venus enters and leaves the sun's disc and the difficulty of establishing simultaneity between two widely spaced observing stations whose longitudes are uncertain—were to continue to be of major concern long after 1761.

Such absence of uniformity resulted, unsurprisingly, in values for the solar parallax derived from the 1761 transit observations that varied widely, over a range of more than 2 arc seconds (from 8.28″ to 10.60″)—clearly a disappointing and unacceptable result.[27] But the 1761 transit, though discouraging, provided a good rehearsal for what followed eight years later. British astronomy, again in the vanguard and still enamored of Halley, was once more inclined to employ his method, this time sending observers out on a long and liberal tether that reached to the other side of the globe. In Europe, the 1769 transit would be visible in its entirety only from Lapland;[28] it was therefore necessary, to procure observations to be compared with those from Lapland, to send an expedition into the Pacific.

By the mid-1760s, Nevil Maskelyne, then the fifth Astronomer Royal at Greenwich, had already delimited a portion of the vast and largely unexplored Pacific Ocean within which it appeared desirable to station a British party to observe the approaching transit (Fig. 2). On the far side of the world, 180° from the meridian at Greenwich, and lying between the latitudes of 5° and 35° south, the trapezoid-like area was neither small nor landless.[29] And it was the serendipitous discovery by Captain Samuel Wallis in 1767 of a warm and inviting tropical island within the area defined by Maskelyne—"an island such as dreams and enchantments are made of"[30]—that prompted the quick return there of HMS *Endeavour,* which sailed in 1768 under the command of James Cook. Although Cook had received secret instructions that were to occupy him in a vain search for

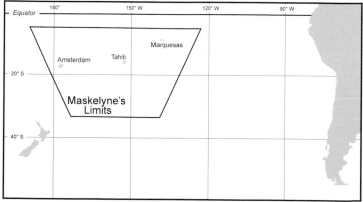

Fig. 2. Maskelyne's Limits

the mythical Southern Continent before his return to England,[31] he also carried with him a copy of the newborn *Nautical Almanac,* fathered by Maskelyne, to which the Astronomer Royal had appended a set of instructions for observing the 1769 transit.[32] And if the latter puzzled him at all, he would have in his company a seasoned astronomer, Charles Green, who had observed the 1761 transit from Greenwich.[33] For Cook's preeminent task and the paramount raison d'être of his voyage was plainly astronomical: He was to proceed to the island discovered by Wallis where, on June 3, 1769, he was to observe the transit of Venus. The island had been called King George's Island by Wallis. The natives called it Tahiti.

Though Tahiti was only one of the numerous sites, including those in its North American colonies,[34] from which the British observed the 1769 transit, it was undoubtedly the most interesting. And it was here that Cook followed a modus operandi that was in all essential respects to be fully imitated in Hawai'i when the next transit—in 1874—provided the justification.

Upon reaching Tahiti in April of 1769, Cook's immediate care was to select a site and build a fort (Fig. 3) from which the transit could be securely observed should the natives turn hostile. And to minimize the risk of missing the transit from bad weather, Cook detached two auxiliary observing parties, one to the eastern coast of Tahiti, the other to Moorea—Wallis' York Island—about 10 miles across the water.[35]

In order to observe the transit itself, all that was needed was a telescope fitted with a micrometer and a pendulum clock set up on shore to give the local time of observation. However, because a knowledge of the latitude and longitude of the observer's location was also desired, it was important that those geographic coordinates be settled.[36] To that end, meridian zenith distances of the sun and select stars were obtained to determine the latitude of the observatory, while lunar distances and eclipses of Jupiter's satellites were observed for the longitude. These observations, which continued for approximately two months, from May (the month before the transit) to July (the month after), established the coordinates of Fort Venus.

Fig. 3. Fort Venus

When transit day came on June 3, Cook and Green, scorched under cloudless skies and laboring under Halley's method, watched the event throughout its duration, more than six hours in the tropical heat that rose to 119 degrees. Although after coming so far they may have considered themselves fortunate for having at least seen the rare celestial display, the scientific merit of their efforts amounted in the end to little. Though they used identical telescopes—reflectors made by the celebrated James Short, each with a 2-foot focus and a magnifying power of 140—they found that their observed times for ingress and egress (the accurate observations of which were the sine qua non for the success of the Halley method) showed wide disagreement. As Cook lamented: "We very distinctly saw an Atmosphere or dusky shade round the body of the Planet which very much disturbed the times of the Contacts particularly the two internal ones."[37] He elsewhere grieved: "It appeared to be very difficult to judge precisely of the times that the internal contacts [at ingress] of the body of Venus happened . . . in like manner at the egress the thread of light was not broke off or diminished at once, but gradually, with the same uncertainty."[38]

The transit observations made by Cook and Green, which were published in 1771 in the *Philosophical Transactions,* included not only a verbal report of ambiguous contacts, but sketches of this vexing phenomenon that came to be known as the "black drop" or "black ligament" (Fig. 4). Having similarly plagued the 1761 transit observations, one author later described it as the matter of the planet appearing to stick to the sun's edge like taffy candy,[39] while another has written of it as if two bodies made of some glutinous material were seen clinging together instead of meeting and parting with a clean definiteness.[40]

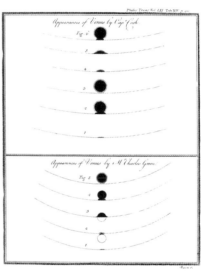

Fig. 4. The "black drop" as seen by James Cook and Charles Green during the 1769 transit of Venus

Because the specter of a black drop cast uncomfortable doubt upon the ability to observe and record the precise moment of Venus' contact with the sun, it remained a topic of considerable concern as the 1769 transit faded into history and the nineteenth century dawned. In fact, in the spring of 1874, George Forbes wrote that the success or failure of all observations of the moment of contact of Venus with the sun still depended upon an understanding of the black-drop effect and that the international astronomical community—including the English, under the leadership of the Astronomer Royal—was vigorously preparing to combat its ill effects as the 1874 transit of Venus drew nigh.[41]

But the transit of Venus technique for extracting the astronomical unit begged an even more general review. One of the practical problems of Halley's method was that it required the precise timing of the moments of contact of the planet with the sun's disc at both ingress and egress—something difficult to realize in practice, even under ideal weather and perfect atmospheric conditions, if for any single observer the sun rose after ingress or set before egress. This meant in effect that for Halley's method to be even potentially promising, observers needed to be stationed where both ingress and egress would be observable. At some stations, this simply required the sun to be above the horizon for the entire duration of the transit. In more extreme situations, the sun might set *after* ingress, travel below the horizon while the transit was in progress, and rise *before* egress.[42] But because observations of these sorts were to be made at *two* stations working in tandem, observations of *four* contacts of Venus with the sun were necessary for the success of Halley's method. To obviate this very real concern, French astronomer Joseph-Nicolas Delisle (1688–1768) had already described an alternative to Halley's method, making it possible to obtain the desired results by merely noting the instant of ingress (or egress) as seen from opposite extremities of a terrestrial baseline (see appendix D).[43] This not only halved the required number of observations of contact for any given station, it also enlarged the number of potential stations where usable observations could be obtained (see Table 2).

In either case, the Halleyan or the Delilean, precisely timed observations were crucial. Inasmuch, however, as the success of Delilean method was additionally dependent upon the ability to accurately determine the longitude of the observing stations,[44] that contingency, unsatisfied during earlier transit observations,[45] would not pass neglected in 1874.

The 1769 transit, it may be said, had resulted in an embarrassment of riches: By the end of 1771, more than two hundred independent (and widely ranging) computations of the sun's distance based upon the 1769 observations had been received by the Paris Academy of Science alone.[46] Still, the 1769 transit results surpassed those of 1761: The value of the sun's parallax had been narrowed to between 8.43 and 8.80 arc seconds.[47] The astronomical unit was at long last being coaxed from its cosmic abyss.

Table 2. The eighteenth-century transits of Venus: observations of internal contacts

Year	Number of stations where internal contact at both ingress and egress was observed	Number of stations where internal contact at either ingress or egress (but not both) was observed
1761	21	81
1769	12	127

Source: Adapted from Harry Woolf, *The Transits of Venus: A Study of Eighteenth-Century Science* (Princeton, NJ: Princeton University Press, 1959). Internal contacts are defined as the first and last instants (at ingress and egress) that the planet Venus appears to be entirely immersed within the solar disc. The (at least prima facie) advantage of Delisle's method over Halley's is evidenced by the quantitative data shown here.

5

· · · · ·

Where the Sun Never Sets

As the 1874 transit approached, interest in the phenomenon among the British astronomical cognoscenti was enlivened by the collective British memory. The chase after the still-elusive astronomical unit was, perhaps, to ordinary citizens not much more meritorious than the chase after the proverbial fox by a pack of well-bred English hounds. It was a purely aristocratic pastime, a sort of intellectual sport to be indulged in only by those who, well fed and well heeled, had the leisure for such delectable delights, a sort of conspicuous consumption with a telescope.[1] But if men of humbler circumstances had little tolerance—and still less leisure— for abstruse astronomical pursuits, they nevertheless might harbor some proper sentiment for national heroes. Horrocks, Halley, and Cook—British icons all—had reputations that outlived the men who made them, reputations that would be exploited on behalf of the 1874 transit.

It was, however, not only British astronomers and British heroes who supplied the nation with the ethos behind the transit chase, though their contribution was large. It was the even larger British view of the world and the British place within it that colored the enterprise. British dominions, now extended to faraway ports visited by exploratory vessels flying the Union Jack and to tiny Pacific islands whose latitudes and longitudes had been fixed by men such as Wallis and Cook, made of Britain an empire where the sun never set. In 1874, this was indeed propitious. It meant that British astronomers, anxious about witnessing the fleeting dance of Venus on the sun, could be stationed wherever Britain and its navy had established a toehold. British colonialism was good for British science.

Eighteen months before the transit, the British journal *Nature* reminded its readers of the proud place occupied by Englishmen in the Venus story, now almost two and a half centuries in the making:

> If national glory can ever be connected with a natural phenomenon, the transit of Venus over the sun's disc may be said to bring peculiar distinction to England. It is in a manner inscribed upon one of the most brilliant pages of our naval history; it led to some of the most remarkable discoveries for which mankind is indebted to our geographical enterprise, and made the renown of our most famous navigator [James Cook]. A hundred and thirty years before Cook, the phenomenon itself was, for

19

the first time in human history, accurately observed in a corner of England, by an English youth [Jeremiah Horrocks], self-taught, and provided with few of the appliances of scientific research.[2]

When, the following year, George Forbes—writing in the same journal—added the legacy of Halley to this proud piece of English history,[3] he was simply displaying a national fervor that was already more than a century old.[4]

By 1874, therefore, England was arguably foremost among those countries that had a reputation to protect by participating in the upcoming transit observations.[5] So it is no surprise that similar appeals to patriotism, honor, duty, and national pride should be conjured, when the time came, by the individual most responsible for superintending the British effort: George Airy, the nation's seventh Astronomer Royal at Greenwich.

By his own reckoning, Airy began to call public attention to the nineteenth-century transit pair as early as 1857.[6] Then, in December of 1868, while apprising the Royal Astronomical Society of preparatory arrangements that he believed would be necessary for the proper observation of the upcoming pair, he reminisced that "the expedition sent into the Pacific for the observation of the Transit of *Venus* in 1769, has always been esteemed as one of the highest scientific glories of Britain in the last century; and I may be permitted to express my hope that it will be surpassed by the efforts which our country will make, with the same object, in the present century."[7]

Airy's desire to see the glories of the previous century surpassed was not merely an impersonal and empty wish. Although the eighteenth-century transit pair had given rise to the first international, cooperative scientific expeditions in modern history,[8] it had not produced results of the precision that his predecessor, Halley, had envisioned. Although it had produced a solar parallax seemingly accurate to the nearest second of arc—a remarkable achievement not possible just one century earlier—still, the difference between a parallax of 8.4 seconds and one of 8.8 seconds is not inconsiderable:[9] The corresponding difference in distance amounts to a gargantuan leap, from Earth to sun, of more than 4 million miles![10]

It was Airy's chief assistant at the Royal Greenwich Observatory, Edward J. Stone, who helped to restore the credibility of the transit of Venus method as a sort of Rosetta Stone for deciphering a long-hidden astronomical secret when, in September of 1868, he rediscussed the results of the 1769 transit observations.[11] And it was not long thereafter that Airy himself was emboldened to write:

> It appears from the calculations of Astronomers that there will occur, on 1874 December 8 and 1882 December 6, Transits of the planet Venus over the Sun's Disk. This phenomenon (which has

not presented itself since the year 1769) is peculiarly favorable for determination of the Earth's Distance from the Sun upon which depend all the dimensions of the Solar System. On account of the importance and interest of this determination, the observations of the two Transits (1761 and 1769), the only ones which have been visible since Astronomy became an accurate science, received the cordial support of the principal civilized nations of the world; and Astronomers now look with hope, for similar assistance in the observations of 1874 and 1882, to their Governments, especially to that of Britain, which from the wide distribution of its colonial possessions may give more efficient aid than any other.[12]

Airy put his appeal into a letter and sent it to the secretary of the Admiralty where he hoped it would find a sympathetic audience. The Royal Navy and the Royal Observatory, Airy knew, had a long-tried professional affinity—a kinship that would soon be tried again, in the service of astronomy and for the honor of the nation.

6

. . . . .

Finding the Longitude

B y 1874, the value of the solar parallax had been investigated by a variety of methods, the transit of Venus method being but one of them. An alternative method discussed by Airy in 1857 but having precedents at least as far back as the sixteenth-century work of Tycho Brahe—observing Mars during its closest approach to the Earth—had been used by a number of investigators, including Stone (at Greenwich) and Newcomb (at Washington).[1] Another method, first used by Laplace and later by Hansen, depended upon the motion of the moon, which is affected by the sun's distance; and Leverrier—codiscoverer, with Adams, of the planet Neptune in 1845–1846—had recently explored the gravitational interconnections among the motions and relative masses of various bodies in the solar system for clues to the sun's proximity. Still another method permitted the extraction of a good estimation of the AU from an emerging knowledge of the velocity of light, and this in two ways: first, from observations of the eclipses of

Table 3. Some values for the solar parallax and the astronomical unit (AU) obtained by assorted methods and by various investigators before the 1874 transit of Venus

Method	Parallax in arc seconds	AU in miles
Transit of Venus, 1769 (Stone)	8.91	91,580,000
Opposition of Mars (Stone)	8.943	91,240,000
Lunar Theory (Hansen)	8.916	91,520,000
Lunar Theory (Stone)	8.850	92,200,000
Planetary Theory (Leverrier)	8.859	92,110,000
Jupiter's Satellites and the Velocity of Light (Foucault)	8.86	92,100,000
Constant of Aberration and the Velocity of Light (Cornu)	8.86	92,100,000

Source: George Forbes, "The Transit of Venus in 1874," Proceedings of the Philosophical Society of Glasgow (1872–1873): 373–394.

Jupiter's satellites made from the Earth at opposite points in her orbit; and second, in conjunction with Bradley's discovery (ca. 1729) of the aberration of light, from a computation of the Earth's orbital speed (from which the length of her orbital path and hence her distance from the sun could be calculated).[2] This methodological phalanx[3] had, by 1874, confined the value of the AU to a remarkably narrow range (Table 3).[4] So, it may be wondered, why should there have been at this historical moment any but the most trivial concern, in England or elsewhere, about the residual ignorance?

The answer to this probing question about the value of knowledge was not found merely in astronomers' high-minded desire to banish human ignorance but in the thundering voice of English utilitarian philosophy[5]—a voice once embodied in Francis Bacon (Fig. 5) and now firmly championed at both the Royal Society in London and the Royal Observatory at Greenwich. It was a voice that demanded to know the *practical* importance of the 1874 transit. And the answer was as thoroughly utilitarian—and as English—as a ship at sea.

Fig. 5. Statue of Francis Bacon at his Cambridge alma mater, Trinity College

When, in 1675, King Charles II established his Royal Observatory at Greenwich, he had his royal eye upon the stars—and his feet firmly anchored in British maritime ambition. Because it had long been recognized that the navigational problem that most afflicted British seamen was the accurate determination of longitude, it was no mere passing fancy that prompted the king, in establishing his observatory, to direct John Flamsteed, his first Astronomer Royal, "forthwith to apply himself with the most exact care and diligence to the rectifying [of] the tables of the motions of the heavens and the places of the fixed stars, so as to find out the so much-desired longitude of places for the perfecting [of] the art of navigation."[6] This conscription of science by government had far-reaching consequences just one century later when Captain Cook, under the auspices of the Royal Society, embarked upon his series of exploratory voyages, accompanied by Greenwich-affiliated astronomers and carrying with him the Royal Observatory's brainchild for longitude-finding, the *Nautical Almanac*. It was at this historical juncture that the matrimonial pairing of positional astronomy with positional geography resulted in the mapping of parts of the world unknown to European communities. Captain Cook—an instrument of that historical moment—then did what Hawai'i-loa could not do: He placed Hawai'i on a map by astronomically pinpointing its latitude and longitude.[7] Hawai'i was now celebrated, however anachronistically, as Cook's "discovery."

The problem of "solving the longitude"—an intimate part of the rai-son d'être of the Royal Greenwich Observatory from the very beginning—lingered on into the nineteenth century. By 1818 the Admiralty had accept-ed full responsibility for the observatory's affairs,[8] and the Astronomer Royal continued to be at the Admiralty's service.[9]

Although Airy, when he first took office, found some of the Admiralty's policies exasperating,[10] he agreed that the observational prior-ities of the Royal Observatory were thoroughly utilitarian.[11] Even when the 1874 transit had passed, he would continue to insist that this was so: "The Observatory was expressly built, for the aid of Astronomy and Navigation, for promoting methods of determining Longitude at Sea, and (as the cir-cumstances that led to its foundation show) more especially for determina-tion of the Moon's motions. All these imply, as their first step, the formation of accurate Catalogues of Stars, and the determination of the fundamental elements of the Solar System."[12] One of the more fundamental elements of the solar system was, of course, the astronomical unit. But what had the AU to do with the moon's motions, and what had the moon's motions to do with determining longitude at sea?

Airy himself might have answered this complex query, for he was nei-ther oblivious to nor ill practiced in longitudinal concerns,[13] and by 1874 nearly two centuries of labor at the Greenwich Observatory had helped to provision the Royal Navy with the necessaries for longitude determination. Although the same navy, Airy realized, would soon be needed to transport British astronomical teams to widely scattered locations around the globe, to provide them and their instruments with proper protection, and to pro-vide—in Hawai'i at least—longitudinal checks of the observing sites,[14] still, to connect the longitude question with both the motions of the moon and a transit of Venus required not a small amount of insight. And it was just the sort of illumination that George Forbes would provide.

In March of 1873, as he awaited his more active participation in the upcoming enterprise, George Forbes read a paper on the approaching tran-sit of Venus before the Philosophical Society of Glasgow.[15] As a post-Newtonian astronomer, he noted that: "The law of gravitation says that the attraction of each body for each other one depends upon the distance between them. The Moon is attracted to the Earth by a force, depending upon the distance of the Moon, which is known in miles. But the Moon is caused to deviate from its natural course on account of the Sun's attraction. This depends upon the distance of the Sun from the Earth, and if this be not known exactly in miles we shall see that it is impossible to apply calculation to foretell the motions of the moon."[16]

Forbes was obviously familiar with the *Nautical Almanac*[17] and with the fact that it contained tables—as it had since Captain Cook's day—pre-dicting the position of the moon at selected intervals of (Greenwich) time. By employing what was called the lunar distance method, these tables could be used, as Forbes knew they were meant to be used, in the determination of longitude.[18] Moreover, Forbes may have by this time already seen a copy of the 1874 edition of the *Nautical Almanac,* printed in 1870, which contained an appendix giving, inter alia, the "Particulars of the [1874] Transit of Venus over the Sun's disc at the stations selected for observation," as well as the familiar tables of lunar distances. For even though the wide availability of chronometers had by this time largely supplanted the lunar distance method for ascertaining longitude, the *Almanac* nevertheless continued to devote some space to its explication (Fig. 6).

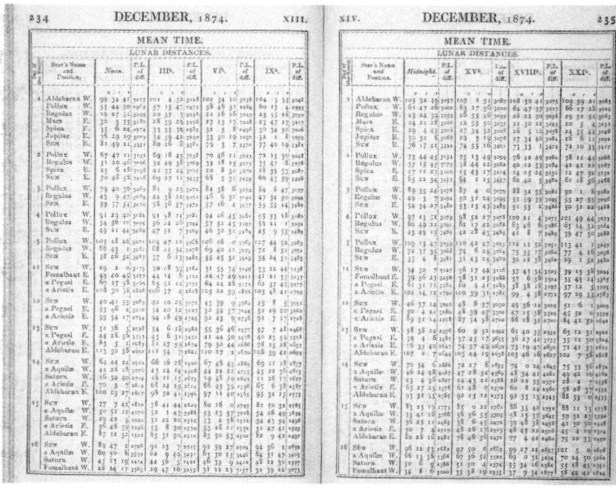
234 DECEMBER, 1874. XIII.
MEAN TIME.
LUNAR DISTANCES.
XIV. DECEMBER, 1874. 235
MEAN TIME.
LUNAR DISTANCES.

Fig. 6. Lunar distance tables from the 1874 *Nautical Almanac*

But the prognostications of the moon's positions given in the lunar distance tables were predicated upon an understanding of the moon's motion—a motion that was predicated in turn upon a correct knowledge of the sun's distance from the Earth and its craggy satellite. Absence of such knowledge, therefore, caused skepticism about lunar distances. But the skepticism could be eased, if not eliminated, by a transit of Venus.

In 1822 and again in 1835, German astronomer Johann Franz Encke, director of the Seeberg Observatory near Gotha, had used the results of the transits of Venus of 1761 and 1769 to obtain a solar parallax of between 8".57 and 8".58, corresponding to a solar distance of approximately 95 million miles. But in 1854 there came an announcement by Peter Andreas Hansen that the observed behavior of the moon—which was affected by solar gravitation and therefore by the sun's distance—required that the solar parallax be larger, and thus the sun's distance smaller, than Encke had supposed. Hansen communicated his doubts to Airy,[19] and eventually tables of the moon's motion produced by Hansen in 1857 were adopted for the calculation of the *Nautical Almanac.*[20]

But the lunar tables remained imperfect. And George Forbes, realizing that this was so,[21] could now make the appropriate connections: "The transits [*sic*] of Venus will aid materially in perfecting the Lunar Tables. The motions of the moon are rendered irregular by the disturbing attraction of the sun. But we cannot determine with great accuracy either the amount or the direction of the sun's attraction upon the moon until we know accurately the sun's distance. Hence if we wish to be able to compute tables of the moon sufficiently correct for the exact determination of longitude, we must employ every means in our power to perfect our knowledge of the sun's distance."[22]

7

· · · · ·

Into the Setting Sun

In October of 1868, eleven years after his address to the Royal
Astronomical Society on the subject of correcting the measure of the
sun's distance, Airy wrote to the hydrographer of the Admiralty, George
Henry Richards. Upon considering the upcoming transit pair from a global perspective for the purpose of selecting appropriate stations of observation, "Owhyhee" was among a small number of places cited by the
Astronomer Royal as suitable for observing, in 1874, the entry of Venus
onto the sun. But what hope was there in actually stationing observers at
those places and in determining their absolute longitudes?[1] So far as the
Admiralty was concerned, Richards told him, there existed no difficulty
whatsoever.[2]

Having received this assurance, Airy again wrote to Richards early
the following month. After noting the difference between the methods of
Halley and Delisle, he affirmed that only the latter could be applied successfully in 1874.[3] The task at Hawai'i would be simple, but critical: to
observe not the entire transit of Venus, but only the ingress of the planet at
a time when the sun was "at a moderate elevation above the horizon, and
sinking." Six months later, after due allowance was made for the expected
participation of foreign and colonial observatories, Airy drew up a short list
of five stations—one each at Hawai'i, Kerguelen, Rodriguez, New Zealand,
and Egypt—to which observing expeditions should be and eventually
would be sent. "Woahoo" was literally at the top of his list.[4]

By this time, Airy had come to realize that sending a party of
observers to Hawai'i was both scientifically attractive and politically convenient. There were three reasons for this. First, Airy understood that the
Hawaiian Islands were "just within the tropics," where, as Forbes was later
to write, "the weather can be depended upon."[5] Cook and Green, after all,
had observed the 1769 transit from Tahiti under cloud-free skies. Was not
Hawai'i's firmament equally sanguine?[6]

Second, Airy realized that the effective application of Delisle's
method required observers to be stationed on nearly opposite sides of the
Earth. Parallactic effects, maximized by the use of the widest practicable
baseline, would cause Venus, which crosses the sun's face from east to west,
to be seen entering the solar disc earlier from one station than from the
other. At the first station (at one end of the baseline), the entry of Venus
upon the sun would be "accelerated," while at the other station (at the

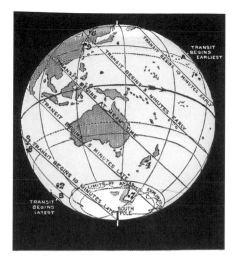

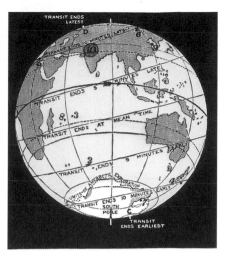

SUN-VIEW OF THE EARTH AT THE BEGINNING OF THE TRANSIT OF 1874

SUN-VIEW OF THE EARTH AT THE END OF THE TRANSIT OF 1874.

1.	Station at	Hawaii.
2.	,, ,,	Kerguelen Island.
3.	,, ,,	Rodriguez.
4.	,, ,,	New Zealand.
6.	,, ,,	Nertschinsk.
7.	,,	(proposed only) at Possession Island.
8.	,,	,, Mauritius.
9.	,,	in North China.

2.	Station at	Kerguelen Land.
3.	,, ,,	Rodriguez.
4.	,,	in New Zealand.
5.	,,	at Alexandria.
6.	,,	,, Nertschinsk.
7.	,,	(proposed only) at Possession Island.
8.	,,	,, Mauritius.
9.	,,	in North China.
10.	The North Indian Region (now occupied).	

Figs. 7 (left) and 8 (right). Parts of the Earth facing the sun at the beginning (left) and end (right) of the 1874 transit

opposite end of the baseline) the same phenomenon would be "retarded."[7] At both stations the sun would be close to the horizon but far enough above it to mitigate atmospheric distortion. Now Kerguelen and Rodriguez Islands—both in the South Indian Ocean, where the sun would be rising at the beginning of the transit—would provide suitable locations for observing the "retarded" ingress.[8] For observing the "accelerated" ingress as the sun was setting, Airy needed a matching station on the other side of the world (Figs. 7 and 8), and he averred that "Owhyhee" and the neighboring islands would be excellent for this purpose.[9]

Airy's third reason, though not strictly scientific, was not insignificant: The British, who had continued to visit Hawai'i since the time of Captain Cook in 1778, had fortified a respectable if not formidable presence there. They had established a consul's office in Honolulu in 1825 and later even sent a bishop, in 1862, to minister to Hawai'i's burgeoning Anglican community—soon to include the high chief (and in 1874, king) David Kalākaua.[10] Hawai'i had reciprocated early by sending two of its own persons of distinction, King Liholiho and Queen Kamāmalu, to England in the 1820s. The flag of the Hawaiian Kingdom had come to incorporate the Union Jack, and under the protection of that flag there lived, among the more than fifty thousand native Hawaiians, a small community of Britons. A census of 1872 placed their number at 619, of whom 381 were living in Honolulu. Among full-blooded foreigners in the Islands, only the Chinese and the Americans were more numerous.[11] Clearly, in 1874 the century-long British presence in Hawai'i had sustained its highly influential position, and the Astronomer Royal could at least imagine the Union Jack fluttering invitingly in the Pacific. Airy therefore evidently took some comfort in knowing that there existed "English society at Woahoo" and thought that good provision would be made for the "Accelerated Ingress" if the British Government would undertake the accurate determination of the longitude of "Woahoo" and the careful observation there of the 1874 ingress of Venus onto the sun.[12]

As seen from a distance, then, the Hawaiian Islands had at least three virtues: their meteorological promise, their geographic location, and their English social propinquities—and these were excellent justifications, Airy thought, for choosing them as a Delilean station.

But it is unlikely that the intentions of the Astronomer Royal were widely known, if they were known at all, on those faraway islands until the Foreign Office was instructed to write to the consul general at Honolulu that it was the "intention" of the British Government to send a party of men to observe the transit of Venus from Hawai'i, and the consul general was similarly instructed "to acquaint the Hawaiian Government accordingly."[13] The news reached the Department of Foreign Affairs in Honolulu in October of 1873 in the form of a dispatch from the British acting commissioner and consul general, Theo H. Davies. Whether the recipient, Charles Reed Bishop, was alarmed, or even mildly surprised, by this cordial imposition, his response was polite if not capitulating: His Majesty's (King Lunalilo's) Government was "pleased" to learn that the Hawaiian Islands had been chosen as a transit of Venus station.[14]

By June of 1874, the *Hawaiian Gazette* was informing Island readers of the pending transit, its anticipated results, and how they were to be obtained and was calling the transit "The Astronomical Event of the present Century."[15] In so doing, it reminded its English-speaking-and-reading audience that even though an accurate measure of the solar parallax may have appeared to some "a very abstruse and purely speculative question," it was not: "All the science of navigation, and indeed all the results of applied astronomy, have sprung from the approximate solution of this very problem. The slight amount of uncertainty which still attaches to the answer, affects the accuracy of the lunar and planetary tables of every nautical almanac, and to a certain degree unsettles all questions of distances in regard to heavenly bodies, and of longitude in regard to places on the earth."

The *Pacific Commercial Advertiser* followed, three months later, with an extended article on Venus, giving a mathematical treatment of the problem of solar parallax, a discussion of the methods of Halley and Delisle—even a description of some of Venus' orbital and physical elements and a mention of Galileo's discovery of its phases—and, perhaps most importantly, a statement of the practical benefits resulting from a successful pros-

Fig. 9. Rear Admiral Benjamin F. Sands, superintendent of the United States Naval Observatory and George B. Airy's correspondent regarding the American interest in observing the 1874 transit of Venus from Hawai'i

Fig. 10. Eight metal chests, now at the United States Naval Observatory in Washington, showing the names of the eight stations to which the United States eventually dispatched observing parties for the 1874 transit of Venus

ecution of transit observations, not only for navigation but "for ascertaining longitudes and defining boundaries."[16] Thus one planet, Venus, was to be used not merely to better locate another planet, Earth, in space, nor merely to better locate places (longitudes) on that planet, but to delimit boundaries upon its surface. This perhaps almost unconscious confluence of two leading passions of Western civilization—the one for Euclidean geometry, the other for territoriality—was spilling out into the Pacific and would not leave Hawai'i unscathed.[17]

Meanwhile, the American interest in observing the transit from the Hawaiian Kingdom curiously came to naught, despite the fact that these two sovereign nations were on the verge of a major treaty that would eventually result in the merger of the two into one. Although the Americans, in deference to Airy's wish that they provide for a Delilean station in the Pacific,[18] thought of occupying Owhyhee,[19] in the end they decided to choose stations where the photographic method of observing the transit could be most advantageously applied. As a result, the eight foreign stations—three in the Northern Hemisphere, five in the Southern—to which the Americans would eventually deploy observing teams were all places from which the entire transit was visible.[20] This, of necessity, excluded Hawai'i (Figs. 9 and 10).

At the last minute, however, Hawai'i was nearly surrendered. In May of 1873, Airy proposed to negotiate with the American Government for the British abandonment of the O'ahu station if the Americans could be persuaded to take it up and work the Sandwich Islands generally. This, he thought, would diminish both expense and trouble and would possibly permit another British station to be established on some island in the South Seas.[21] But George Airy, the landlubber, was quickly disillusioned by George Richards, the seasoned seaman. Not all islands, the astronomer was reminded by the hydrographer, afforded proper shelter for a ship. Some were eternally buffeted by winds, while others had only "a problematical existence." Besides, it would be a shock to British gentility— downright bad manners—to leave an observing party for several months on such "inhospitable rocks." And furthermore, Richards grimaced, there was in Airy's proposal an intolerable offense to proper patriotic sentiment: The British, who had just the previous year (1872) lost some attractive islands— the San Juan—to the Americans, had been pushed far enough: "The Americans as they forced us out of San Juan and have forced us into acquiescence in any views they may take will gladly shunt us out of the pleasant Isles of the Pacific on to barren Southern Rocks where if we don't fail from fog and sleet we shall probably fail from not being able to get a footing on the land. Some of our own would-be Astronomers are taking the same line."[22] The Americans had already heaped humiliation on the British, Richards was implying, and he personally had had enough.[23] Airy could do little but surrender to such ex cathedra reasonings, and he pledged thenceforth to subordinate his thoughts to the establishment of auxiliary stations at Kerguelen and at the Sandwich Islands.[24]

In good time, two such auxiliary stations would be established in the Sandwich group—and at sites well known even to Englishmen who had never so much as set foot upon a ship's deck. One would be at Waimea, near the very spot where Captain Cook had first made landfall in 1778.

The other, just north of the ominous waters of Kealakekua, would be the destination of George Forbes.

8

· · · · ·

The Prime Mover

Fig. 11. George B. Airy

As the management of the British effort to observe the 1874 transit of Venus would expectedly devolve upon its prime astronomer, it is difficult to imagine anyone better equipped for that office—by aptitude, industry, or habit—than George Biddell Airy (1801–1892), who, in 1835, accepted the post of Astronomer Royal, England's seventh (Fig. 11).

The prolific talents of Airy manifested themselves at an early age, and as a youth of ten he stood first in Byatt Walker's school at Colchester.[1] His scientific studies, while yet a boy, ventured into optics, chemistry, astronomy, and fluxions (calculus), but he had as well a taste for literature and a prodigious memory; while still in school, he could repeat at one examination 2,394 lines of Latin verse.[2]

Matriculating at Trinity College, Cambridge, in 1819, Airy graduated in 1823 "first among the first" as senior wrangler[3] and first Smith's prizeman,[4] far outdistancing his nearest competitor. A fellow of Trinity by 1824, he published, in 1826, his *Mathematical Tracts on Physical Astronomy*—and it immediately became a textbook at the University. In that same year, and at the age of only twenty-five, he was elected to the chair once occupied by the inimitable Newton: that of Lucasian Professor of Mathematics. He soon became, in 1828, Plumian Professor of Astronomy and director of the Cambridge Observatory; and in 1831, for his various researches in optics, he was awarded the Royal Society's Copley Medal.

The quantity of his labors and the number of honors received by him during his lifetime were truly monumental, almost beyond belief, and have rarely if ever been equaled. He published books on *Gravitation* (1834), *Trigonometry* (1855), *Partial Differential Equations* (1866), *On Sound and Atmospheric Vibrations, with the Mathematical Elements of Music* (1868), and his *Popular Astronomy* (1848) passed through twelve editions. He contributed 377 papers to journals and scientific collections, in addition to 141 official reports and addresses and other papers. His paper on suspension bridges, contributed in 1867 to the Institution of Civil Engineers, was honored with the Telford Medal. He served several terms as president of the

Royal Astronomical Society and he was, from 1872 to 1873, president of the Royal Society. Among the countries conferring him with orders were Prussia, Sweden, and Brazil, and in 1872 he succeeded Sir John Herschel as one of eight foreign members of the French Institute.

Airy's tenure as Astronomer Royal, which lasted forty-six years, was extraordinarily productive, and he completely reequipped the observatory at Greenwich with instruments designed by himself.[5] One admirer, a professor of engineering at Cambridge, recalled that:

> Sir George Airy was one of the most remarkable men, indeed I think I may say the most remarkable man, whom I ever met. In every part of his thoughts he was the most absolutely original person with whom I ever came in contact . . . the whole of the Observatory was full of his inventions—doors which shut by contrivances of his own, arrangements for holding papers, for making clocks go simultaneously, for regulating pendulums, for arranging garden beds, for keeping planks from twisting, for every conceivable thing from the greatest to the smallest. On all there was the impress of an original and versatile mind, bubbling over with inventiveness. His conversation ranged over everything of human interest, historical, religious or scientific, and his ideas had the immense merit of being always couched in the most simple and intelligible language. He was a colossal-minded man.[6]

It was at Greenwich, too, where this extraordinary individual undertook the enormous task of preparing for the 1874 transit of Venus. The entire control of the various British expeditions—of which there were five, including the Hawai'i contingent—was in his hands.[7]

But it was exactly because of Airy's high-profile position as Astronomer Royal that his perceived foibles and failures became as much a part of the historical record as his perceived accomplishments. Not yet a dead and distant Carlylean hero, he could hide himself from neither friend nor foe as the 1874 transit of Venus approached. And as he gave counsel and made decisions, he became, ex officio, a target of criticism.

One man who repeatedly took aim at Airy was Richard Proctor (Fig. 12).[8]

Fig. 12. Richard Anthony Proctor

A member, with Airy, of the Royal Astronomical Society and RAS secretary in 1874, Proctor could wield a pen with noticeable effect. And in 1874, shortly before the transit, he published a book that openly criticized the Astronomer Royal.

It was not Proctor's first book, nor would it be his last. But it was one of his more acclaimed works, and before the 1870s were out it would go through several editions. Proctor's *Transits of Venus,* in fact, presented such a well-articulated study of the conditions of the nineteenth-century transit of Venus pair—including, importantly, a careful discussion of where the methods of Halley and Delisle might be most advantageously applied—that it came to be described as "the best popular exposition of the nature and use of that phenomenon" that was then available.

But *Transits* was much more than an exposition. It was an argument—or more precisely, at least in its latter parts, it was the recapitulation of several arguments. For within its pages Proctor was urging, as he had urged the Astronomer Royal several times before, that there were advantages to be found in Halley's method—a method sometimes discredited in its raw, original form, but a method that Airy had "too hastily assumed" would be inapplicable to the 1874 transit.[9]

Proctor's book, complete with numerous illustrations and as carefully laid out as a legal document, was a masterful amalgamation of factual evidence and persuasive argument. Beginning with a discussion of the historic transits of the seventeenth and eighteenth centuries, followed by a separate chapter devoted to transit conditions, Proctor gave much of his last chapter—on the then-approaching transits of 1874 and 1882—to a criticism of Airy. He took issue, in particular, with Airy's early examination of the circumstances of the two transits, an examination he judged to be reckless. Airy's 1857 alert to the RAS of the approaching transit pair[10] had been so "roughly" prepared, Proctor thought, that it had no "scientific weight"[11]—and yet Airy continued for more than a decade to promulgate one of its blunders. "When at length," Proctor wrote, "in 1868, he [Airy] published what purported to be a detailed description of the circumstances of the two transits, and of the duties not of English astronomers only, but of astronomers generally with respect to the transits, he remarked that Halley's method had been *shown* to fail totally in 1874."[12] But this, as Proctor had already argued (and was now cogently demonstrating in his book), was a mistake—and given Airy's authoritative position, a potentially disastrous one. "In particular," he continued, "I found that Halley's method, instead of failing totally in 1874, could be applied under highly favourable conditions."[13]

Though such inquiries proved "distasteful to the Astronomer Royal,"[14] Proctor persisted—in some measure, to good effect. John Adams, director of the observatory at Cambridge, would himself come to realize the merits of Halley's method and by 1873 would swing his weight to Proctor's side.[15]

But by the time it appeared in print, Proctor's *Transits* was more an instrument of public criticism than it was a helpful treatise on transit matters. And it surely was not an objective appraisal of the office of Astronomer Royal—or, less obliquely, of Airy's own competence in fulfilling the duties of that office. But Airy—who parried Proctor's verbal pugilism by sarcastically characterizing him as a wonderful "scribbler"[16]—did seem to recognize the intelligence of Proctor's critique, even if he did not relish its display. And he probably needed from Proctor's book no reminder such as this: "If . . . Delisle's method were to be frustrated by bad weather at the Sandwich Islands . . . then ingress observations would fail" altogether.[17] By 1874 several nations, including the British, would occupy Halleyan stations. Hawai'i simply would not be one of them.[18]

9

· · · · ·

Cambridge Connections

J ust as the rise of modern science in England could not have stood apart from the work of the Royal Society, nor from the inspiration given to that work by such highly educated men as Francis Bacon (see Fig. 5), so too the professionalization of astronomy in England and its institutionalization at the observatory at Greenwich under a system of royal patronage could not have stood apart from the grooming of astronomers royal at the universities of Oxford and Cambridge (Table 4). Cambridge in particular produced several men who brought, via the Greenwich byway, a subtle but distinct British identity to Hawai'i's astronomically studded history.[1] And it was at Cambridge, more than anywhere else in England, where the entire family of the country's most celebrated navigator, James Cook, was by the nineteenth century best etched into the national memory (Fig. 13).

Table 4. Beginning in the seventeenth century and continuing almost without interruption since the eighteenth, Great Britain's most public and arguably its most coveted astronomical post, that of Astronomer Royal, has been filled by Cambridge-educated men. Of the fifteen individuals who have occupied the post since 1675, ten have been educated at Cambridge. They (and, if a Cambridge-educated man, his affiliated college) are given here in chronological order.

1. John Flamsteed, Cambridge (Jesus)

2. Edmond Halley, Oxford

3. James Bradley, Oxford

4. Nathaniel Bliss, Oxford

5. Nevil Maskelyne, Cambridge (Trinity)

6. John Pond, Cambridge (Trinity)

7. George Airy, Cambridge (Trinity)

8. William Christie, Cambridge (Trinity)

9. Frank Dyson, Cambridge (Trinity)

10. Harold Jones, Cambridge (Jesus)

11. Richard Woolley, Cambridge (Caius)

12. Martin Ryle, Oxford

13. Francis Smith, Cambridge (Downing)

14. Arnold Wolfendale, Manchester

15. Martin Rees, Cambridge (Trinity)

IN MEMORY
of *CAPTAIN* JAMES COOK, of the ROYAL NAVY,
one of the moſt celebrated Navigators, that this,
or former Ages can boaſt of; who was killed by
the Natives of *Owyhee*, in the *Pacific Ocean*, on the
14th Day of February, 1779; in the 51ſt Year of his Age.

Of Mr. NATHANIEL COOK, who was loſt with the
Thunderer Man of War, Captain *Boyle Walſingham*,
in a moſt dreadful Hurricane, in October, 1780;
aged 16 Years.

Of Mr. HUGH COOK, of *Chriſt's College*, CAMBRIDGE,
who died on the 21ſt of December, 1793; aged 17 Years.

Of JAMES COOK, Eſq: COMMANDER in the ROYAL NAVY,
who loſt his Life on the 25th of January, 1794; in
going from *Pool*, to the *Spitfire* Sloop of War, which
he commanded; in the 31ſt Year of his Age.

Of ELIZ.ᵗʰ COOK, who died April 9ᵗʰ 1771, Aged 4 Years.
JOSEPH COOK, who died Sept.ᵗ 13ᵗʰ 1768, Aged 1 Month
GEORGE COOK, who died Oct.ᵗ 1ˢᵗ 1772, Aged 4 Months.

All Children of the first mentioned CAP.ᵗ JAMES COOK by
ELIZABETH COOK, who survived her Husband 56 Years, &
departed this life 13ᵗʰ May 1835, at her residence Clapham Surrey
in the 94ᵗʰ Year of her Age. Her remains are deposited
with those of her Sons JAMES & HUGH,
in the middle Aisle of this Church.

Fig. 13. The Cook Family Memorial inside Great Saint Andrew's Church, Cambridge

Captain Cook's contemporary, Nevil Maskelyne—fifth Astronomer Royal at Greenwich and father of the *Nautical Almanac*—had himself been educated at Cambridge's Trinity College, as had the eponym for the Sandwich (Hawaiian) Islands, First Lord of the Admiralty and fourth Earl of Sandwich John Montagu. When, following Cook's death at Kealakekua Bay in 1779, George Vancouver—who had accompanied Cook on the ill-fated voyage—returned to the Pacific in the 1790s, his appointed astronomer

36

William Gooch would, with Maskelyne's blessing, carry still another set of Cambridge credentials into the Pacific via Greenwich—only to be murdered, like Cook, on a beach in Hawai'i (Fig. 14).[2]

But before the days of royal astronomy at Greenwich—the beginnings of which preceded George Airy's transit of Venus work there by two centuries—England produced few astronomers whom history cares to remember. Among those few, however, were several Cambridge men: Edward Wright, John Dee, Thomas Digges, William Gilbert, John Bainbridge, and Jeremiah Horrocks—all of them contemporaries of Kepler and Galileo, and all of whom made their contributions.[3]

Men of such breeding were exceptional in their day, as astronomers then were largely made outside the universities at either Oxford or Cambridge. They could be made, for example, at London's Gresham College,[4] where, given the widening access to printed books,[5] regular courses in astronomy had been available from 1598. But these courses were mainly practical in intention: subordinate astronomy designed primarily for men in other professions—mariners, cartographers, instrument makers, and others for whom astronomical knowledge had a distinctly utilitarian and not merely an academic value.[6]

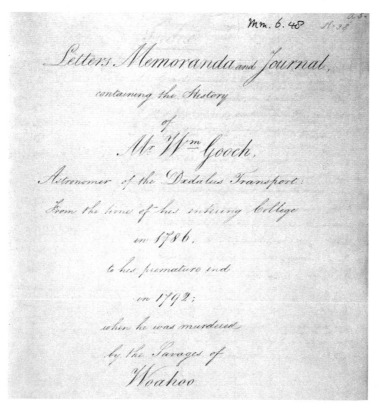

Fig. 14. The papers of William Gooch, now held at the Cambridge University Library

This situation changed only slowly. Even though both Oxford and Cambridge established chairs in astronomy—the Savilian at Oxford and the Plumian at Cambridge—around the years 1619 and 1704 respectively,[7] there were still no clearly delineated avenues leading to careers in astronomy in England right into the seventeenth and early eighteenth centuries, and a university education generally remained better suited for the professional training of ecclesiastical and legal rather than scientific minds.[8] For astronomy in particular, the practical mechanical skills and the knowledge of mathematics and optics that had galvanized the work of the autodidactic Horrocks and Newton might have been garnered in a variety of ways, inside or outside academia.[9] Astronomy, though long recognized as one of the seven liberal arts,[10] was still largely what Horrocks himself had called a mere "ornamental" pursuit,[11] not the matter of a widespread and learned profession.[12]

John Flamsteed therefore became somewhat of a pioneer in 1675 when he accepted the first full-time professional position in astronomy established in Britain.[13] Flamsteed, the first Astronomer Royal at Greenwich, was a Cambridge man.

But so too was George Airy. And when Airy inherited Flamsteed's position in 1835, he was not the first—nor would he be the last—Cambridge-trained man to occupy the post. So Airy, upon assuming his responsibilities at Greenwich, simply followed and furthered, in a manner, a Cambridge tradition—even advancing it by strengthening his observatory staff with Cambridge-trained personnel.[14]

In fact, English astronomy had long before Airy's day twice exported Cambridge's good name abroad: first to Ireland in 1792 in the person of John Brinkley (1763–1835), the first elected Astronomer Royal for that country and a graduate, like William Gooch, of Caius College; then onto the African continent in 1820 in the person of Fearon Fallows, the first Astronomer Royal at the Cape of Good Hope and a fellow of St. John's College.[15] If, when Thomas Henderson, Fallows' successor, gave up his work at the Cape to become Scotland's first Astronomer Royal in 1834, English astronomy became more firmly implanted on foreign soil than ever before, it had also become—in the very year of Fallows' appointment to the Cape—freshly invigorated at home under the aegis of the newly founded Royal Astronomical Society,[16] of which body Airy would eventually serve as president.

Meanwhile, the study of astronomy at Cambridge was itself being strengthened. By the 1820s, a new observatory to succeed the recently dismantled facility atop Trinity's Great Gate was rising from a site on Madingley Road. By 1828 Airy, then Plumian Professor at Cambridge, could report that in the opinion of all the astronomers who had seen it, both English and foreign, it was "better adapted to its purposes than any similar building in Europe."[17] The study of scientific subjects in general was, furthermore, in the ascendant; and soon a university degree in the natural sciences—though not in astronomy per se—would become available at Cambridge for the first time.[18]

But Airy, a product of an earlier and more strictly mathematical curriculum, probably would have remained favorably disposed toward his alma mater as an institutional incubator for England's astronomical elite even without such developments. Not only did it cultivate men of respectable rank in society; but, he thought, it also produced men of high mathematical attainments and patient and industrious habits—all desirable traits in the astronomical profession.[19] So whatever he thought of the strictly "Physical Astronomy" that had formed a part of his own Cambridge education in the early 1820s,[20] Airy was inclined to extol its other intellectual and moral strengths. The fact that it was as a student at Cambridge that he had learned, perhaps for the first time, of the transits of Venus was incidental.[21]

What other men, especially men without university credentials, may have thought of the Cambridge experience was a different matter. David Gill (1843–1914), a watchmaker-turned-astronomer and a close friend of George Forbes, had his own opinion; and some years after observing the 1874 transit of Venus with Lord Lindsay at Mauritius, he would offer it.

In 1879 Gill would accept an appointment as Her Majesty's astronomer at the Cape of Good Hope where he would become "the most significant Astronomer Royal" ever to work there.[22] But with neither the benefits nor the encumbrances of a university degree, Gill's view of astronomy school back in England was untainted by schoolboy nostalgia; and in 1897, when one Bryan Cookson sought his counsel with respect to pursuing a career in astronomy, Gill would candidly remark:

> There is [still] no good school of Astronomy in England. At Cambridge you can have the necessary outfit of mathematics, and no doubt at Oxford also—in fact, you have probably enough of mathematics to take up the rest for yourself.
>
> For practical work the Greenwich system . . . has never made an astronomer. The chief assistants are selected as young men with a sound mathematical but no practical training. They enter into chief positions where they have to superintend men who know much more about practical work than they do, and they have to pick up what they can of a hard and fast hidebound system—which they are taught to regard as unquestionably superior to all others.[23]

As 1874 approached, therefore, Airy knew that there were no astronomers alive in England—or anywhere else—qualified to observe the upcoming transit, if by "qualified" is meant experienced in observing the phenomenon or even in using all the relevant instruments. His exigent task, therefore, was to find and recruit promising personnel, outfit them with properly (even if experimentally) made instruments of observation, and rigorously train them in the use of those instruments. Although he was, in the event, to recruit mainly from outside academia—and, in some cases, from outside England—he continued to cast a backward glance toward Cambridge, where he found promising candidates even among those who vaunted neither professional credentials in astronomy nor even strong academic training in the discipline. Airy, after all, had an insider's view of Cambridge. If a man with Cambridge connections expressed the necessary interest, there was reason to believe that he also had the necessary talent; if this was Airy's inference, he was at least partially correct.[24] And in the case of Leonard

Fig. 15. Leonard Darwin, ca. 1875

Darwin (Fig. 15), the requisite mixture of interest and talent—and the Cambridge tie—was easily found.

Born into a family of distinguished Cambridge men, Leonard Darwin[25] (1850–1943) was the son of naturalist Charles Darwin, the great grandson of poet Erasmus Darwin, and the brother of astronomer George Darwin. The penultimate of five sons,[26] Leonard's long life, spanning nearly a century and highlighted by three astronomical adventures, was full of interest. In 1868, at the age of eighteen, he entered the Royal Military Academy at Woolwich; and it was during his years of service with the Royal Engineers (RE, from which he retired in 1890) that he did his most memorable astronomical work. He was twice sent to the Pacific for transit of Venus observations, first in 1874 and again in 1882; and in 1886 he was a member of the British solar eclipse expedition to Grenada under the direction of Sir Norman Lockyer.[27] His active work in the RE and in astronomy then at an end, he became in succession, first, a member of Parliament (from 1892 to 1895); then, president of the Royal Geographic Society (from 1908 to 1911); then, after the death of his distinguished cousin Sir Francis Galton (the father of eugenics), president of the Eugenics Education Society (serving from 1911 until 1928); then, finally, an honorary doctor of science at Cambridge in 1912.[28] In 1926 he published his definitive book, *The Need for Eugenic Reform*,[29] and—perhaps still mindful of his earlier endeavors in astronomy—contextualized his reflections with a suggestively entitled chapter, "Eugenics and the Riddle of the Universe."[30]

Until Leonard's work, the Darwin family's interest in astronomy, though perhaps latent in Charles,[31] had gone, like a vigorous but sadly neglected seed, largely unwatered. For although it was George who, having graduated from Cambridge (Trinity College), was to return there in

1883 to become Plumian Professor of astronomy and experimental philoso-phy,[32] it was Leonard who would observe almost a decade earlier a transit of Venus from the Pacific.

Leonard's budding astronomical talents had come under scrutiny in the summer of 1872 in an oblique and curious fashion. As a young man of twenty-two, he had expressed an interest in the approaching transit with an obeisant letter to the Astronomer Royal (Airy) that was less than thor-ough.[33] His father, believing that Leonard had qualifications that had not been properly placed before Airy's attention, quickly sent a testimonial let-ter to Airy's son, Hubert, on his own son's behalf, deferentially requesting that Leonard's unsung praises be politely noted.[34] The letter had the desired effect. Leonard Darwin would be assigned to the New Zealand sta-tion for the 1874 transit—and soon afterward would be in Hawaiian waters having his very own encounter with the Sandwich Islands, a group about which his father Charles could only write, the *Beagle* having bypassed Hawai'i altogether four decades earlier.

But if Charles Darwin by this gesture had given direction to his son's scientific aspirations, the gesture was not unreciprocated. Charles' *The Expression of the Emotions in Man and Animals*—a sequel to *The Descent of Man* (1871)—would appear that very year, 1872, and Leonard, who trained in photography with the Royal Engineers, had already recom-mended a photographer for the book's illustrations.[35] Yet *Descent* may have had—and would perhaps soon have again—more than just a casual inter-est to Leonard, especially those parts that would include his father's spec-ulations on the causes of the declining population among native Hawaiians; since Captain Cook's arrival, their numbers had been reduced from an estimated four hundred thousand to fewer than sixty thousand. Those figures, supplied to Charles Darwin in 1874 by the Hawai'i-born Titus Munson Coan, would lead the author of *Descent* to pessimistic thoughts about the eventual extinction of the Hawaiian people. But even before Coan's data arrived from New York for Charles Darwin's perusal, Leonard appears to have provided his father with essentially the same numbers from the Naval College at Greenwich. How Leonard himself may have obtained those figures is not clear; but if, when he did, he still had no inkling of the true causes of the population decline in Hawai'i or about the alarm that it was raising there in the 1870s, a post-transit of Venus trip aboard the *Mikado* would eventually furnish a firsthand answer.[36]

Leonard's ship would not reach Honolulu Harbor until after transit day. Before his arrival, however, a total of three Cambridge-trained men, observing the transit of Hōkūloa from two separate islands in the Hawaiian chain, would already have made their presence felt. Of those three, the man of highest aptitude and greatest distinction was George Forbes.

10

· · · · ·

The Sandwich Island Seven

GEORGE FORBES

Fig. 16. George Forbes

George Forbes (Fig. 16) was only twenty-five when he arrived in Hawai'i in September of 1874 as a member of the British observing team.[1] Born on April 5, 1849, in Edinburgh, where his father James David Forbes held a chair in Natural Philosophy, Forbes had matriculated at Christ's College, Cambridge, and in 1871 had emerged with a degree in the Mathematical Tripos. A man of versatile talents—a traveler, a journalist, an inventor, and an electrical engineer, as well as an astronomer devoted to the search for an ultra-Neptunian planet—he became professor of Natural Philosophy at Anderson's College, Glasgow, in 1872.

Following his transit of Venus work in Hawai'i, George Forbes conducted research on the velocity of light, and when electric lighting began in England in the 1880s he went to London as an adviser or manager of one of the then-formed companies. After working at Niagara Falls from 1891 to 1895, where he was involved in the ambitious plans to harness the falls' hydroelectric potential, he went on to survey the Huka Falls in New Zealand in 1896 and the cataracts of the Nile in 1897–1898, with a view to their electric exploitation.

Made a fellow of the Royal Astronomical Society in 1873 and of the Royal Society in 1887, he was also an honorary member of the Franklin Institute of Philadelphia and of the American Philosophical Society. His written work included *A History of Astronomy* (1909), *Puppets: A Work-a-day Philosophy* (1911), and a biography of his friend and fellow Scotsman, astronomer David Gill (see Fig. 17, inset).

Although George Forbes was to serve in 1877 as a special correspondent for the *Times* during the Russo-Turkish war and even invented a range finder used by British gunners in the Boer War (1899–1902), his soldierlike gallantry would clearly manifest itself before his return to England from Hawai'i in 1875. After he died in 1936 at the age of eighty-seven, it was written of him that the code of honor exhibited by his father James—a sense of right that amounted to chivalry—was likewise characteristic of his father's son:

> George Forbes thought much of his work and little of his reward; had he been a mercenary man he could scarcely have failed to enrich himself, more or less, by his pioneer work at Niagara. As it was, old age found him a very poor man, living at one time in a shed (as he liked to call it) built mostly by his own hands at the edge of a Highland wood . . . [and where] he was surrounded by books, the better part of his father's library [Fig. 17]. When he ceased to read because his eyes grew dim, piety and honour forbade him to sell his father's books, and he gave them all to St. Andrew's University. . . . These books, some four thousand in number, are of great value. . . . The sale of these books would have brought him comfort, almost wealth, but money had no place in his thoughts. To suggest of some great enterprise (as was once done in his hearing in the Club) that "there was money in it", was to move him to anger, and draw from him a not unmerited rebuke.[2]

Some years before the transit of Venus, Forbes' scientific talents had already come to the attention of influential men, and by the summer of 1872 his candidacy for a professorship at Anderson's University had elicited the strong support of a multitude of academics in Scotland, Ireland, and England. Several Cambridge men wrote testimonials on his behalf: James Stuart, fellow of Trinity College; Charles Kirkby Robinson, master of St.

Fig. 17. George Forbes in "The Shed" at Pitlochrie (Pitlochry), ca. 1929, and his friend David Gill (inset)

Catherine's; John Fletcher Moulton, fellow of Christ's College; and George Gabriel Stokes, Lucasian Professor of Mathematics. John C. Adams, director of the Cambridge Observatory, was impressed by Forbes' "active & original mind constantly on the watch for new ideas." William (Lord Kelvin) Thomson—long a family friend[3]—deemed him "well fitted" for the post by virtue of his experience and training in mathematics, experimental physics, and observational astronomy and certified his "very great zeal for science." Warren De la Rue was taken by his "astuteness" in conducting original research. And all three—Adams, Thomson, and De la Rue—were confident that his ability to expound his ideas well and with clarity would serve him well as a teacher. On September 23, 1872, after more than twenty testimonials had flooded in supporting his candidacy, Forbes was sent a telegram informing him that he had been unanimously elected to the post. Among those letters was one that, though similar to the others in its laudatory tone, served as a unique prelude to events that were soon to unfold. The letter came to the trustees of Anderson's University from the Royal Observatory at Greenwich, and it was signed by George Airy.[4]

Forbes had already spent some time (Airy noted in his letter) at the observatory preparing himself for the transit of Venus observations and had already offered himself as a candidate in the overall British effort. But besides this general wish, he had one more specific—one that he had already privately disclosed to Airy: to be dispatched to the Pacific, where he might observe the "volcanic phenomena" of the Sandwich Islands.[5]

Although Airy committed himself to the idea only slowly and with caution,[6] by October of 1873 he had sent Forbes a fateful note: He was now being considered for the auxiliary station on the island of Hawai'i "under the shade of the great Mouna Lowa [Mauna Loa]."[7]

HENRY GLANVILLE BARNACLE

The island of Hawai'i easily had room for a second astronomer, and Forbes' assigned observing mate there was Henry Glanville Barnacle.[8] Born at Knutsford, Cheshire, in 1849, the same year as Forbes, he was to outlive the latter by two years, dying in 1938 at Perth, Australia, at the age of eighty-nine. Although he too was a Cambridge man and a fellow of the Royal Astronomical Society, he proved for Forbes to be an otherwise incongruous, discontented, and troublesome partner.

Barnacle had matriculated at St. John's College, Cambridge, in 1869 and took his degree in 1873 in the Mathematical Tripos. How he may have heard about Airy's need for transit of Venus observers is uncertain, but soon after graduation and with less than a year to go before transit day, he sent a letter to Airy from Knutsford, where yet another Cambridge graduate—his own father, in fact—happened to be the parish vicar. Offering himself as a candidate in the transit enterprise and saying that he not only possessed his own telescope but had already done "a great deal of Astronomy, both Theoretical and Practical," he was also careful to alert the Astronomer Royal, twice over, to his Cambridge upbringings.[9]

This proffer of talent to a Cambridge man by the Cambridge son of a Cambridge man was not unlike Leonard Darwin's similar—though more subtle—appeal to a respectable educational breeding. And again, the mention of proper Cambridge relations apparently had the desired effect on the Astronomer Royal, who replied the very next day: "I think it likely that we should be glad to avail ourselves of your offer to join the Expedition for observing the Transit of Venus,"[10] suggesting either the Sandwich Islands or Kerguelen's Land as options to Barnacle, who responded with alacrity.[11]

Airy still knew little about his new candidate, and Barnacle was quick to reassure him of his qualifications, reiterating his love for astronomy and his acquaintance with telescopic observing; affirming his physical health; expressing his desire to become well practiced in photography and thus of greater value to the expedition; mentioning, by the way, that he was a good drawer, both neat and exact; and even enclosing a recent photograph of himself (Fig. 18). In short, it was a good piece of salesmanship, and even included the names of several personal references at Cambridge.[12]

Fig. 18. Henry Glanville Barnacle

One of those references was Wm. H. H. Hudson of St. John's, to whom Airy posted a letter requesting confirmation of Barnacle's qualifications. Hudson's reply, penned the day before Christmas, opened with a sentence that Airy should have seen as a red flag: "It is only fair to say that M^r. Barnacle is not a man of high mathematical knowledge." Still, he was better qualified than most: He possessed a greater knowledge of astronomical facts, Hudson believed, than many men who were merely acquainted with astronomical theory; he could painstakingly and faithfully carry out instructions; and his evident familiarity with a telescope, together with his fondness for making astronomical observations, could be of "great advantage" to him on the sort of expedition he wished to join.[13]

Within a month, Airy—anxious to have his chosen observers trained at Greenwich before their departure to distant parts—wrote to Barnacle saying that he would be glad to have him at work there as soon as he could come.[14]

Henry Glanville Barnacle commenced his apprenticeship at the Royal Observatory on January 30.[15] And whatever reservations Airy may have had about this blooming but still untested candidate were soon cast upon the waters, to heave up many months later in the Hawaiian Islands.

John Walter Nichol

A far less troublesome addition to the Sandwich Island contingent—and a traveling companion with whom George Forbes probably had a greater affinity—was the young Scotsman, John Walter Nichol (1843–1878).[16]

Born in Edinburgh and the son of a teacher of mathematics in the high school of that city, Nichol received his earlier education at the Edinburgh Institution and subsequently attended lectures at the university there. At the close of his curriculum, he was engaged by Piazzi Smyth—successor to Thomas Henderson and second Astronomer Royal of Scotland—to assist in the reduction of the Edinburgh observations that formed the basis of a catalog of stars published there, and for three years he worked at the Edinburgh Observatory with Smyth. In May of 1874, shortly before his departure from England as a member of the Hawai'i-bound expedition, Nichol would be elected a fellow of the Royal Astronomical Society, but by mid-1873 he had already come to Airy's attention in an oblique if predictable fashion: through the embrace of the Cambridge network.

When Airy assumed his position as Astronomer Royal, he had necessarily vacated his position as Plumian Professor of Astronomy at Cambridge—a position that in 1883 was to be filled by George Darwin, Leonard's brother. Between the tenures of George Airy and George Darwin, the Plumian chair was occupied by James Challis (1803–1882);[17] and in July of 1873, Challis sent a letter to Airy for the purpose of bringing under his notice an "energetic and intelligent young man" from Edinburgh who had called upon him in Cambridge and who was on the "look out for more active employment such as the Transit of Venus Expedition may be supposed to afford."[18] Challis had received a letter from an Edinburgh professor (Kelland) recommending Nichol for active work, and Challis was acting as a go-between.

At this time, however, with almost a year and a half to go before the transit, Airy was inclined to be circumspect. He now had a number of candidates—"quite as many as are required," he thought—among young navy officers and students at the Greenwich Naval Hospital and was inclined to think that the government would prefer, as far as possible, selecting from them. He was reluctant, therefore, to encourage Nichol's candidacy.[19]

Nichol was, however, steadfast in his desire and ready to make the required sacrifice. He wrote to Challis asking him to communicate his circumstances to the Astronomer Royal: "As . . . I happen to have some small means to live upon and wish to extend my acquaintance with the subject," he wrote to Challis, "I should prefer going on the Expedition." He understood that it would be necessary for him to resign from his position at the Royal Observatory at Edinburgh and simply hoped that there might be "some suitable appointment" available to him upon his return.[20]

Challis transmitted Nichol's communiqué to Airy, and after a two-and-a-half month incubation it received a reply: Airy wrote to Nichol and, without mentioning which one, offered him a position on one of the transit expeditions. Nichol accepted the offer without delay.[21]

Francis E. Ramsden and E. J. W. Noble

Airy's intuition that naval officers would fill a large number of places on the five separate British expeditions was accurate. Among the twenty-two observers appointed to the five stations, nearly a third (seven in all) were members of the Royal Navy, and several others came from other branches of military service, with at least one representative of the national militia at each station. The Royal Navy was represented at four of the five sites, Egypt being the lone exception. Three stations—Egypt, Rodriguez, and New Zealand—had three appointed observers each. Kerguelen had six. Hawai'i drew the greatest number of assigned observers—seven—including the largest number of civilians—four. The three remaining members of the Hawai'i team all had military credentials.[22]

Representing the British Navy was Lieutenant Francis E. Ramsden, R. N., whose chief duty on transit day was to document the transit photographically. Though Ramsden's "Photographer's Journal," kept at Honolulu, still survives, there is among the otherwise voluminous papers of George Airy little surviving correspondence with the photographer himself, and therefore little is known about the man.[23]

Representing the Royal Marine Artillery on the Hawai'i contingent was Lieutenant E. J. W. Noble. Although Airy indicated early on that the soldier Noble would observe from Kaua'i with the civilian Richard Johnson,[24] he was found on transit day in Honolulu with Lieutenant Ramsden—and, like Ramsden, under the watchful eye of an officer of higher rank. If Noble kept a journal, either personal or official, on transit matters, as did several other members of the expedition, its fate is unknown. And perhaps because of his soldierly near-anonymity, or perhaps because of his lack of Cambridge affiliations, his correspondence with the Astronomer Royal was, like Ramsden's, seemingly limited to the sparseness of businesslike memoranda, and the voice of history barely whispers his name.[25]

George Lyon Tupman

But whispering and going gently into the night was not the lot of a military man of higher rank: the chief of the transit observations in Hawai'i, George Lyon Tupman (Fig. 19).[26]

Born on September 7, 1838, at Boulogne, Tupman was educated at the Royal Naval School, entered the Royal Marine Artillery as second lieutenant in 1855 at the age of seventeen, and by 1873 had risen to the rank of captain. Having made an early offer of his services to the transit effort, he was soon entrusted by Airy with a large portion of the superintendence of the preparations and was eventually named head of the entire five-district enterprise. Although he would himself be dispatched to Hawai'i, every observer in every other district would be responsible to him. He in turn would be responsible, through Airy, to the government.

Fig. 19. George Lyon Tupman at Honolulu

Tupman had taken an interest in astronomy from his youth, and one of his early written works was a catalog of meteor radiants based mainly on his own observations in the Mediterranean. Though he was elected a fellow of the Royal Astronomical Society in 1863, his scientific interests extended beyond astronomy and into geology, microscopy, natural history, and archaeology. On October 26, 1876, two years after his transit observations in Honolulu, he married Miss Rebecca G. Wetherill of Philadelphia.

Tupman's most important contribution to the science of astronomy was his work in connection with the nineteenth-century transit of Venus pair. He was effectively appointed to the 1874 expedition by Airy in April 1872 and commenced his work at the Royal Observatory at Greenwich on May 15 of that year.[27] By 1873, he was appointed to instruct the members of the 1874 observing teams in the course of training that they were required to undertake at Greenwich, and upon his return to England after the 1874 transit, he remained at Greenwich to superintend the voluminous reductions of the observations made by the various British parties, a task that occupied several years. Back in the Pacific shortly thereafter, he observed the 1882 transit from New Zealand, and upon returning to England he set up the Hillfoot Observatory at Harrow, from which place he continued his astronomical pursuits, observing comets, minor planets, occultations, and faint stars on the meridian. He died on November 3, 1922, at the age of eighty-four.

RICHARD JOHNSON

With less than a year remaining before the transit, George Airy was still recruiting observers for the overall British effort. News of vacancies had already crept outside the hallowed halls of the Royal Observatory to the vicarage at Knutsford, where it had found an attentive and anxious listener. It had infiltrated the mildly foreign soil of England's immediate neighbor to the north, where the long shadow of Cambridge University had similarly fallen with well-nigh predictable results. Now, by early 1874, the news had spread westward across the Irish Sea to the capital city of the emerald land to prick the ears of a teacher and scholar at a well-known Irish college. And the day immediately following the beginning of Barnacle's work at Greenwich, a letter of introduction was crafted there and sent off to the Astronomer Royal. It came from the pen of Richard Johnson (1840–1894).[28]

Johnson, a native of Dublin, had entered Trinity College in 1862, had become a scholar in Classics by 1867, and by 1874 had been teaching experimental physics and astronomy at Trinity for five years. His letter to Airy said that he was "very willing" to fill one of the transit of Venus vacancies—even though, he confessed, he was "slightly short-sighted."[29]

Airy's reply was both prompt and encouraging, assuring Johnson that his ocular affliction "would probably be quite unimportant," and offering him an option: Would he prefer to observe at a near station—Alexandria, perhaps?—or a more distant station, such as the Sandwich Islands?[30]

Johnson's expressed preference for a distant station[31] was quickly accommodated. A place could be found for him in the Sandwich Islands, Airy believed, but it would be necessary for him to come to Greenwich soon for three months' required practice: The expedition to the Sandwich Islands would sail early in June.[32]

Johnson accepted Airy's offer with alacrity.[33] He would sail in four short months for Hawai'i. But even shorter—and remarkably so—had been his passage under Airy's initial screening. From the day of his introductory letter to the day of his appointment to the expedition, barely a week had passed. There now was, clearly, little time for hesitation.

11

· · · · ·

Practice at Greenwich

Planning and preparing for the British observations of the 1874 transit of Venus—an event that itself would begin and end in a fraction of a day—required several years' labor. Individual observers needed to be selected, organized, and trained. Instruments—telescopes, transit instruments, photoheliographs, chronometers, and their accessories—needed to be built, bought, or borrowed. Materials for buildings had to be acquired, and huts for sheltering personnel and equipment had to be constructed. Forms for entering and reducing the observations had to be prepared and printed. And then all these—people, instruments, buildings, and materials—had to be shipped to foreign parts without loss or injury. Though it was a herculean task, one that centered on transit day but begun long before it, its success could be largely attributed, George Forbes thought, to three sources: the Astronomer Royal (whose "generalship [was] quite unparalleled in the annals of Science"); the Admiralty (who "liberally supported" Airy "on all points"); and Captain Tupman (who spent "three years in training himself and . . . other observers").[1]

But the quality of scientific manufactures in England, and not simply of the men who could deftly wield those manufactures, was likewise critical. And in the nineteenth century such manufactures—telescopes and their accessories—as were necessary for the success of the transit of Venus enterprise were more readily available than ever before.[2] By 1869 the first telescope-producing factory in England, erected in 1855 in the city of York by Thomas Cooke, had birthed the world's largest refracting telescope (of 25-inch aperture), and soon thereafter several Cooke telescopes, though considerably smaller, would be in Honolulu for the 1874 transit of Venus undertaking. George Airy would no longer need to wait, as he had waited during his time at Cambridge, "years" for something as small as a 4-inch lens. Nor would he need to look much beyond London for the altazimuths and transit instruments that the 1874 enterprise would require: Troughton & Simms, now well established on Fleet Street and ready to please such a major customer as the Astronomer Royal, supplied not only these but, for the Cooke telescopes, double-image micrometers as well. High-quality optical glass was, of course, required for such purposes, but after about 1848 the importation of it was not. It could be gotten directly from Birmingham, where the Chance Brothers had located a well-respected glass-manufacturing firm—the same firm to which Airy, wishing to add

50

astrophotography to the British 1874 effort, would turn for the provision of the desired glass plates.[3]

In 1869, preparations for the transit were, by Airy's account, finally begun "in earnest." Barely two months after reading his transit-related paper (on December 11, 1868) to the Royal Astronomical Society, Airy sent correspondence[4] on the subject to the First Lord of the Admiralty, the Rt. Hon. H. E. Childers, M. P., and was soon asking the Admiralty's permission to prepare and purchase instruments. Permission, along with £10,500, was granted in June.[5]

By 1870, preparations were in full swing. Airy was now off and running, purchasing and ordering equipment[6] and soliciting and obtaining the timely support of J. R. Hind, superintendent of the *Nautical Almanac*. The 1874 edition of that book (printed in 1870) would include—at Airy's bidding, but through Hind's efforts—several pages of tabulated data on the upcoming transit as it would be seen at the numerous stations selected for occupation by the participating scientific powers of Europe: France, Russia, and the North German Confederation, as well as Great Britain. The local mean time of internal and external contacts, the altitude and azimuth of the sun, and other "particulars" calculated for forty-six stations, including Honolulu, would be set forth in an appendix and would be ready for the press by November.[7]

By 1871, several treasured pieces of transit-related hardware had been brought safely into Airy's possession. He now had, for each of his five chosen stations, an equatorial telescope, an altazimuth, and a transit instrument, many of which—including all of the last—were new. By the following year, the portable wooden observatories for the altazimuths (observatories that would feature revolving domes) would be complete, as would be a set of first-class clocks (to be used in tandem with the transit instruments). Just as importantly, promising personnel from both military and civilian ranks would begin to appear in harness at Greenwich in the persons of Tupman and Forbes.[8]

Forbes' apprenticeship at Greenwich, which began in April of 1872, was not altogether auspicious. Airy was early inclined to be backbitingly cynical and suspicious of his new associate from the north. He impugned Forbes' working habits.[9] And he questioned Forbes' leadership skills. Already wary of employing together on a single task both civilians and military servicemen,[10] he told the secretary of the Admiralty that Forbes—though he might possibly be useful if held in strict subordination—could not be trusted, as could Captain Tupman, with the command of a station.[11]

Tupman, however, was not as misanthropic, and he cautioned Airy that it was "very unlikely" that they would be so fortunate as to secure the services of other "gentlemen" who could match Forbes' qualifications.[12] Having had the matter thus brought into focus for him, Airy was soon telling Forbes, almost apologetically: "You slipped away so quickly that I had no opportunity of saying to you that I had heard from Captain Tupman how much he was pleased with your command of the instruments astronomical and photographic, and how glad he is to have your services."[13] Airy soon realized, if he hadn't already, that Forbes would probably not only enjoy an observing assignment on the island of Hawai'i, but that he could also manage it well.[14]

If Forbes' preparedness for a transit assignment and his ultimate approval by Airy was bolstered by his long if intermittent days at the Royal Observatory, Airy could not have been as comfortable with the readiness of others who came to the task less well qualified, and he required of other candidates at least three months transit-related practice at Greenwich.[15] Though this commitment of time to such an important undertaking was far from severe, the practice regimen under Tupman's superintendence had several casualties, and by September of 1873 at least a half-dozen lieutenants who had stepped forward for transit of Venus work had either volunteered their retirement from the enterprise or were informed of their "mistake" and asked to give up altogether.[16] Remarkably, none of the Hawai'i-bound observers were among the relinquished: Tupman and Forbes were all but aboard by 1872; Noble and Ramsden by the summer of 1873; Nichol by the fall of that year; and Barnacle and Johnson by early 1874. All seven men would pass their apprenticeships at Greenwich, some—such as Forbes—demonstrating both aptitude and accomplishment.[17]

But in 1873, Forbes' Hawaiian destiny was yet to be decided. As preparations at Greenwich continued, whether or not the Honolulu station would be enlarged and strengthened by the inclusion of auxiliary stations was, in the spring of that year, still in abeyance. The essential astronomical equipment was now nearly all ready and all the portable buildings, except those for the photoheliographs, were finished. The skeleton forms for calculations had been prepared. And Airy had even begun to collect the scientific books that the transit of Venus observers would require in the course of their work. But the arrangements for—and even the selection of—those observers were still incomplete.[18]

The number of trainees preparing themselves for a possible place at one of the five British stations was, however, growing; and as the year passed, both civilian and military observers were assembling at the Royal Observatory for instruction and practice with the various instruments. This was especially true of an ad hoc device invented by Airy: a working model of the transit (Fig. 20).[19] In action by October, Airy's model was capable of exhibiting the transit phenomena in their "true angular magnitude and velocity,"[20] and it quickly attracted widespread attention. From the many officers at the nearby Naval College to the director of the Cambridge Observatory, John Adams; from the astrophotographers Warren De la Rue and Pierre Janssen to the director-general of the Ordnance Survey, Sir Henry James[21]—word of Airy's invention traveled outward. Not long after the news reached Scotland, George Forbes appeared again at Greenwich and before the end of October had written a multipage report on his own

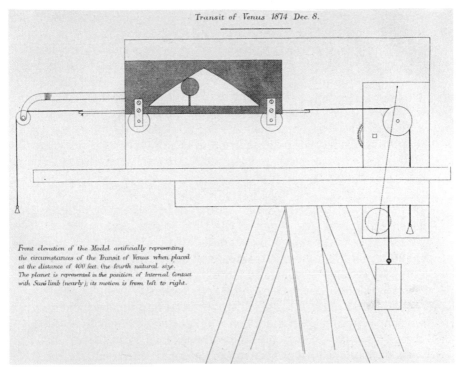

Front elevation of the Model artificially representing the circumstances of the Transit of Venus when placed at the distance of 400 feet. One fourth natural size. The planet is represented in the position of Internal Contact with Suns limb (nearly); its motion is from left to right.

Fig. 20. Airy's transit of Venus model

practice with Airy's ingenious contrivance.[22] But the practice was important. To this both Forbes and Airy agreed. Airy, in fact, would come to place such faith in the utility of his invention that, at Forbes' suggestion,[23] he would eventually have one sent to Hawai'i along with instructions regarding its continued use.

Just before the termination of their training at Greenwich, Tupman's assessment of the preparedness of the would-be transit observers was in general positive, and he wrote to Airy from the Royal Naval College reporting that all of them—with one exception—were able to work independently at all the instruments. The exception was Henry Barnacle.[24]

But Barnacle was a latecomer to Greenwich—and a civilian son of a vicar besides. And he had been set adrift among military and professional men of status and accomplishment. So when he began to encounter what Tupman simply called "difficulties," including interruptions from other observers, it should have been evident to Tupman that Barnacle's social integration was as much a matter of concern as his scientific training.

Barnacle's own journal recounts some of the elements of the Greenwich practice regimen and reveals some possible occasions of difficulty and frustration.[25] Work with the transit of Venus model, photographic practice, observations of clock stars, checking for instrumental errors, computing, reading and note taking, making altazimuth observations, and practice dismantling and rebuilding a transit hut—these were among the tasks that kept him occupied six days a week, the seventh day, Sunday, routinely being a day of rest. But to a careful reader, Barnacle's journal reveals even more: the more written into it by another's hand—the hand of George Airy.

Had Airy's tenure at Greenwich been briefer than it was, or had his sole task and his sole accomplishment been the superintendence of the British 1874 transit of Venus enterprise, his reputation for managerial and organizational prowess would have been well deserved. But so too would have been his notoriety for paternalism and fastidiousness—idiosyncrasies that, though well exampled in Barnacle's journal, were also well lampooned by an observatory assistant:

> [Airy's] love of method and order was often carried to an absurd extreme, and much of the time of one of the greatest intellects of the century was often devoted to doing what a boy at fifteen shillings a week could have done as well, or better. The story has often been told, and it is exactly typical of him, that on one occasion he devoted an entire afternoon to himself labelling a number of wooden cases 'empty', it so happening that the routine of the establishment kept every one else engaged at the time. His friend De Morgan jocularly said that if Airy wiped his pen on a piece of blotting-paper he would duly endorse the blotting-paper with the date and particulars of its use, and file it away amongst his papers.[26]

The professional relationship between George Airy and Henry Barnacle was, both in its earlier and its later manifestations, a considerably troubled liaison and one that at least three men—Tupman, Forbes, and Airy—came to lament. Indications that trouble lay ahead came early. Barnacle, conceding to Airy's wish that observers keep journals, began his on the day he commenced work at Greenwich. Less than a month had passed, however, before Airy, like a glowering schoolmaster, was correcting that journal by entering comments therein: "The entries might be made to occupy much less space, which is generally convenient. The writing would be more legible if closer. No margin to be left at the right hand," he wrote. And: "On all following leaves, rule a marginal line and a top line as shewn on next leaf. Leave a blank line after every day, and place the date in the margin." He would then initial his comments, authoritatively, "GBA."

Soon, lines and dates were placed as requested. Barnacle was obedient. He would be allowed to go to Hawai'i.

12

· · · · ·

Astrophotography

B efore Galileo turned his telescope toward the heavens in 1609, astronomy was largely taught and learned by means of words, numbers,
and diagrams, but with few if any naturalistic representations or *pictures* of the heavenly bodies. Excepting Leonardo's few drawings of the
moon, memorable and well-executed pictures even of Earth's nearest celestial neighbor seem to have been rare before the seventeenth century. The
addition of the telescope—and later the camera—to the astronomer's tool
kit changed all that, but the resulting tumescence of raw data could be dis-
comfiting, and the questionable epistemic status of *pictures* in the newly
equipped discipline would continue to smart well into the nineteenth century. Indeed, dispute about the faithfulness of astronomical pictures as representative of astronomical reality was already abroad by 1647, the year
that witnessed the publication by Johannes Hevelius of his *Selenographia,*
the first treatise devoted to the telescopic appearance of the moon. In it
Hevelius took aim at Galileo, whose illustrations of the moon as they had
appeared in his *Siderius Nuncius* (1610) were impugned, Hevelius claim-
ing—perhaps somewhat unfairly, Galileo having died five years earlier—
that the book's author must have lacked a sufficiently good telescope, been
inattentive to his observations, or been ignorant of artistic principles. When
Hevelius' own representations of the 1661 transit of Mercury came under
attack by Thomas Streete, Hevelius, still much alive, had to fight to escape
discredit. But any easy transformation of astronomy into a picture-laden
science had been staggered by duels such as these, and the advent of
astrophotography two centuries later would not eliminate them.[1]

Airy's early planning for the 1874 transit of Venus did not include
astrophotography.[2] The joining of a camera to a telescope was still somewhat of a novelty, and it was a completely untried partnership for transit of
Venus observations.[3] What sort of optical distortions were to be expected
from a camera-telescope? What further distortions would be produced in
the shrinking of a collodion film,[4] which received its impressions when in a
wet state but which would be scrutinized and measured when in a dry
state? And, considering the required precision of the transit observations,
could a newly compounded mechanical eye, still in the experimental stage,
outperform the collective biological eye of a cadre of well-trained observers?

The year 1839 had marked the beginning of the photographic era. It
was in that year—Airy's fifth as Astronomer Royal—that the word "pho-

tography" was coined[5] and that the photographic process developed by Louis Jacques Mande Daguerre (1787–1851) was published by the Paris Academy of Sciences. But to astronomers, the daguerreotype must have seemed as awkward as it was primitive. It required exposure times of twenty to thirty minutes and access to a photochemical laboratory, and even then it produced only a single—and reversed—image. Within two years, however, William Henry Fox Talbot (1800–1877) patented in England a process that allowed a man to make reproducible photographs on paper with exposure times of as little as sixty seconds or less. The wet collodion process, conceived by Frederick Scott-Archer (1813–1857), quickly followed in 1851. It involved spreading a thin coat of collodion on a glass plate, sensitizing the plate in a silver nitrate bath, and, while still moist, placing the plate in the camera to make the exposure. But although exposures of only a few seconds were required, this was still much too slow for transit of Venus purposes—and there was the added inconvenience that the plates had to be developed and fixed almost immediately, a process requiring a portable darkroom or tent. The development in the 1870s of the dry plate—produced by a gelatin emulsion poured on a glass plate and allowed to dry—helped to mitigate these concerns. It required an exposure time of less than a second.[6] And it obviated the need for the immediate development of photographs by potentially excited or distracted observers.

The newborn dry plate process, which came to be used in the 1874 British transit of Venus astrophotographic efforts, was, like an infant, promising but precarious. And this had already been foretold by events in France thirty-five years earlier: When the astronomer Francois Arago announced Daguerre's invention to the Paris Academy, he had admitted that scientists had no adequate theory to explain it, citing "the positive inability of the combined wisdom of physical, chemical and optical science, to offer any theory of these delicate and complicated operations, which might be even tolerably rational and satisfactory."[7] Indeed, Airy himself objected early on to the employment of photography in the transit expeditions and later came to accept it only as "a valuable adjunct to the system of eye-observation."[8] His skepticism was not ill founded. Any expectation that a "photo-machine" could observe a fleeting celestial event better than the eye of an astronomer and could record the truths of Nature without the intervention of individual bias—such an expectation in the 1870s was premature.

The camera had already been turned toward the sky, it is true; and by 1851 the photographic record had already come to include images of the sun, the moon, the solar spectrum, and some of the brighter stars. But the bald acceptance of a photograph as a scientific document; the admissibility of an artifact as evidence for a natural fact; its ability or inability to represent Nature unadorned; the problems inherent in a photograph's faithful reproduction; and the issues surrounding its legitimation as part of the investigative process—all these annoying brambles about appearance and reality should have provided, like a row of longstanding philosophical hedges, some properly prickly precautions against the mere prima facie credibility of sky pictures. Still, between the years 1839 and 1875—that is, between the daguerreotype and the transit of Venus—the *fixity* of the data promised by such pictures, even if not of proven reliability, was enough to entice hopeful men, and George Airy was one such man. So too was Airy's collaborator, Warren De la Rue.[9]

Warren De la Rue (1815–1889) was born in London and educated in Paris. Although he published his first papers in the late 1830s in the areas of chemistry and electricity, by 1850 he had submitted his first astronomical contribution—a drawing of Saturn—to the Royal Astronomical Society. His interest in astrophotography was stirred by two daguerreotypes of the moon taken at the Harvard Observatory and displayed at the Great Exhibition of 1851, photographs that attracted great interest among British astronomers because of their clarity and because of their close correlation with telescopic views. When Archer's development of the wet collodion in the same year led to a period of exploration and experimentation, De la Rue trained himself in Archer's method and soon produced the first collodion print of the moon. But there were difficulties with the moon as a subject fit for photography. Which type of telescope—a reflector such as the one used by De la Rue or a refractor such as those destined for the British 1874 transit of Venus observations—would give the clearest image? And how could any telescope be mounted and driven to accurately compensate for the ever-varying velocity of the moon in the heavens during the time required for a wet plate exposure? It was not until 1856 that De la Rue solved the latter problem. His successfully designed driving clock resulted in photographs that were both clear and impressive.

But the stage was merely being set during the 1850s for an even greater endeavor. It was during this period that De la Rue began corresponding with Airy. And by the time he sent Airy examples of his lunar photographs, Airy had already incorporated photography into the regime at Greenwich in the form of a self-recording machine for registering magnetic and meteorological observations. Ever eager to eliminate inconsistencies in accounts and descriptions of astronomical observations and to diminish the reliance that had to be placed on the mere observer, Airy foresaw the promise of astrophotography as a tool for standardization. Then came the British eclipse expedition of 1860.

For the 1860 effort, Airy organized the expedition and the Admiralty funded it, while De la Rue prepared and carried out the photographic operations. A portable observatory, partly to contain a photoheliograph and partly to serve as a photographic room, was constructed under De la Rue's direction, then dismantled for the journey to Spain where the eclipse was observed. Airy did his part by recruiting a ship from the Admiralty, the *Himalaya,* to transport the astronomers and their equipment to Spain.

Many of the elements of the 1860 enterprise—the passing of an object in front of the sun, the pioneering use of photography in recording the phenomenon, the authoritative role of De la Rue, the overall superintendence by Airy, the construction and transport of a portable observatory, and the timely assistance of the Admiralty—were to likewise buttress the 1874 transit of Venus campaign. And, as in 1860, the transit of Venus of 1874 was to be an undertaking that realized both the aspirations and the limitations of astrophotography.[10]

Concerned about the technical difficulties of photographing the transit as well as the immense cost, Airy wanted reassurance that photography could succeed before spending time and expense to include it. He obtained this reassurance from De la Rue. Issues that had been raised by the eclipse of 1860—concerning, for example, the shrinking of the photographs—were raised again. But by De la Rue's confidence in the promise of photography, together with the introduction by Captain W. Abney of the Royal Engineers of a dry-plate process[11]—and a welcomed surprise delivered up by Pierre Janssen—Airy was disarmed. And with De la Rue's endorsement of both the Abney and Janssen additions to the project and his agreement to act as its photographic advisor, Airy successfully lobbied the Admiralty for £5,000 to "fortify" (though not to replace) the eye observations of the transit with photography.

In 1873, the year after Airy had at last conceded that provision should be made for the application of photography,[12] five photoheliographs were executed for the English Government by the celebrated optician John Henry Dallmeyer[13] under De la Rue's direction.[14] In order to capture photographically the instant of Venus' contact with the sun on transit day, a clever invention by Janssen—the photographic revolver, or "turning wheel"—would be attached to the photoheliograph.[15] The Janssen device would permit up to sixty pictures,[16] each measuring a half inch wide and an inch high, to be taken in quick succession around the edge of a circular

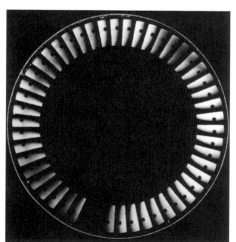

photographic plate at one-second intervals, the plate completing one rotation within a period of one minute (Fig. 21). It was hoped that one of these photos would reveal the moment of Venus' contact with the sun to the nearest second of time, thus obviating the possible, even likely discrepancies among observers in noting the same phenomenon.[17]

With these developments underway, the engaging of a photographic teacher was sanctioned;[18] and in good time, Airy could report that all the observers selected for the upcoming transit effort had

Fig. 21. A series of exposures made with the Janssen turning wheel

undergone a course of training in photography—first under a professional photographer (Reynolds) and subsequently under Captain Abney, whose new dry-plate process, Airy reported, was to be adopted at all the British stations.[19]

At three of the five stations—Rodriguez, Kerguelen, and New Zealand—photography, it was thought by one writer in *Nature,* would be well suited, as the entire transit would be visible from those sites.[20] Hawai'i would not enjoy such an advantage. Besides, any photographs of the transit taken there would need to be obtained with the sun at a low altitude, thus increasing the likelihood of atmospheric distortion. But despite any residual skepticism concerning their possible scientific value, Airy's orders to the members of the expedition—that after the photoheliograph had snatched its images of Venus on the sun and photographic prints had been made, the photographic plates were to be "carefully packed and jealously preserved"[21]—were historically momentous. For although photography had been introduced into the Hawaiian Islands by the 1840s, there had been little or no use of the photograph there for purposes other than personal or scenic portraiture.[22] The first known instance in Hawai'i of the application of photography to the process of scientific data gathering would occur in 1874, when a fleeting Venus became frozen in time on a glass plate.

13

· · · · ·

Supplies

T he British transit of Venus project was not only risky but expensive.
Salaries for personnel needed to be set within the bounds sanctioned
by the national government, and Airy's duties as the national superintendent of the operations would have been severely hampered had such
salaries not been successfully negotiated.[1]

The task of equipping and provisioning the five British stations was
likewise no mean achievement.[2] The astronomical apparatus for the
Hawai'i station alone would include three transit instruments (one each for
O'ahu, Kaua'i, and Hawai'i) and more than a half-dozen telescopes. Then
there were the clocks and chronometers, the compasses and micrometers,
the reflecting circles and the artificial horizons (and the mercury necessary
for their proper use). And even though there would be but one photoheliograph, it would come with the cumbersome appendage of a well-con-
structed darkroom complete with shelves and cupboards, drawers and a
sink, funnels and "india rubba [sic] tubes," and an assortment of chemicals—collodion (bromized and plain), sulphate of iron, alcohol, ether,
cyanide potassium, bromide potassium, nitric and sulphuric acid. And
because the Astronomer Royal expressly prescribed a method for cleaning
the corrosion from the graduated circles of instruments with a "soft silk
handkerchief . . . wrapped round the top of the finger dipped into a little
sweet oil and rubbed very gently on the corroded part,"[3] the Sandwich
Island observers would be outfitted with a proper supply of silk handkerchiefs with which to pamper their delicate instruments.

To supplement the astronomical equipment, the Meteorological
Office would generously supply an assortment of barometers, thermome-
ters, hydrometers, and rain gauges and a set of instructions. Airy's own
"Instructions to Observers," together with copies of the *Nautical Almanac*
for the years 1874 and 1875, a set of Admiralty charts, refraction tables,
books on logarithms, and astronomy texts and catalogs would help stock
the expedition's library.

Much of the expedition's work would need to be recorded on paper
of one kind or another, and for this it would be supplied with a dozen or
more different kinds: scribbling, foolscap (cross-ruled and plain), cartridge,
note, letter, foreign letter, blotting, copying, drawing, brown, litmus, and
photo. There would be three kinds of envelopes, an assortment of pens, ink-
stands, and ink (both red and black). And to help complete the stock of sta-

tionery items, there would be copybooks, memorandum books, pencils, and erasers—along with tape, scissors, pins, and three kinds of string: stout, medium, and fine.

Because the expedition would be required upon arrival in Hawai'i to erect and labor within temporary structures, along with the pure scientific equipment there would go building tools: saws, chisels, crowbars, files, screwdrivers, pliers, table vices, soldering irons, hammers, nails—implements of metal that only a century earlier would have been much coveted by stone-age Island natives.

Nor would the expedition lack the accoutrements of English domesticity: knives (table, butcher, and carving), forks (table, carving, and flesh), and spoons; cooking stoves and washbasins; coffee pots and teapots; chairs and stools, bedsteads and mattresses, blankets and sheets; candles, lanterns, lamps, and oil—all would be shipped to Hawai'i. And not just oil for lamps: The astronomers would also bring their own salad oil—together with sauces, herbs, and spices; salt, pepper, and mustard; curry powder, yeast, and vinegar; pickles and raisins; biscuits and bottled fruits (cherries, black currants, red currants, plums, gooseberries, raspberries, rhubarb); almonds and tapioca; figs and dates; butter; and, for hygiene, soap.

And if there were any lingering suspicions that English anatomies would too soon wither in the tropical heat, such sufferings would not emanate from a shortage of well-chosen beverages: wine, brandy, whiskey, orange bitters, ale, Guinness Stout, breakfast claret, dinner sherry, champagne, and more would be supplied. And, lest a simple oversight lead to the denial of the merited libations, a supply of corkscrews would also be sent along.[4]

14

· · · · ·

Gifts

In January of 1873, as transit preparations continued at Greenwich, an adventuresome traveler from George Forbes' native country arrived in Honolulu. Journeying alone, this middle-aged maid from Edinburgh was escaping her homeland for reasons of health and was to spend, like the transit team that was to follow her a year later, six unforgettable months in Hawai'i. Eventually both a distinguished traveler and the first female fellow of the Royal Geographic Society, she would publish such accounts of her travels that they would become minor classics. One would describe her experiences in Hawai'i, where she traveled the Islands by ship and by horseback, from the volcanic fountains of Kīlauea to the fern forests of Kaua'i. Under the title *The Hawaiian Archipelago: Six Months among the Palm Groves, Coral Reefs, and Volcanoes of the Sandwich Islands,* her book would be published in 1875 in London and would be reprinted many times thereafter.[1]

Fig. 22. Isabella Bird

George Forbes knew the woman, at least from afar. Her name was Isabella Bird (Fig. 22). But it was most unfortunate that Bird's account of her experiences in Hawai'i was not sooner available to Forbes and other members of his transit team. Her understanding of Island society, her detailed accounts of Hawaiian geology and botany, her insight into the Islands' sugar industry and its desire for a reciprocity treaty with the United States, her sightings in Hawaiian waters of both British and American "national ships" (a mere euphemism, she thought, for men-of-war), even her description of the Honolulu hotel that would eventually provide a temporary home for members of the transit of Venus expedition—all would have been timely and useful pieces of information to the seven astronomically inclined *malihini* (newcomers) who would soon find themselves immersed in a series of similarly strange scenes on an archipelago extolled by Bird as verdant, fragrant, delicious, sensuous, salubrious, intoxicating.

Forbes in particular would have found especially noteworthy that chapter of her book describing a visit made by King Lunalilo to Hilo, where the king was welcomed with a spectacular *ho'okupu*, an inveterate Hawaiian ritual of gift giving to an *ali'i* (chief) as a sign of honor and respect. Many native Hawaiians traveled to the occasion, some from as far away as 80 miles, all the women wearing flower leis and not a man, woman, or child coming empty-handed. Hundreds of live fowls and hogs; two tons of sweet potatoes and taro; clusters of bananas; and a cornucopia of yams, coconuts, oranges, onions, pumpkins, and pineapples—these, together with leis made of both flowers and feathers, were the *ho'okupu* gifts to Hawai'i's king.

A similar though less lavish *ho'okupu* would be given on the opposite side of the same island in the following year, 1874, to Isabella Bird's star-struck countryman. But although the recipient of that *ho'okupu* would not be as accustomed as a Hawaiian chief to the magnanimity—or the diet—evidenced by the public display of gift giving witnessed by Ms. Bird, he would nevertheless be, in 1874, a momentary chief of things astronomical—and thus in need of some understanding of ritual exercises in a strange land. He would confront soon enough the Polynesian pabulum ceremoniously laid at his feet. But what should he, a respectable gentleman from Scotland, bestow in turn upon the people of Hawai'i?

On May 26, 1874, a week before Forbes' departure from Liverpool, Isabella Bird, now becoming an increasingly sophisticated lady of some reputation, wrote to him from Oban, Scotland, answering these concerns by proffering a list of gifts for Island residents:

> My dear Sir
>
> It is always pleasant to leave some trifling gift as a remembrance with strangers, and in some quarters on the islands, where white people are very poor but insist on giving one accommodation without remuneration, it is really essential. I suppose your gifts must be neither heavy or expensive so I will just suggest any of the following articles, some of which may appear a little queer to your ideas, but would be very acceptable to anyone out of the Capitol.
>
> For any lady ½ a dozen of those "Windsor Scarfs" which are 4/s [4 shillings] a dozen in blue pink and mauve.
>
> Mounted photographs of the best Madonnas, Ecce Homos and Holy Families.
>
> Any of Scotts Poems bound in tartan or white Scotch wood or any portable articles in either.
>
> Any of the innumerable stands or easels for Cartes, or cabinet photos in Austrian gilding morocco or white enamel.
>
> For a gentleman a good knife or better still one of those picnic knives in case which when separated makes a knife and fork
>
> Portable metal drinking cups which draw out. I only saw 2 on the islands.

Plain strong English riding whips, that kind made of plaited things of leather thick at one end and tapering to a whipcord lash.

Bottles of eau de cologne are much valued

Those pretty ornamental cord board flat cases of stationery would make nice presents, as paper and envelopes are enormously dear on the islands, and these two would delight the natives, as well as bright ribbons (2 yards) and bright bandana handkerchiefs. White pocket handkerchiefs please the natives very much too (both sizes) and scizzors.

Hoping some of these suggestions may be useful

Believe me
Very Sincerely Yours
Isabella L. Bird[2]

15

· · · · ·

Instructions

T he seven astronomers bound for Hawai'i would depart from
Liverpool in June, six months before the transit, laden with nearly
100 tons of goods. But they would not escape from their fatherland
without the additional baggage of fatherly advice: Airy's multipage
"Instructions to Observers," just completed in May.[1]

Airy's list of instructions was neatly divided into thirteen sections, each
with its appropriate rubric, and each divided into numbered subsections.

The first section listed the twenty-two observers appointed to the five
chosen districts and indicated how those observers were to be subordinat-
ed. The Sandwich Islands, designated as District B, had three subdivisions:
at Honolulu, Tupman was chief and Nichol and Ramsden were observers;
at Owhyhee (Hawai'i), Forbes was chief and Barnacle was observer; and at
Atooi (Kaua'i), the chief would be Johnson and the observer Noble. In addition to these men, Tupman, who was the general chief of District B, was to
have under his direction three noncommissioned officers or privates of the
Corps of Royal Engineers.

The second section of Airy's instructions required that Tupman write
to the Astronomer Royal at every opportunity with up-to-date reports. It
noted that all books, papers, journals, and notes of observations and calculations related to the expedition were the property of the British
Government and were to be delivered up to Tupman, for deposit at the
Royal Observatory at Greenwich, no later than the day of the observer's
return to England; and further, that observations and calculations were as
a general rule to be written out in duplicate, so that two copies could be
transmitted back to England, each by a different channel. The government
reserved to itself the right of publication of all papers relating to the transit
enterprise.

Section three dealt with the disposition of the huts, instruments, and
stores; and here Airy required that catalogs be made "in the greatest
detail"—and in triplicate—of all movable items, great and small, including
the sequentially numbered parts of the portable buildings. As the purpose
here was to provide a means of ascertaining loss, Airy demanded in addition that another triple set of catalogs be made regarding the external marks
on and the dimensions of boxes and other cargo as they would appear in
transport, in carriages or on ships. And, as with Barnacle's journal, he was
fastidious about the catalogs' details: "Ample room should be left on the

sheet of paper," he wrote, "and vertical columns should be ruled, one for every embarkation, debarkation, or transfer of any kind, room being left at the top of the column for the names of locality, or ship, or carriage, &c., and for date." Transfers of cargo were to be witnessed by an appointed observer who was to mark a "tick" in the catalog for each item. Tupman would be responsible for periodic examinations of the buildings, instruments, and stores. Though the astronomical instruments and their fittings were to be brought back to England "without the smallest omission," other items could be left behind if their value was deemed insufficient to compensate the expense of return transport.

Section four provided instructions for the early conduct of the observers upon arrival at their appointed destination. Here, the chief's first two concerns would be to establish proper relations with "principal persons" and then to select an astronomically appropriate observing site. But, Airy warned, it would probably also be "necessary in an inhabited country [such as Hawai'i] that the [observation] place adopted should be an inclosed space, surrounded by a good wall, and under constant guard"—a warning that would not go unheeded. The foundation of the pier for the transit instrument (and its accompanying clock-tripod) was to be established "without delay." Other instruments and huts could be erected as soon as practicable. Finally, Airy wanted the position of the observing station so defined that it could be recovered "at any future time."

Parts five and six of Airy's instructions set forth the regimen for making observations with the transit instrument and with the altazimuth, observations that were necessary for the determination of the longitude and the latitude. The transit instrument, which was to be checked twice daily for its error of level, was to be employed "on every practicable day" to observe a half dozen or more stars for time. Those observations were then to be fully reduced and the error and rate of the transit clock ascertained. All other clocks and chronometers were to be compared with the transit clock on a daily basis. The transit instrument was to be used as well to observe "every practicable" transit of the moon across the meridian, while the zenith distance of the moon was to be observed with the altazimuth. Zenith distances of stars near the meridian were also to be observed with the altazimuth and those observations immediately reduced for the purpose of determining latitude. Airy also thought it desirable that a distant meridian mark be fixed and observed daily, as the combination of star observations and meridian mark observations would provide a trustworthy method of giving a "zero of azimuth" and, thus, an accurate north-south line.

The adjustment of and practice at the telescopes was briefly treated in part seven of the instructions. Of particular concern to Airy here was the comfort of the observer; and he suggested that the seat at the equatorial telescope(s) be so arranged "that the observer's body and head will be in easy position, especially for the Transit of Venus."

Part eight of the instructions dealt with the working model of the transit, about the general use of which, Airy could hopefully if not confidently write, the observers would by now "scarcely require instruction." He nevertheless urged the observers to remain familiar via the model with the various phenomena at contact, including the black drop, and with the expected times of these appearances; and he urged that their practice observations include work with a double-image micrometer.

Practice with the photoheliograph and its attached Janssen must be kept up, Airy insisted in part nine; and at least one photographic print on paper should be made from each day's practice. The precise photographic procedure on transit day was described in part eleven: The Janssen was to be mounted at the appropriate moment, the winch turned, the seconds counted, and the series of exposures made. When "the crisis" (at contact) was past, the Janssen was to be dismounted and the sun pictures begun. Complete sun pictures were to be taken throughout the duration of the transit—at intervals, Airy suggested, of about two minutes—and for every picture, the time was to be recorded "with the utmost accuracy" by the photographer and his assistant working in tandem and using a chronometer that had been compared with the transit-clock. The photographic plates were to be diamond-scratched with numbers. As soon as practicable, three prints were to be made of every photograph; and then the glass plates were to be "most carefully packed and jealously preserved."

The more general observations of the transit of Venus were treated in part ten. While at least four persons were required at the photoheliograph, at least two were required at each telescope—and there must be, in addition, "several persons to guard against intrusions." If there were any lingering doubts as to whence those ghostly persons might appear, Airy did his best to banish them: "If . . . [a] British ship is lying in the neighbourhood, the officers and others of the crew will undoubtedly give their best assistance." At least two hours before transit time, sentinels were to be placed to prevent the approach or admission of strangers. With regard to the behavior of the principal observer(s) at the telescopes, Airy wrote a characteristically paternalistic prescription: He "will have his eye at the telescope . . . his body and his head . . . in convenient and unstrained positions, and . . . both his hands . . . at liberty." The observer's assistant, Airy thought, needed similar admonition: For recording data such as times or micrometer readings, he must have "a book in a convenient position, and a pen or pencil whose point is verified as fit for clear writing." The chief would order "Silence!" as the critical time neared. To the first perhaps hastily made written record of the transit observations could be added details from memory after the fleeting phenomenon had passed. Then the various entries in the observing book were to be copied in triplicate without damage to the originals, which were to be "carefully preserved."

Part twelve of the instructions required that the chief of District B, Captain Tupman, have his headquarters and his fundamental determination of longitude by altazimuth at Honolulu. From Honolulu, Tupman was to send chronometers to and from Hawai'i and Kaua'i for the purpose of determining the difference between their longitudes and that of Honolulu, availing himself of the services of British or local ships. If other observers of the transit of Venus were located in the Hawaiian archipelago, Tupman was ordered to assist them in ascertaining their longitude(s) relative to Honolulu, Airy noting that it was "very desirable, for other wants as well as for the Transit of Venus, that these longitudes be accurately determined." And although Airy was not hopeful of making "chronometric communication" with San Francisco, he did not rule out the possibility of Tupman making a longitudinal connection with that city.[2]

At the time of the transit, Airy noted in the last part of his instructions, the British commissioner and consul general at Honolulu would be Major J. Hay Wodehouse. It was Wodehouse to whom Tupman was to refer for diplomatic communications.

16

· · · · ·

Military and Political Maneuvers

I n 1874, diplomatic communications between Britain and Hawai'i had been barely a half century in the full fire. For the half century before that, they had been sputtering at best. Relations between the two island nations, kindled by Captain Cook, had been vigorously stoked sixteen years later when, during a visit by Captain George Vancouver to Kealakekua Bay in 1794, Hawai'i's King Kamehameha I formally ceded the island of Hawai'i to Great Britain.[1] What followed, however, in the wake of a visit to England in 1824 by Kamehameha's successor King Liholiho and his queen, Kamāmalu, better demonstrated the tenuous nature of the British-Hawaiian flame. After the royal couple contracted measles during their visit and succumbed, their bodies were respectfully returned to Hawai'i aboard the British frigate *Blonde,* under the command of Lord George Byron, cousin of the poet. But preceding the *Blonde* and the royal remains by a few short weeks came Richard Charlton, the first British consul commissioned to the Sandwich Islands. Charlton's appointment was a tacit recognition of Hawai'i's independence, Britain never having acted to ratify Kamehameha's cession to Vancouver.[2]

Fig. 23. The tomb of Lunalilo ka Moi (Lunalilo the King) in the Kawaiaha'o Churchyard in Honolulu

Hawai'i was still an independent kingdom when Charlton's post was filled by James Hay Wodehouse. Appointed to the office in 1866,[3] Wodehouse, a royalist sympathizer, retired only after the forced abdication of Hawai'i's last monarch, Queen Lili'uokalani, and eventually returned to England in 1897.[4] In the interim, and in the midst of considerable political and economic uncertainty in the Islands, the 1874 transit of Venus brought to Hawai'i, as if directly from a London stage, its own inimitable cast of characters and its own high drama.

On February 3, 1874, eight years after the beginning of Wodehouse's tenure, Hawai'i's penultimate king, Lunalilo, died after a reign of only

Fig. 24. King David Kalākaua

thirteen months and was buried in Honolulu at the Kawaiahaʻo Churchyard (Fig. 23), literally steps from where the British astronomers would set up their transit of Venus observatory in seven short months. As Lunalilo had not named a successor, the issue passed to Hawaiʻi's legislature, which, on February 12, elected David Kalākaua (Fig. 24) as Hawaiʻi's next—and last—king. When the result of the vote was announced, a riot ensued at the legislative chambers in Honolulu, instigated by the supporters of Kalākaua's rival to the throne, Dowager Queen Emma, who had lost the election by a wide margin. Property was destroyed. At least one man died. Island law enforcement officials were unable—or unwilling—to still the pandemonium. And Hawaiʻi's militia was feeble. Amidst the tumult, however, Kalākaua, Charles R. Bishop (minister of Foreign Affairs), and John Dominis (governor of Oʻahu and brother-in-law of Kalākaua) asked U.S. minister Henry A. Pierce and British commissioner Wodehouse for military assistance. One hundred and fifty men were marched into town from the U.S. warships *Portsmouth* and *Tuscarora* that lay in Honolulu Harbor. Seventy or eighty came from HMS *Tenedos*. By the next day, the town was quiet, and Kalākaua took the oath of office. But lasting peace was still not assured, and the appearance of the *Tenedos* in Hawaiian waters would continue, to some eyes, to be a welcome sight.[5]

Minister Pierce, an erstwhile Honolulu businessman, was an ardent fan neither of Hawaiʻi's native population nor the new native king. He gloomily predicted, from Kalākaua's election, a decline in the prosperity of the fragile island kingdom, intimating perhaps most especially a weakening of the economic position of "foreigners" precariously positioned among native Hawaiian "tigers" capable of violence. No sooner, then, had Kalākaua ascended the throne than eighty merchants and others petitioned Pierce for protection; and on his recommendation, the U.S. Navy assigned five warships to visit Honolulu in strict rotation.[6]

But the American sailors would not be alone in the neighborhood. As early as January of 1874, as one Honolulu newspaper was printing information on the approaching transit, it was already noting that in the Pacific Ocean and stationed on the line of observation that extended from India to New Zealand there would be, for one purpose or another, more than thirty ships of war.[7]

The British transit of Venus expedition would itself arrive in Hawaiʻi in September, courtesy of the British Navy. Before it reached Honolulu, fifty supporters of the Anglophile Queen Emma who had rioted in February would be tried—and forty jailed. In the meantime, King Kalākaua, who had pledged himself and his government to "the advancement of agriculture and commerce," would be planning a trip to the United States to bring his personal influence to bear on the question of a reciprocity treaty—a treaty that would allow Hawaiian sugar to enter the U.S. market duty free, and a treaty that Kalākaua hoped would be possible without the cession of the much-coveted Pearl Harbor. He would be the first reigning Hawaiian monarch to leave the Islands since Liholiho had gone to London a half century earlier to have his eyes forever closed by a foreign disease. He would produce results both potent and historic.[8] Astronomically, however, his trip could not have been more poorly timed.

It was against this unsettled—and unsettling—backdrop that British commissioner Wodehouse, more full of concern for Hawai'i's continued independence as a sovereign nation than of her role in the approaching astrodrama, wrote these ominous words to the Earl of Derby:

> Honolulu
> April 30. 1874.
>
> My Lord,
> I have the honour to inform Y L [Your Lordship] that the trial of the rioters of the 12th of Feb . . . passed off quietly. . . . [But] As the present position of Affairs cannot be regarded as settled & as an admiral of well known annexationalist proclivities, wh: [which] he has made no scruple of concealing, has just been app^{d} [appointed] to the command of this station & who it is said will make Honolulu his head quarters, I think it very advisable that the English Naval Flag . . . be displayed here as frequently as possible, as an evidence of the continued interest taken by HMG. [Her Majesty's Government] in the welfare & independence of the Sandwich Islands. . . .
>
> The "passive presence" of the Brit flag at the present juncture w^{d} [would] be invaluable.
>
> It follows as a matter of course I may remark that if the Hawaiians see only one flag in there [sic] waters & that the flag of a power wh: [which] they credit with a desire to "swallow them up," they will come to the conclusion that England does not care what becomes of them & will prepare themselves for their fate.[9]

Wodehouse's premonitory warnings of the rise of a palpable American influence in Hawai'i, especially in the absence of an English naval flag, were to be repeated less than a year later, as the last of the transit of Venus party, after a six-month sojourn in the Islands, was preparing to depart.

17

· · · · ·

A Royal Reception

In June of 1874, Venus, having passed superior conjunction several months earlier, was approaching greatest eastern elongation (see appendix C, Fig. C.1).[1] Now prominent in the western sky at sunset time, this resplendent planet, the brightest of the anciently denominated *wandering stars,* would have easily attracted the attention of the seven-member British transit of Venus team as they crossed the Atlantic, in two contingents, beneath dark and star-filled skies. Barnacle, Noble, and Ramsden—all under the charge of George Forbes—embarked from Liverpool aboard the steamship *Illimani* on June 3, laden for their task with 64 tons and 146 boxes of goods. The remaining baggage and the other members of the expedition—Tupman, Johnson, and Nichol—followed aboard the *Britannia* when it weighed anchor from the same port two weeks later on June 17. After passing through the Straits of Magellan, the two vessels called at Valparaiso, Chile, where the traveling cargo, both human and material, was transferred to HMS *Scout.* From Valparaiso, both Tupman and Forbes wrote to Airy, Forbes reporting that the transfer of the baggage from the *Illimani* to the *Scout* had been accomplished without any loss or breakage, Tupman groaning that the final leg of the journey to Hawai'i would probably be somewhat delayed as the expedition's baggage aboard the *Britannia* had been buried under a quantity of cargo in the hold of the ship![2]

Fig. 25. Transit of Venus party, Honolulu

At last, on August 4, the *Scout,* captained by Ralph P. Cator, embarked for Honolulu with the full transit of Venus party including the seven astronomers, three sappers,[3] and one private servant. The *Scout*—which was not unfamiliar with Hawaiian waters, having been anchored at Honolulu alongside the American warships *California* and *Benicia*

Fig. 26. The Hawaiian Hotel

when Isabella Bird arrived in January of the previous year[4]—was a 1,461-ton vessel built in 1856 and carried a 275-man crew.[5] Together with HMS *Tenedos* and HMS *Reindeer,* the *Scout* would provide invaluable service to the transit party during the upcoming months.

After a five-week journey, the *Scout* anchored in Honolulu Harbor at 5 P.M. on September 9. The following day, the transit party (Fig. 25) disembarked and took their billet at the Hawaiian Hotel (Fig. 26) and Tupman, following Airy's instructions, forthwith began his attempts to establish good relations with "principal persons" of the town. Airy's earlier intimations that an English expedition would be well received in Hawai'i were almost prescient, and Tupman would within a week write to the Astronomer Royal with much happy news:

Hawaiian Hotel, Honolulu
1874 Sept 17

My dear Sir,

It is with very great pleasure I write to inform you of the safe arrival here of the H.M.S. "Scout" bearing the whole of the "Transit" Expedition. We arrived Sept. 9, having made a very quiet and quick passage of 35 1/2 days.

I immediately called upon Major Woodhouse [*sic*], Her Majesty's Commissioner, who kindly conducted me to the Minister of the Interior, the Governor of Oahu and other officials and persons of distinction, all of whom accorded me a courteous welcome and expressed their desire to afford every possible assistance to the Expedition.

The Hawaiian Government was pleased to allow all our stores to be landed without examination & free of all duties and allowed them to be temporarily located in the Customs House Stores. I need hardly say that this courteous action greatly facilitated our operations.[6]

At the time of the expedition's arrival in the Islands, King Kalākaua had occupied the throne a mere seven months. But the neophyte monarch was by no means a newcomer to astronomy. Educated at the Royal School in Honolulu as a youth, he had received instruction there in the *Rudiments of Natural Philosophy and Astronomy,* authored by the well-known Yale author and pioneer in the study of meteor showers, Denison Olmsted.[7] Chester Smith Lyman, later Olmsted's colleague at Yale, had also taught at the Royal School in the 1840s during Kalākaua's student days there and while in the Islands had even made (as Tupman would soon discover) some useful astronomical observations.[8] Now, some three decades later, as Professor Lyman prepared for his own transit-day observations in far-away New Haven, King David Kalākaua was about to re-enter his life under circumstances that no one could have anticipated.

King Kalākaua evidenced, early on, a considerable personal interest in the transit of Venus operations. Within the very first week of their presence in Hawai'i, the members of the expedition were formally received by the king at his palace in Honolulu. Tupman's letter continues:

> At His Majesty's request we were all presented to him, Sept 15. I considered it my duty to express our thanks to His Majesty for the nature of our reception here—the cordial welcome and generous assistance accorded us by His Majesty himself, his Ministers and every one with whom we had been brought into contact. His Majesty was pleased to read an exceedingly graceful reply, expressing the pleasure our visit gave him, and his earnest wish to assist us to the utmost.

The expedition's presence in the Islands soon created a stir in the local newspapers, as well as in private correspondence. Before the end of September, James Wodehouse would provide the earl of Derby with the latest transit news from the other side of the world, including a newspaper extract from the *Hawaiian Gazette.* He would also furnish an explanation for King Kalākaua's remarkable conduct: Not only had the king taken such "great pleasure" in the return to Honolulu of HMS *Scout* that he had placed a house of his own at Captain Cator's disposal, but, after Wodehouse had personally thanked him on behalf of the British Government for the courtesies accorded to the transit party, he had replied: "I am under obligations to The Queen for selecting my Islands as one of the points of observation."[9]

The transit of Venus operations in Hawai'i clearly could not escape their political context; and had a man with Wodehouse's eyes and ears furnished the earl of Derby with a description of the gathering at the palace on September 15, he likely would have portrayed it as more of a political whirl than as an event charged with scientific meaning. The credentials of the individuals in attendance would have made such a portrait easy. The honorees were not, after all, wholly British scientists. They were British military men. And they were met and matched at the palace by men of a distinctly nonscientific sort: Nahaolelua (minister of finance), Green (minister of the Interior), Stanley (attorney general), Dominis (governor of Oʻahu), Kanoa (governor of Kauaʻi), Allen (chief justice), Judd (colonel), and Prendergast (major)—these—along with the king, his brother (Prince Leleiohoku), and his brother-in-law (Archibald Cleghorn)—were among the men who greeted the transit team and its naval escort.[10]

Under the circumstances, and considering the credentials of his own entourage, it was much to his credit that Kalākaua managed a salutation that was both "exceedingly graceful" and scientifically informed:

> It gives me great pleasure to receive you and the members of the expedition sent by Her Majesty Queen Victoria to observe the approaching transit of the planet Venus across the Sun's disk. I have requested My Ministers, and through them all the officers of My Government, to grant you every facility in their power, in carrying out the very important objects which you have in your charge. I trust you will not hesitate at once to inform them of anything that you may require to facilitate your operations.
>
> It will afford me unfeigned satisfaction if My Kingdom can add its quota towards the successful accomplishment of the most important astronomical observation of the present century, and assist, however humbly, the enlightened nations of the earth in these costly enterprises to establish the basis of astronomical distances.[11]

When a local newspaper made the king's words public, friendly though formal efforts at rapprochement seemed well underway. But what was privately written was another matter. And whatever Captain Tupman may have initially felt about Kalākaua's informed and respectful demeanor, his privately recorded sentiments toward Hawaiʻi and its king would begin to sour in the days ahead.

18

· · · · ·

The Observatory at 'Āpua

After his successful social foraging, Captain Tupman's next official concern was the selection and fortification of some appropriate site(s) for observing the impending transit. But numerous friendly hands again extended assistance and advice, and soon Tupman could tell Airy:

> After consultation with numerous residents, well able to advise in the matter, I saw no reason to alter the original choice of Honolulu itself for the Head Station. Some difficulty was experienced in finding a suitable place of observation, as I considered it of great importance that the observers should be lodged very close to the instruments; and house accommodation is rather limited. However we have been enabled to rent a cottage [Fig. 27] belonging to the Princess Ruth, Governess of Molokai, capable of accommodating the Head Station observers, and adjoining some land owned by His Majesty the King who has kindly given us permission to erect our instruments Etc. and enclose as much land as may be necessary.
>
> The site is probably as good as could be found on the Island and . . . it is admirably suited to the purpose.[1]

Fig. 27. Honuakaha Hale, the temporary quarters of the Head Station observers in Honolulu

Tupman was properly impressed by his good fortune. The site offered by Kalākaua was an "open piece of grass land in the district called Apua . . . south of Punchbowl Street and west of Queen Street"[2] and boasted an area of approximately 1,600 square yards. Here, not far from the waterfront, an observatory could command an unobstructed view of the southwestern sky where the setting sun, on the day of the transit, would be visible to within "half a degree of the horizon."[3]

On September 14, Tupman began the task of enclosing the land with a wooden fence, erecting sheds, and laying off the meridian. Digging deeply, he would eventually strike coral beneath some 4 feet of light sandy soil, and the foundation for the astronomical instruments would be laid atop a bed of marine skeletons.[4] Soon a well-equipped astronomical observatory—complete with a transit instrument, a photoheliograph, an altazimuth, two equatorial telescopes, several clocks, and a platform for observing the transit of Venus model—would appear on the Honolulu plain (Figs. 28 to 40); and water, a critical item for photographic and other purposes—including fire protection—would be accessed by pipes from the road nearby.[5]

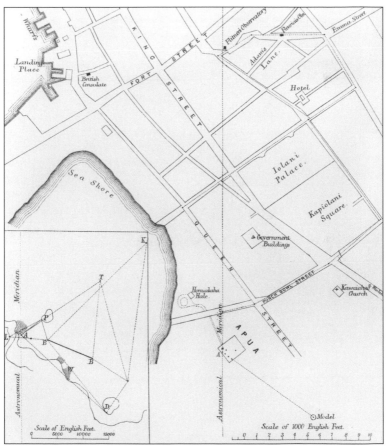

Fig. 28. The location of the observatory at ʻĀpua. The Flitner and Fleuriais observatories are seen to the north, just east of the astronomical meridian. The inset (lower left) shows the position of the observatory relative to some principal points of the Government Trigonometrical Survey: P is Punchbowl, T is Tantalus, K is Konahuanui, D is Diamond Head, and W is Waikīkī.

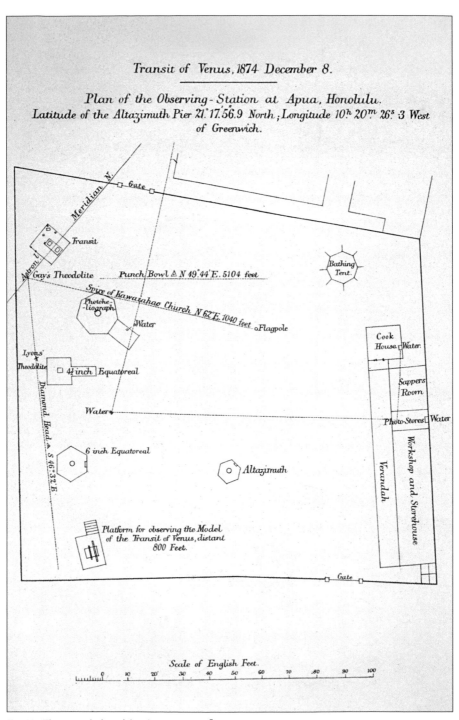

Fig. 29. The ground plan of the observatory at 'Āpua

Fig. 30. Modern survey mark on the summit of Diamond Head

Fig. 31. The model stage (left), the 6-inch equatorial hut (right), and the altazimuth hut (right foreground) as seen from within the observatory at ʻĀpua

Fig. 32. The Long Shed. Fronted by a veranda, this building included, under a single roof, a sappers' barrack, a storehouse, and a workshop. The smaller detached shed on the left was the cookhouse. Note the water hose in the foreground.

Fig. 33. The bathing tent, cookhouse, and sappers' barrack (left to right)

Fig. 34. Practice with the transit of Venus model at Honolulu

Fig. 35. The transit instrument and its companion clock

80

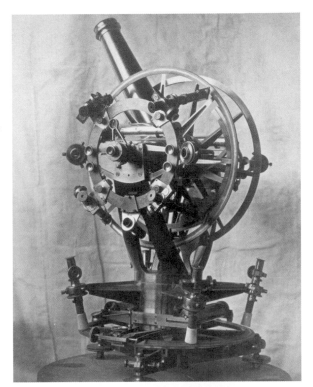

Fig. 37. An altazimuth by Troughton & Simms for Station E

Fig. 36. The clock used to record Tupman's observations of internal contact

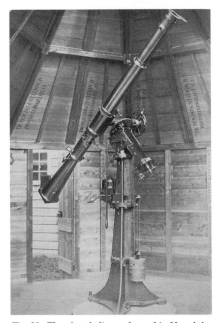

Fig. 38. The photoheliograph used in Honolulu

81

Fig. 39. The 6-inch refractor by T. Cooke and Sons

A rigorous practice regimen soon became the order of the day at Honolulu,[6] and among the assortment of tasks with which Tupman kept his men busy was the continued practice with the transit of Venus model (Fig.

34). A stage was erected within the observatory enclosure and a table placed on top. The model itself stood in horse pastureland outside the enclosure at a carefully measured 800 feet from the front edge of the table, the distance between them having been taken multiple times over the flat and grassy terrain.[7] When the 6-inch and the 4.5-inch telescopes were removed from their mountings and laid on the table with their objectives projecting a little over the edge, their distances to the model could be known to within a fraction of a foot. By using a mirror mounted on a separate tripod, an assistant could reflect sunlight through the triangular opening in the model, past the sheet-brass image of Venus, and into the

Fig. 40. Tupman at the telescope in Honolulu

telescopes, which, as they lay on the table atop the distant stage, were some 8 or 9 feet above the ground. A roof of rushes protected the on-stage observers and their instruments from the direct and fierce illumination of the tropical sun, while a wood and canvass screen provided a shady shelter for the man at the model.

As at Greenwich, practice with the model at Honolulu demonstrated no material difference among the various observers' appreciation of the exact moment of contact, no matter which telescope was employed, provided that the magnification was 100 times or better. Suitable experiments found that the time of internal contact as observed from the telescope was within a small fraction of a second of the true time of contact at the mechanical model.[8]

Photographic labors produced similar success—and several bonuses—as Ramsden, using the photoheliograph from the stage, practiced exposing Janssen plates on the model with good results.[9] But he did this only after he had turned his camera elsewhere. And by the time the camera had completed its inspection of the scene at 'Āpua, an assortment of gratuitous but well-aimed photographs would be produced, giving an unmatched pictorial record of the Honolulu proceedings.[10]

19

· · · · ·

The Adversities of Nature and Society

For the seven telescope-toting natives of the temperate British Isles, adaptation to the tropical Sandwich Isles was a physical requirement, whatever the psychological hazards to a polite display of English equanimity. Tupman's first letter to Airy had already contained a muffled complaint about the heat—and this despite the fact that the expedition had arrived in Honolulu only two weeks before the autumnal equinox, not at the height of a tropical summer. "I find it very trying running about all day in the sun," he had written on September 17, "but it is the only way of getting the work done."[1]

The wooden huts at 'Āpua, once erected, provided some shelter but little respite from the penetrating heat. For the photographic work, this was a particularly alarming circumstance; and Tupman, finding the heat of the darkroom "intolerable," finally had it covered with a roof of rushes.[2] Although other structures, including the transit hut, were similarly cooled (Fig. 41), a single roof for the photographic room was not enough. The photographic chemicals continued to suffer from the unaccustomed warmth

Fig. 41. Photo hut and transit hut covered with rushes to counter the tropical heat

Fig. 42. Coconut tree crashes down within 6 feet of the transit clock

until a second roof of rushes, erected over the first, reduced the temperature another ten degrees.[3]

But Mother Nature was not so easily subdued. In Nu'uanu Valley—just a short distance from Honolulu Harbor—she was simply biding her time and refitting her arsenal. Before October was out, she would produce enough wet weather to transform a hot town into a steamy one. And in the weeks and months to follow, she would regularly give Tupman good cause for his private—and frequently repeated—lamentations over her moist outpourings.[4] In November, she was especially generous in this respect, unleashing at Nu'uanu a cumulative rainfall of 23.99 inches. It was the wettest month of 1874 at that location[5]—and it was more than wet at the observatory nearby. On one occasion, more than a foot of rain pummeled the 'Āpua site within a twenty-four-hour period,[6] and Tupman's sagging disposition grew increasingly droopy under the dependable inundations. "We had a terrible southerly storm," he sighed to Airy, "from Nov 17 to 22 inclusive with incessant heavy rain." On the night of November 20, rain fell at the rate of an inch an hour for more than twelve hours. The water at the observatory rose to knee deep until the floors of some of the huts began to float. It wasn't until morning that the sappers, perceiving the danger, cut a big trench from the middle of the ground and under the fence. It took the water two hours to run off.[7]

But such elemental floggings were now becoming routine. Earlier in the month, on November 2, a sudden gale of wind had nearly crushed one of the observatory's most critical parts, toppling a coconut tree over 90 feet in length. Cutting the palings of the observatory enclosure in two places, the towering behemoth had bludgeoned down within 6 feet of the transit clock, nearly eliminating the "Time department"[8] (Fig. 42).

Throbbing heat, merciless rain, indiscriminate wind, pulverizing palms: If Nature had big surprises, she also had little ones—mosquitoes. Having come to plague this Pacific paradise only after the arrival of Captain Cook, they were now poised to exact a sort of Montezuma's revenge upon Cook's nineteenth-century cousins.[9] And when it came time to sit quietly engaged in the required mathematical calculations and computations, a miniature army of buzzing bloodsuckers made the work "almost impossible." Nichol's face and hands became a feasting place, covered with sores; and Ramsden couldn't sit at the table five minutes.[10]

But if Nature could be indelicate in her disruptions, so too could society—especially one that was, to European eyes, both technologically impoverished and scientifically ill informed. Tupman, now caught up with his men as in the opening scenes of a burlesque, couldn't restrain a growl. "Numerous inhabitants," he wrote to Airy, "imagine we have come all this way on purpose to satisfy their curiosity to see Saturn's Rings and Jupiter's belts through a telescope."[11] And if the commoners could be this bad, the king could be even worse. As early as September 21, His Majesty had already paid a private visit to the observatory and inspected the work going on[12]—a mere prelude, as it proved, to the numerous regal interruptions that would occur over the next several months. And although Tupman thought that the obtrusiveness of unwanted visitors—ministers of state, foreign representatives, captains of men-of-war, and, perhaps most especially, members of the royal family—wasted a great deal of valuable time, he felt obliged to "give up work" for many of them, and he did.[13] Even so, the visit of October 3 must have caused his teetering equanimity to be especially tilted: "His Majesty paid us a private visit in the evening and remained 2 hours. He proposed that as soon as all the Instruments were mounted we should throw open the grounds to the public for a week at a charge of a dollar or so a-head and he would send his Military Band down every day!"[14]

Whether or not such suggestions were given or taken seriously, Tupman understood that he and his scientific cohorts were the king's guests in the king's backyard. And so, on the afternoon October 31, and despite the fact that it "poured with rain the whole day without a moment's cessation," some 150 ladies and gentlemen, having obtained tickets through "influential persons," were admitted to the observatory grounds[15]—and a little corner of Honolulu, where some high-minded men were now encamped to make "the most important astronomical observation" of the nineteenth century, thus became to Tupman's great annoyance a site for simple-minded merrymaking.

20

· · · · ·

Measuring Heaven and Earth

B ecause the precise location of the transit of Venus station in Honolulu was a major concern to the success of the overall enterprise, much care was taken in the determination of its geographic coordinates—coordinates that were established astronomically, though they had a genuine down-to-earth application that extended well beyond the fleeting events of 1874. Indeed, the obsession with the concept of location that had teased Captain Cook across Polynesia in the eighteenth century, with its mathematically seductive alliance between *positional astronomy* and *positional geography,* was now rising ominously in the mid–North Pacific like a twin-headed femme fatale.

As a mathematical discipline, positional geography may be divided into the three subdisciplines of navigation, surveying, and cartography. But all such geographic disciplines were, historically, subordinates of astronomy, the most advanced and prestigious of the mathematical sciences at the time of the European Renaissance.[1] Because the methods and instruments of astronomy formed the foundation of these other mathematical sciences, the navigational and cartographic talents displayed by Captain Cook in 1778 when he happened upon the Hawaiian Islands at the tail end of Europe's Age of Discovery had resulted from this long mathematically inclined tradition, a tradition that was as geometric as it was geographic. It was a tradition that was to continue into the nineteenth century, as the 1874 transit of Venus demonstrated, again, not only the paramount importance of astronomy to mundane concerns but the increasing attention paid, in Hawai'i, to one of its more practical and socially divisive derivatives: surveying. For in Hawai'i, as elsewhere, land measurement—literally "geometry"—would imply land division.[2]

With great punctiliousness, then, the geographic coordinates of the observatory at 'Āpua were determined—but not only to secure the desired celestial measurements. There were terrestrial purposes as well, and they were clear: They were to serve as "a point of reference for the Trigonometrical Survey of the kingdom of Hawaii undertaken by the Government of His Majesty King Kalakaua."[3] This survey, which began only in 1870,[4] was by 1874 deemed to be in good hands. It had been placed "under the able management"[5] of an erstwhile professor of astronomy at O'ahu College, W. D. Alexander (Fig. 43).

The principal objects of the Government Survey were three in number:

Fig. 43. Professor William DeWitt Alexander, surveyor general

(1) To construct an accurate general map of the Hawaiian Kingdom (the existing maps, having been founded on the original charts of Cook and Vancouver, abounded in "gross errors"); (2) To fix permanently and accurately a large number of points of reference upon which local surveys could be based and by which they could be interconnected; and (3) To produce a map of each district *(moku)* and show the contents and boundaries of its principal subdivisions *(ahupua'a* and *'ili)*. In sum, the Government Survey, "being founded on accurate trigonometrical and astronomical measurements," was intended as a survey of the "landed property" of the kingdom. But it was a foreign system of land division, subdivision, and distribution. The Great Mahele of 1848, during the reign of Kamehameha III, had already resulted in contentious land apportionments. Because of the lack of surveyors in the Islands at the time, the division *(mahele)* had been made without any islandwide survey whatsoever. Now, as the Islands were being surveyed, measured, and divided up with mathematical precision—and with a determination heretofore unknown in Hawai'i—an even further muddling of property lines was the predictable result. Much of the land in the kingdom, including most of the *ahupua'a* (slices of land that extended, ideally, from the mountains to the sea), had never been previously surveyed at all, while the *kuleana* (small pieces of land awarded to the common people) had been surveyed without uniformity, in a hasty and fragmentary manner, and by incompetent surveyors with inferior instruments; and the existing chaos had brought forth "much troublesome uncertainty and litigation." The confusion and discord, the antipathy and land grabbing consequent upon the parceling of Hawai'i's tiny amount of real estate was to continue into the 1870s and beyond.[6]

Still, by early 1874, Surveyor General Alexander was already anticipating the arrival of the transit of Venus expedition, expecting that it would render "invaluable assistance" to the Hawaiian Government Survey by obtaining and sharing latitude and longitude measurements "with a degree of accuracy never before attained in these islands."[7]

The assiduity that would characterize the efforts of the transit of Venus expedition in the determination of latitude and longitude had already been set forth in Airy's instructions to the expedition's members; and the instruments that they brought to Honolulu—especially the transit instrument, the altazimuth, and the multiple timepieces—were strongly indicative that the simple observation of Venus against the sun was not their sole concern. This was no better evidenced than when, with the assistance of James W. Gay, surveyor of Honolulu, the British transit of Venus station at 'Āpua was connected by theodolite and chain to two other observatories in downtown Honolulu, only one of which—that belonging to David Flitner—could be readily found.[8]

The precise whereabouts of Honolulu's other observatory was more problematic. Six years earlier, between October and December of 1868, M. G. Fleuriais, a French naval officer interested in determining Honolulu's longitudinal distance from Paris, had made a series of astronomical observations from downtown Honolulu, the results of which were published in the 1872 edition of *Connaissance des Temps,* France's counterpart to England's *Nautical Almanac.*[9] But by 1874, Fleuriais' observatory had all but disappeared.

Tupman instituted a search, and within a few days surveyor Gay hit paydirt. Writing to Tupman from the British Club of Honolulu, Gay hinted of the existence of a valuable ruin of coral, brick, and wood just discovered beneath the city's streets.[10] The foundations of Fleuriais' transit pier were still recognizable, resting upon coral, 5 feet below the surface. Using a theodolite and chain, Gay ran a traverse along the streets from the observatory at 'Āpua to Fleuriais' pier—and Flitner's nearby—and then back again by a different route (see Fig. 28). The three observatories were now interconnected to within a foot or less.[11]

Tupman, cognizant of the importance of his discovery, took proper precautions to preserve it. To prevent the site from being lost, he built upon it a small square pier of brick and cement up to within 18 inches of the surface of the ground and deposited "a bottle containing a paper."[12]

The recovery and reconstruction of Fleuriais' observatory site proved to be an excellent investment. The longitude figure derived therefrom was of "great value,"[13] and the expenses, including the cost of hired labor, had amounted to only $16.[14]

As for David Flitner's observatory, it had more than a simple surveyor's connection to the British transit of Venus work, and Flitner was himself to become a welcome addition the transit enterprise. Known for his business (Fig. 44) of selling nautical instruments and charts, adjusting sextants and quadrants, repairing fine watches, and, perhaps most importantly, rating chronometers "by observations of the sun and stars, with a transit instrument accurately adjusted to the meridian of Honolulu,"[15] Flitner would

Fig. 44. David Flitner's business in Honolulu

eventually lend six chronometers to the transit of Venus expedition to assist in the longitude operations.[16] He would visit the observatory at ʻĀpua.[17] And he would observe the transit of Venus from Waikīkī. Tupman appreciated and cultivated Flitner's friendship and even spent some time at his observatory—an observatory that had a curiously interesting history, one of which Tupman himself was not fully aware.

Fig. 45. Chester Smith Lyman

The story of Flitner's observatory began in 1845 when another man, E. H. Boardman, established a transit instrument in Honolulu to assist in the work of rating chronometers. The instrument, imported and expensive, was sheltered by a small observatory building modeled after a Grecian temple. Situated near the corner of Union and Hotel streets, it subsequently became the property of David Flitner. But the longitude of Flitner's Observatory (as it had become known by the 1860s) had been established in the 1840s with such accuracy that in 1874 it was still being used by Hawaiʻi's surveyor general. More remarkable still, the man responsible for helping Boardman establish the longitude of his observatory with such precision, C. S. Lyman (Fig. 45), had become such a friend to Hawaiʻi's royal children that he would soon see one of them—David (now King) Kalākaua—at his New Haven home.[18] But he would also soon see something else by which history would better remember him. Twenty-eight years after visiting Hawaiʻi, in December of 1874, and as the British observing team in Hawaiʻi awaited the appearance of Venus against the sun, Lyman, by then a professor of astronomy at Yale, would be observing the same planet from a Yale observatory.[19]

21

· · · · ·

Kailua-Kona

When, shortly after the British expedition's arrival in Honolulu, Tupman wrote to Airy from the Hawaiian Hotel, he mentioned that the cottage belonging to Princess Ruth—Honuakaha Hale—would soon be occupied by the Head Station observers, but that the observers destined for the auxiliary stations would remain at the hotel.[1] This arrangement could not have been the cause of any grievous lamentation by those so assigned, for the Hawaiian Hotel was easily the more sybaritic of the two. In January of the previous year, Isabella Bird had written to her sister from the same hotel, describing her temporary domicile as "the perfection" of a hotel: a long, stone, two-storied house with its never-closed door and its two deep verandas festooned with clematis and passion flowers set amidst the welcoming embrace of ocean and mountain scenery, tropical trees, rainbows, scented breezes, starry skies, and other sensuous charms. Complete with a delicious dining room serving strangely exotic vegetables, fishes, and fruits and possessing a racially varied staff—German, American, Hawaiian, Chinese—the recently built Hawaiian Hotel seemed to Ms. Bird to be the great public resort of Honolulu, enlivened with English and American naval uniforms, health seekers from California, whaling captains, tourists, and townspeople percolating through its confines.[2] It was into this enchanted scene that Bird's fellow Scot, George Forbes, had been momentarily plunged; and it was from the Hawaiian Hotel that he would write a dreamy letter to James Clerk Maxwell on the daunting subject of action-at-a-distance and its cosmological implications.[3]

But Forbes had little time for such impracticalities as the month of October drew to a close. Information regarding suitable ancillary observing sites on islands other than Oʻahu had been secured; and although several alternatives—Kealakekua Bay (Hawaiʻi), Haleakalā (Maui), and the island of Niʻihau—were considered, the choice in the end settled upon Kailua-Kona (Hawaiʻi) and Waimea (Kauaʻi).[4]

Henry Barnacle was destined to depart with Forbes for the Kailua-Kona station in early November, and by the last week in October the portable transit instrument[5] assigned to them was being dismantled and readied for transport aboard the *Scout*. Earlier, the same instrument had been erected in the garden of the Hawaiian Hotel so that Barnacle might have what Forbes deemed some still-needed practice.[6] But the practice had been of little avail. Barnacle's observations continued to be unsatisfactory, and "his reductions showed such ignorance of the elements of astronomy," Forbes wrote privately in his journal, "that I gave up thought of wasting time by attempting to instruct him."[7]

But by now Forbes' unflattering assessment of Barnacle's practice at the transit instrument had found a parallel in his practice elsewhere, and Tupman had mused in private: "Mr. Barnacle is apparently out of his mind. Nothing will induce him to discontinue playing the same tune over and over again on the piano forte. I doubt if I ought to send him back to England immediately, as it is almost impossible to get any work of him & no faith can be placed in anything he says."[8] Still, Tupman's ambivalence—and his indecision—persisted.

On the morning of November 2, King Kalākaua boarded the *Scout* to say good-bye to Forbes and to give him two letters: one from himself to the Honorable Simon Ka'ai at Kailua, the representative of that district; the other from Princess Ruth to the custodian of her house at Kailua-Kona, the princess having granted permission to the transit party to use her residence there.[9] Then, shortly after 10 A.M., the ship carrying the Forbes-Barnacle team weighed anchor and proceeded under steam out of Honolulu Harbor, where she had been moored since her arrival on September 9. At daybreak the following day, the vessel made land off the island of Hawai'i and, after a brief layover at Hilo, at last dropped anchor on November 5 at Kailua-Kona, where the ship's crew hoisted out and landed the transit of Venus gear.[10]

George Forbes had at last arrived on the island of Hawai'i, where he was to live for the next three months "under the shade of the great Mouna Lowa," and where—so the Astronomer Royal hoped—he would not be "assassinated" like Captain Cook.[11] But it was an assault of a decidedly more gentle sort that came to menace Forbes within the very first week of his stay. "The place is rather uncivilized," he wrote to Tupman. And there were "no white men" living in the vicinity—though the natives were "all very civil, and willing to oblige so long as we do not wish them to work." Still, his chief difficulty was in getting provisions. "There is no meat to be had here . . . [and] hardly any vegetables. Jim [a native interpreter] cannot even get Poi and he needs it so much that I went to considerable trouble to get him some." But the greater shock was yet to come, and Forbes was soon adding a postscript to his letter:

> Since writing the above we have had a great ceremony here. All the natives belonging to the Governess arrived from the country on horses carrying with them fruits & vegetables. They assembled at the house and we received them in State. They laid down their fruits etc at our feet & then shook hands & passed on. Then I had to make a speech which was translated to them. They stared a little & then went away. There were over a hundred of them. It was rather amusing. As a result of this I send you now by the [steamship] Kilauea some of our surplus stock. I daresay you won't thank me for it.[12]

About 150 residents "from all the country round" had gathered at Forbes' doorstep in *ho'okupu* style. Each bearing a gift, they had collectively lavished the transit party with oranges, plantains, coconuts, watermelons, pumpkins, sweet potatoes, eggs, fowls, and fish.[13] For the young *malihini,* such a public outpouring was unforgettable, diverting his attention at least momentarily from the astronomical to the gastronomical. But Forbes had not lost sight of his greater purpose and dutifully reported that although there was to the northeast a high mountain—Hualālai—that often attracted clouds, the nights were "always clear." As for his temporary residence, the house of Princess Ruth, he described it as "large & cool . . . [and] enclosed in about an acre of land by a stone wall."[14] And even if sparsely furnished and "wholly unfit for Europeans,"[15] it was palatial by Island standards and stood solidly and comfortably on the shores of Kailua Bay (Figs. 46 to 48).

Fig. 46. Hulihe'e Palace, Kailua-Kona

Nearby, and just to the southeast, Forbes would erect his transit instrument and telescope. As at the 'Āpua station in Honolulu, James Gay would survey the site and connect the transit pier with surrounding objects.[16] And for better guarding the valuable government instruments and property under Forbes' charge, Captain Cator, at the suggestion of British commissioner Wodehouse, would agree to provide a British flag.[17]

Meanwhile, at Kealakekua Bay, an estimated 12 miles south of Forbes' observing station, Cator and Wodehouse would be providing the island with much more than a flag.

A place of melancholy interest to British subjects since Captain Cook's death there in 1779, Kealakekua had continued to attract English voyagers to the bloody site. In 1825, Lord Byron, upon returning the remains of King Kamehameha II and Queen Kamāmalu to Hawai'i from England, com- manded HMS *Blonde* to Kealakekua where a simple monument of oak and copper was erected to Cook's memory. And in 1837, a similarly rude memo- rial—a simple inscription on a copper plate affixed to the stump of a coconut tree—was placed by the crew of HMS *Imogene.* But neither object befitted the memory of England's most famous explorer. And it was not until 1874, in the wake of the transit of Venus operations, that the situation was satis- factorily rectified.[18] For along with Forbes and Barnacle and the astronomi-

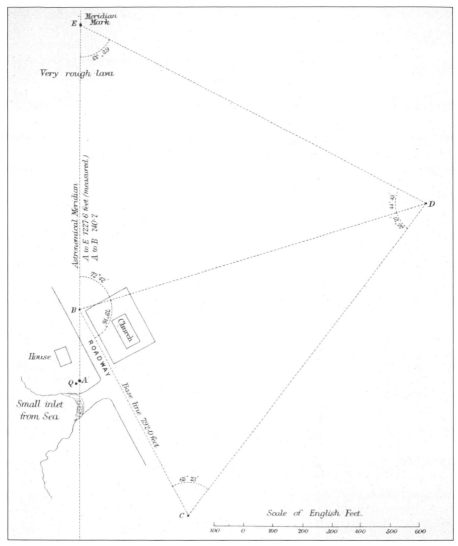

Fig. 47. The site of the auxiliary station at Kailua-Kona. Q marks the position of the equatorial telescope and A the transit instrument. The "House" is Hulihe'e Palace. Just across the road stands Moku'aikaua Church, the steeple of which can be seen in Fig. 46.

Fig. 48 (right). Transit of Venus monument at Hulihe'e Palace

cal cargo, the *Scout* had carried from Honolulu British commissioner Wodehouse together with the gear to be used for the erection of a new monument.[19] And on November 6, the day following her arrival at Kailua-Kona, the ship had landed the construction materials at Kealakekua Bay.

94

IN MEMORY OF
THE GREAT CIRCUMNAVIGATOR,
CAPTAIN JAMES COOK, R N.,
WHO
DISCOVERED THESE ISLANDS
ON THE 18th OF JANUARY, A.D 1778
AND FELL NEAR THIS SPOT
ON THE 14th OF FEBRUARY, A.D. 1779.
THIS MONUMENT WAS ERECTED
IN NOVEMBER A D 1874
BY SOME OF
HIS FELLOW COUNTRYMEN.

Fig. 49. The Cook Memorial at Kealakekua Bay, with inscription (inset)

Wodehouse's reasons for making the trip were twofold: "To render by my presence at the spot all the assistance in my power to Professor Forbes and the party which had been selected to observe the Transit of Venus from Kailua . . . and, as Chairman of the Executive Committee of Cook's Memorial Fund, to superintend the erection of a monument near the spot where the 'great discoverer' met his untimely end."[20]

When, on November 14, the new Cook Memorial (Fig. 49) was unveiled, one hundred years of British presence in Hawai'i became glorified in concrete.[21] Kealakekua Bay now sheltered and sanctified a monument to the man whose astronomically attuned ability had, one century earlier, pulled the Sandwich Islands into the orbit of the British Empire.[22]

Back at Kailua-Kona, Forbes and Barnacle were contributing their own efforts to Britain's astronomical legacy. The transit instrument, erected on a brick pier founded on solid rock, stood firmly against a violent sea that was breaking on the rocks only 20 yards away. Forbes' telescope (see Fig. 50) was mounted nearby and a platform constructed for Barnacle's.[23]

As the month of November continued, so too did the generosity of natives with edible presents.[24] But all was not well. Work—even casual con-

Fig. 50. The Lee equatorial used to observe the 1874 transit of Venus from Egypt. The telescope used by George Forbes at Kailua-Kona was similar to the Lee.

96

versation—with Barnacle was a joyless imposition; and Forbes, anticipating further difficulties, had already begun maneuvering to make some of the astronomical observations easier, just in case he had to do them by himself.[25] For a brief while, the void was filled by a friend of Captain Cator's who had come from Valparaiso aboard the *Scout*. Were it not for him, Forbes told Tupman, "I should not have a soul to speak to."[26] The soul's name was Charles Lambert. But Lambert, all too soon, was only a memory:

Nov 20. Friday. Mr Lambert & I went to bathe this morning before breakfast, as usual. The sea was very rough. We anticipated no danger as we were both fair swimmers; & the Hon: Simon Kaai, the only other person on the beach foresaw no danger. A very strong under-current from the shore had set in. The wind suddenly got up & the sea with it. . . . Mr Lambert appears to have been immediately overwhelmed by the size of the waves. He was much exhausted when I reached him, swallowing water with every wave until I turned his face to the shore. I seized him under the left armpit by my right hand, & struck out for the shore. By watching the rocks on my left, I perceived that instead of making way I was being drifted out. A crowd of natives who were collected on the shore saw our danger, but did nothing for some time. There was a channel among the rocks on my left; If they had pointed this out to me I could have taken Mr Lambert there. As it was, my only duty was to keep Mr Lambert's head out of the water with the back of it to the waves. I did not give up swimming towards the shore, though I made no way. Two natives came out for about five minutes & then left us. Eventually a canoe was launched with great risk. At the same time a native called Kaea relieved me of Mr Lambert's body (he had now been dead some minutes). The bottom of the boat was stove in, but we got to the shore in it. All means of resuscitation were attempted in vain. We had been in the water ³/₄ of an hour.[27]

Later that day, Barnacle rode to Kona to make funeral arrangements. The following morning, twelve men working in turn bore the coffin containing Lambert's corpse into Kona town where an English clergyman, Mr. Davis, was awaiting them and where the body was buried.[28]

Forbes, distracted and wearied, now did no astronomical work for three days, his own account of the events of November 20 having been modest, if not self-effacing, as he was "almost insensible himself when rescued by the natives."[29]

But his transit-related afflictions were not yet at an end. Even while attending to the burial of his friend, trouble had arisen, and Forbes wrote:

Since our return from [the site of Lambert's burial at] Kona I have been annoyed to find that on the day of the funeral . . . the native, called Jim, whom Captain Cator left with us as interpreter, behaved in a very bad way. He stole a bottle of brandy and gave it to the natives that live near us, & then brought them into the house & distributed our beer amongst them. I also found the box of the R. A. S. [Royal Astronomical Society] repeating circle broken, and some cigars missing. Since the women whom he brought to the house left it in a state of intoxication, and since the man's conduct was very generally talked about, it was necessary to take some steps. Mr Kaai the sheriff of this place assisted me, & brought the women whom Jim had treated to brandy &c. They affirmed that he had done so, &, as this was not his first offence, I told him that he must leave by the next boat for Honolulu; although it inconveniences us considerably to have no interpreter.[30]

Jim was prosecuted the next day by the government authorities; not only had he given liquor to the natives, which was forbidden by law, but evidently, after another man had informed the authorities about the incident, Jim had seduced the man's wife. He was fined $10.[31]

Meanwhile, preparations for the transit continued. Barnacle, having been sent to Honolulu to attend to the possible return of Lambert's body to his home, would not return until December 2, and Forbes, now left alone without a friend, a colleague, or an interpreter, pursued his work in glorious and disconsolate solitude.

But the dullness of daily routine was relieved by his own ingeniousness, and by late November Forbes had erected a 20-foot spiral-spring seismometer—his own invention. Intended not only to indicate the presence of an earthquake but to measure its vertical component, Forbes thought his invention might also prove astronomically useful in accounting for any instrumental errors that might arise from that geological cause, the island of Hawai'i being, as he well knew, in an active volcanic state.[32]

If some of Forbes' hours were filled with misfortune, others were—when not frustrated by cloudy weather[33]—simply laborious and routine. He adjusted the transit instrument. He regularly observed "clock stars" for time. He obtained shots of the noonday sun (using the RAS's repeating circle as an "improved" sextant) for the determination of latitude. And he observed meridional transits of the moon for the purpose of inferring his longitude. But it was from such drudgery that there came the numbers he knew he needed: latitude, 19° 38' 23" north; longitude, 10h 24m 1.7s west.[34] George Forbes had his location.

22

· · · · ·

Waimea

The task of observing the transit of Venus from Hawai'i's second auxiliary station was given to Richard Johnson, who left Honolulu on
November 6 aboard the schooner *Odd-Fellow.* He was accompanied
by a Honolulu carpenter, a cook, and a marine, as well as by navy
Sublieutenant R. H. Wellings of the *Scout,* who would act as his observing
assistant. The cargo included instruments, stores, lumber for fencing, bricks
and cement for the piers of the transit instrument, and, for longitude determination, three chronometers protected in a padded box.[1]

Early the following afternoon, the vessel dropped anchor off Waimea,
Kaua'i, where Captain Cook had first made landfall in Hawai'i in 1778 and
where Johnson now began his efforts to establish himself in a strange place
and among strangely friendly people: "At about 12^h 30^m P. M. we cast
anchor abreast of this town, or rather Native Village. . . . The schooner lay
three quarters of a mile or thereabouts off the shore, and then a boat was sent
[carrying us and our gear] within twenty yards of the beach, and there
anchored. Natives, or as they are called, Kanakas, next waded through the
surf and carried us ashore in their arms like so many children."[2] If this were
not enough to immediately disarm Johnson and his cohorts, such unabashed
aloha only prefigured what was to come. The auspicious welcome continued:

> When I had been safely deposited on the strand along with M^r
> Wellings I went to look for a Mr Knudsen, who is the principal
> white man on the island, and who promised in Honolulu,
> where I met him, to assist me in every way he could in estab-
> lishing my station. I met him a short distance from the landing
> place whither he had come to meet me. . . . I discussed with him
> the possibility of obtaining a house to live in on the island. He
> informed me there were three places, all equally good for the
> observation of the actual Transit of Venus and for the observa-
> tion of Pole stars . . . in which I could have a house.[3]

Because it was on the leeward side of the island, protected from the
northeast trade winds and hence less liable to clouds and rain, and because
it had only very low hills to the north, Johnson decided to place his station
right there at Waimea rather than at any alternative and less favored site.
He rented a house on a hill half a mile inland and some 80 or 90 feet above

the beach, close to the ground he had selected for his observing site. The rate was $15 a month. Within a few days he could report to Tupman at Honolulu that all the gear had been safely landed and that the chronometers—which he and Wellings had personally carried up the hill—were going well.[4]

The day immediately following his arrival, Johnson marked out the hillside ground he intended to have enclosed. He also marked the positions of his transit instrument and telescope. By November 10 he had hired some local hands to dig the holes for the transit piers,[5] the foundation of which was laid upon red volcanic clay, 6 feet below the surface of the ground.

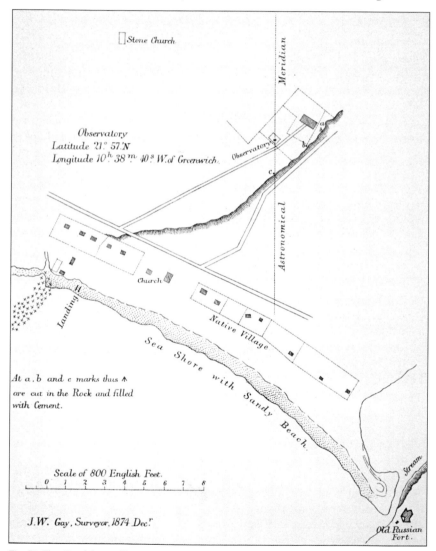

Fig. 51. The site of the auxiliary station at Waimea

In due course, Johnson's observatory would be fenced in and its position plotted by the same man who rendered similar services at both the Honolulu and Kailua-Kona sites, surveyor James Gay.[6] The latitude of the site would be obtained from the mean value of twenty-two noontime observations of the sun's upper limb made by Sublieutenant Wellings, using an ordinary navigator's sextant and a mercurial horizon. The longitude would be gotten via chronometric comparison with Honolulu. The resulting values would be: latitude 21° 57.2' north, longitude 10h 38m 39.8s (±2s) west (Fig. 51).[7]

Additionally, as at the Honolulu site, and in accordance with Airy's instructions, prophylactic measures would be instituted in order to preserve a knowledge of the precise location of Johnson's observatory (Fig. 52). Its remote position—on the margins of an obscure Polynesian village, almost a hundred feet above the sea, and half a mile inland—could be recovered, it was surmised, from this description: "Near the edge of the rocky cliff overhanging Valley Road, 35 feet E.S.E. from the S. corner of the dwelling-house, a mark [in the shape of an arrow] . . . has been chiselled in the rock and filled with cement. . . . Two similar marks were cut in the rock on the edge of the cliff to the S.W., distant 90 and 346 feet respectively from the above-mentioned mark, and distant 174 and 199 feet respectively from the transit pier."[8]

From the first of these three marks, compass bearings were taken to four places: (1) to Johnson's transit pier, 231 feet distant; (2) to a "sharp peak" in the Kaua'i mountains; (3) to the Old Russian Fort; and (4) to the highest peak of "Lehau Island."[9]

By Friday, November 13, the foundation of the transit piers was completed and work commenced on the fencing around the grounds. After the transit hut was erected, pieces of sackcloth were nailed along the edges of the hut's doors and joints to prevent permeation by the fine red volcanic dust—dust "so penetrating," Johnson later wrote, "that it finds its way everywhere." This done, and a mosquito curtain having already been hung around his computing table, Johnson could at last consider himself well sealed against blowing or blood-sucking intruders.[10]

But if Richard Johnson, as well as he was able, kept airborne annoyances at a distance, he was necessarily more cordial to the people of Kaua'i. He hired and paid—though not without negotiating "honest" wages—several men, even though he could not understand their language, nor they his, and even though they declined to work on Sundays. He employed a man to carry fresh water up to the house from the Waimea River and another to launder his clothes; and though neither task paid princely sums, they were simple and undemanding ones that, while relieving the astronomer of dollars, also relieved him of domestic chores. Of the workmen he himself employed, he learned their native names—"Puhimoku, Halo, Alohaikeao, Leoiki, Mahu"—and even tried to understand their meanings. But even as he concluded that their names were not simple descriptors of the bearer's physical or mental qualities, he had already discovered that, by whatever

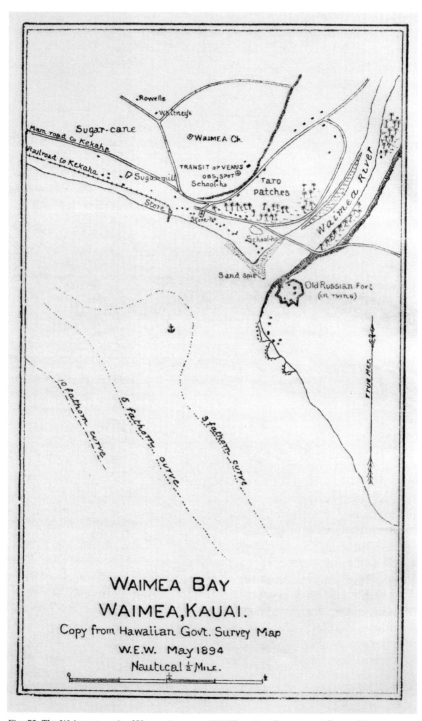

Fig. 52. The Waimea transit of Venus site on an 1894 Hawaiian Government Survey Map

names they were called, not all of Kaua'i's native residents were as honest and innocent and plain-dealing as Mr. Knudsen had reported them to be. His own early experiences on the island had, in fact, uncovered some exceptions to Mr. Knudsen's rule. "As far as my present experience goes," Johnson had written of the "Kanakas" on November 7, "they are all of the same kidney."[11] He would simply have to adapt as best he could.

The sun continued to rise over the island on schedule, and observations of that luminary (for time) went on with almost uninterrupted regularity, the weather initially being much more cooperative than on O'ahu. But the happy weather, which Johnson described as "very fine" and which persisted for ten days, deteriorated on November 17. Rain fell the next day. The rusty dust turned to red mud. A *Kona* wind blew from the southwest. The telescope shook. On November 23, Johnson required nearly the entire night to observe a mere five clock stars and Polaris and thought the clouds "simply abominable." Though some astronomical observations were made over the next week, the weather did not show decisive improvement until December 1. It was then to remain good through transit day.[12]

On November 25, the Cambridge-trained clergyman Robert Dunn (1839–1902) arrived from Honolulu to supplement the Johnson-Wellings team. Dunn, who would remain in Hawai'i until 1876, had been in the Islands for almost nine months before sailing to Waimea and, having already practiced with the transit model at 'Āpua, was prepared to assist as far as he was able in the British effort.[13]

On Thursday, December 3, a telescope from Tupman—a 2.7-inch altazimuth by Dolland—arrived via the schooner *Odd-Fellow* for Dunn's use. Like Johnson's 3.5-inch equatorial by the same maker, it was the property of the Royal Observatory at Greenwich.[14]

The following day, in addition to conducting telescopic practice on sunspots, Johnson made for the clergyman a diagram of the position and relative size of Venus on the sun. Special preparations on Dunn's behalf continued right up to transit day: Johnson measured the powers of the eyepieces attached to his telescope; he obtained the services of navy Sublieutenant Warleigh, of HMS *Reindeer,* for the purpose of taking time for Dunn during the actual transit; and in order to avoid confusion on transit day between his own official and duty-bound observations and Dunn's gratuitous ones, he arranged for Dunn to observe the transit from a tent pitched outside the observatory enclosure. Dunn returned the favor by photographing the instruments in situ and, at Johnson's request, took some photographs of the Kaua'i station in order to show its position with reference to the neighboring hills.[15]

Transit day, December 8, was now imminent. As the sun rose that morning—first in Kailua-Kona, then seven minutes later in Honolulu, then seven minutes later still at Waimea—the three-station British team, now spread across the Hawaiian archipelago over more than 3½ degrees of longitude, watched the blinding host and eagerly awaited its planetary guest.

23

· · · · ·

An Absentee King

Back in Honolulu, a cascade of surprises continued to drop at the feet of Captain Tupman. In mid-November, and with less than a month remaining before the transit, King Kalākaua, in the company of Prince Leleiohoku and many ladies of the court, sashayed into the observatory at 'Āpua. The transit of Venus model was obligingly worked for them and they were shown the moon and other objects in the telescopes. But Tupman, who had come to scorn visitors as "an intolerable nuisance," now had scant choice as he watched kingly munificence, Janus-faced, turn to kingly importunity. "Savages," he blurted into his journal.[1] Still, the king was undeterred. The very next day, November 16, was his birthday. The *Scout* bent to him a 21-gun salute. And King Kalākaua celebrated unswervedly by taking his wife, Queen Kapi'olani, and a host of followers to the observatory, where they remained for two hours![2]

But for the Merrie Monarch, the approaching transit was—as it had been for British royalty of the preceding century— just a pleasant and entertaining diversion.[3] His prime focus in late 1874 was, in fact, not at the telescope at all but upon pressing economic issues that were much more critical to his kingdom than mere astronomical ephemerae. And when transit day finally dawned in Honolulu, King Kalākaua was nowhere to be seen.

On November 17, the day immediately following his thirty-eighth birthday and exactly three weeks before transit day, Kalākaua left Honolulu, not to return for nearly three months. The object of the king's trip, as Captain Cator had already suspected two months earlier, was money—and not just any money, but American dollars. What the king would be looking for in faraway Washington, indeed what some Island residents had been seeking for a long time now, was a way to circumvent American tariffs on Hawaiian goods—principally sugar, its greatest commercial crop—with a well-forged Reciprocity Treaty.

The prospects and the mutual benefits of such a Reciprocity Treaty had been discussed before and in 1874 would be discussed again, this time with Kalākaua in America's capital city to leverage his personal presence on the debate. For Hawai'i, the main value of such a treaty would be economic and would depend upon the market value of Hawaiian sugar. For the United States, the treaty's value would be both strategic and (as later events would prove) far reaching and would lie in the important privileges it granted to Pearl Harbor.

Though Kalākaua's concession of Pearl Harbor was made neither readily nor willingly,[4] the king was evidently more than ready and willing to undertake all the personal discomforts, as well as the personal hazards, associated with a long journey to a foreign country in order to secure prosperity for his economically strapped kingdom. His sister, Lili'uokalani, acknowledged as much many years later in this panegyric to her brother:

> Kalakaua valued the commercial and industrial prosperity of his kingdom highly. He sought honestly to secure it for every class of people, alien or native, in his dominions, making it second only to the advancement of morals and education. . . . Kalakaua's highest and most earnest desire was to be a true sovereign, the chief servant of a happy, prosperous, and progressive people. . . . He freely gave his personal efforts to the securing of a reciprocity treaty with the United States, and sought the co-operation of that great and powerful nation, because he was persuaded it would enrich, or benefit, not one class, but, in a greater or less degree, all his subjects.[5]

The signing of the Reciprocity Treaty in January 1875 would eventually be called "the most important event in the last twenty years of the Hawaiian Kingdom"—a kingdom that would survive but a few years beyond Kalākaua's death in 1891. Although it did not go into effect until the following year, 1876, the treaty would put Hawai'i's fragile economy on a firm basis by permitting Sandwich Island sugar to enter the United States duty-free. It would also direct the Hawaiian Islands—the green gem of the North Pacific, and much coveted—away from their long-standing flirtations with England and toward their consummate embrace with the United States.[6]

Before leaving Washington, Hawai'i's king would be introduced to America's president Ulysses S. Grant and would be received by the houses of Congress in joint session. Before returning to Hawai'i, he would pay a visit to the Connecticut home of his former teacher, the astronomer C. S. Lyman;[7] and in California he would personally call in on the dying James Lick, benefactor of the then nascent Lick Observatory.[8] But as astronomically punctuated as this sojourn was, Kalākaua's absence from the Islands as 1874 drew to a close was not without consequences for the transit of Venus operations, and as the sun ascended into Honolulu's skies on December 8, social confusion descended onto a tiny kingdom. It was not entirely unexpected. On November 26, Lili'uokalani had written to the king with intimations of political instability:

> My dear Brother
>   I had no idea that in the absence of one man there should be such a vacancy and I must say that when you went away

there was a feeling of want for a man whom you could look up to and feel he had a head over us all. The Prince [Leleiohoku] is regent but the people are not acquainted with him and therefore have not the love for him they have for you. It will take time and perseverance on his part to gain it.

    . . . Every thing seems to be peaceable & quiet, but I think the soldiers are very slack and needs [*sic*] a little more discipline in the palace. People can go in and out without [a] pass word. . . . But everything is quiet. We have the Scout, Reindeer, [and] Tenedos, [and] there is a report that the [USS] Tuscarora is in.[9]

If these were worrisome days for the king's sister as well as for the king, they were no different for the British astronomers. But reckless insecurity, such as that observed by Lili'uokalani at the palace, would not be allowed to infect the transit proceedings. Stout wooden fences, fortified by the presence of stout British marines from the *Scout,* the *Reindeer,* and the *Tenedos,* would see to it.

24

· · · · ·

Military Fortification

A t 7:30 A.M. on the morning of Sunday, December 6, ten days after Lili'uokalani's letter to the king, the *Tenedos* left Honolulu bound for Kailua-Kona. The *Reindeer* followed at 2:10 P.M., steaming away for Waimea. Both vessels arrived at their destinations the following day, where Captains Van der Meulen of the *Tenedos* and Anson of the *Reindeer* made arrangements with Forbes and Johnson for the protection of their observatory grounds.[1]

Airy's instructions were quite specific regarding the conduct of operations on transit day: "If . . . [a] British ship is lying in the neighbourhood," he had written, "the officers and others of the crew will undoubtedly give their best assistance." British ships had already provided men to assist at the auxiliary stations in the actual astronomical observations: Lieutenant Bigge of the *Tenedos* was with Forbes, and Sublieutenant Wellings of the *Scout* was with Johnson. But additional men would be more than welcome on transit day—most especially, as Airy had warned, "to guard against intrusions" and, even more specifically, "to prevent the approach of strangers for at least two hours before the critical phenomenon."[2] The astronomers, not expected to undertake the task of policemen themselves, could call upon the British militia to provide this service.

At Kailua-Kona, December 8 dawned bright and clear. George Forbes, in near accordance with Airy's instructions, arranged with Captain Van der Meulen to have eight marines, four at a time, posted around the observatory grounds from an hour before the transit until sunset. The task of the sentinels was both to ward off strangers and to ensure absolute silence. Whether or not they were necessary, such precautions were wise. Although curious natives crowded around, they kept a respectable distance and perfect silence was easily obtained. "They were not in the slightest degree troublesome," Forbes wrote, "[and] caused no disturbance whatever."[3]

A sunny tranquillity likewise saluted Waimea, where Richard Johnson saw his guards posted in their proper places and in due time on the eventful day—one "most lovely," he wrote, "[with] not a speck on the sky anywhere." And if the weather on Kaua'i was cooperative, the residents were no less so, as Johnson had a *kapu* (taboo) placed on the grounds for the day and had "no trouble at all with the Kanakas."[4]

Meanwhile, in Honolulu the day of the transit fell upon Captain Tupman with much excitement—not all of it welcome. Awash in a kingdom with an absentee king, Tupman and company were forced to cope with not a few enthusiastic but misguided subjects who, carrying with them the delusion that they could gain easy access to the telescopes or would at least be permitted entry to the observatory on this historic occasion, brought a pathetically festive appearance to the ʻĀpua site, threatening to transform the pending celestial drama into an ill-timed comedy or, worse, a thoughtless calamity. In the absence of the king, two of Hawaiʻi's queens—Kapiʻolani and Emma—anticipating possible unrest in downtown Honolulu, stepped forward in an attempt to maintain public order. British commissioner Wodehouse, on behalf of Captains Tupman and Cator, appealed to the Hawaiian Government for permission to land a small band of men from the *Scout* to be available in case of need and to keep the ground around the observatory clear.[5] By early afternoon, Honolulu's astronomical playground for royalty had taken on the unfriendly appearance of a military fort (Fig. 53); and Tupman, whose journal struck up the day with a few quick notes of joyful anticipation, was quickly overtaken by serious business:

> 1874 Dec 8 A superb cloudless day. Our joy is great. . . . H. M. Queen Kapiolani sent a messenger to say that Silence had been ordered throughout the Royal grounds & would be observed. . . . At 2h a detachment of 12 Marines and a Sergeant came from H.M.S. "Scout" to keep the ground. They were posted round the enclosure, with orders merely to prevent talking or noise. There was a general feeling among the Native population that the

Fig. 53. "The Transit of Venus: Waiting for Contact at Honolulu"—an artist's rendition published in the *Illustrated London News* on January 23, 1875

observatories would be open to the public on this day. H. M. Queen Emma communicated this to Major Wodehouse in the morning. It was quite true for many hundreds of natives came to the gates about 3 o'clock in their holiday clothes! The sight of the red coats, however, had the desired effect.[6]

25

· · · · ·

All Honolulu Was Awake

Outside the quiet sanctuary at 'Āpua, the general public was astir. Three days earlier the *Pacific Commercial Advertiser* had reminded its readers in Honolulu that the long-awaited day was fast approaching and that the transit, which would commence shortly after 3 P.M., would positively not be postponed on account of the weather.[1] For nearly two months there had not been a day, the newspaper reported, that would have afforded satisfactory transit observations; and less than a week before the transit, Tupman was still bemoaning the heavy and seemingly endless rain.[2] Now the long succession of inclement days that had plagued the British effort seemed to threaten its defeat when, on the eve of the long-anticipated event, masses of clouds still obscured the western horizon. But on the morning of December 8, the weather turned around—and the *Advertiser* turned effusively romantic:

> As the day dawned, early risers looking over land and sea, and observing only light masses of vapor on the misty mountain-tops, and a soft, sweet, calm air, with just breeze enough to fan our city's rich umbrageous foliage into soft rustling kisses among its leaves, whilst resplendent shafts of light shot clearly into the heavens from the top of towering Tantalus, then hope sprang up and mounted triumphant with an unclouded sun in order to observe our sister planet make her centennial solar call.[3]

Like the *Advertiser,* the Hawaiian-language newspaper *Ka Nūpepa Kū'oko'a* was keeping its own audience abreast of transit-related news. It was now poised for its own transit-day story (which it would eventually print on December 12).[4]

No one among Hawai'i's reading public, native or foreign, was as well equipped as the British scientific team for the approaching event. But neither were they entirely unprepared for a rare view of *Hōkūloa i mua o ka lā* ("Venus in front of the sun"), for the delectation of which a telescope was not necessary:

> During the day, there was a very general demand for broken panes of glass and bottles, which were smoked and held in

readiness for looking at the sun. . . . The natives were as busy with their preparations for astronomical observations as the white foreigners. Little kanakas were going about the streets with pieces of blackened glass in hand, for the purpose of looking as they said at the *Hokuloa,* the morning star, go through the sun.[5]

And if the deployment of pieces of smoked glass as primitive solar filters seemed worthy of readers' attention, so too, thought the *Advertiser,* was the history of Venusian transits, and most especially the place occupied in that history by Captain Cook—or, as "savage" eighteenth-century Hawaiians knew him, the god Lono:

It was curious to listen to the remarks and speculations of natives whose savage fathers had never suspected this occasional moving spot on the great light of day. They knew that Lono, or Capt. Cook, the discoverer of their isles had come to these seas to observe a star in the sun, and it had been predicted in his day that it should be seen again more than a hundred years afterwards on this day, with the hour, and the minute, and the very second specified. And now there were tens of thousands throughout these isles looking upwards to prove the truth of this century old prediction.[6]

Still, if the unprecedented excitement that now descended upon the Islands from the heavenly vault was being fanned into sentimental heat by the bellows of public newspapers on public streets, it was captured with more restraint in the private journals of some of Honolulu's prominent citizens. Archibald Cleghorn (King Kalākaua's brother-in-law) and Dwight Baldwin (the American missionary) were two such men. Cleghorn would call the day of the transit nothing other than "Splendid."[7] And Baldwin's journal entry for December 8, brief as it was, would have no rivals:

Tues. Dec. 8. This was the day for the Transit of Venus.—4½ hours in passing over the Sun—only the first half to be seen here, because it w^d begin at 3^h..5^m..3^s pm, & the sun w^d set at 5..18. All Honolulu was awake to the event. The Eng. Astronomers (Capt. Tupman at their head) had been here since Sept. 10th making preparations to observe the Transit. We had had a succession of storms, & feared the clouds might hide the Transit. On the contrary, the whole day was very fair, & especially the West in the afternoon—not a cloud to be seen, except a low stratum along the W. horizon.[8]

26

. . . . .

Hōkūloa i Mua o ka Lā

At an estimated longitude of 10h 24m 1.7s west of Greenwich, Kailua-Kona witnessed sunrise on the morning of December 8 approximately 7 minutes 24.6 seconds before the day dawned at the ʻĀpua station in Honolulu. Venus, approaching inferior conjunction as it quickly closed in on the sun from the east, rose shortly after. Above Kailua-Kona, the morning sky was bright and clear.[1] Forbes and Barnacle were ready.

Among the several officers from the *Tenedos* who were there to assist, Lieutenant H. C. Bigge was to aid Forbes with the management of the Hodgson telescope, attending to the driving clock, the clamps, the sunshade, and other parts of the instrument. Lieutenant J. M. Lloyd was appointed to take time by the sidereal clock located inside the transit hut; from his position, he would be able to see Forbes directly at the telescope—12 feet away through the doorway of the hut—and thus accurately record the time of Forbes' observations. Barnacle was supplied with a lieutenant who took time with a chronometer. An acting sublieutenant was instructed to stand by as a messenger-in-waiting. The cordon of marines was deployed, each man being given a certain space to watch to prevent the natives from approaching too near. Simon Kaʻai supplied a bilingual native to act as an interpreter for the marines, should it be necessary.[2]

The hundreds of natives who gathered around to watch from a distance caused no disturbance, and everything appeared favorable until about 2 P.M. But despite the laborious and careful preparations, no man had the power to dissipate the meddlesome clouds that descended from the mountains. As they came and went, Forbes was able to observe both the sun and Venus. But just before the critical moment, a very heavy cloud passed over the sun, hiding it from view (Barnacle estimated) approximately five long minutes. When next seen, the dark disc of Venus was, alas, already well on the sun. Internal contact had been missed.[3]

On the island of Kauaʻi, Richard Johnson was more fortunate. After seeing his sentries posted and after arranging things for Mr. Dunn's convenience, Johnson went with Sublieutenant Wellings into the enclosed observatory grounds, where he took up his post about fifteen minutes before the expected time of external contact. Then, with an eyepiece magnifying 130 times, he peered through his telescope at the heavens as Venus slowly bit into the sun, Wellings noting the time and Dunn, with his smaller instrument blowing in the wind, observing the spectacle from a short 60 yards away. The critical moment neared. But there was no black drop! More surprising still, twelve minutes before internal contact the entire disc of Venus became distinctly visible and Johnson, observing the gradually changing juxtaposition of planet and sun, was able to estimate the time of internal contact to within 9.3 seconds. Vis-à-vis the well-rehearsed practice on the model that had permitted a far greater accuracy, this was somewhat disappointing, but Forbes and Barnacle could only have wished for as much.[4]

Meanwhile, midway between Forbes on their east and Johnson on their west, Tupman's team on the island of O'ahu took their proper positions on center stage as the day's drama unfolded. At 1 P.M., the astronomers lunched with Commissioner Wodehouse and three officers of the *Scout*—Lieutenants Clapp, Oldham, and Shakespear(e)—all four of whom would partake of the afternoon's excitement from within the observatory grounds. Then, at 2 P.M.—barely an hour before the high-spirited crowd appeared at the entrance—the contingent of marines arrived in their sobering red coats. Finally, a little after 2 the observatory gate was locked and silence enjoined. Every observer went to his station.

Tupman began by posting himself at his own telescope, the 4.5-inch equatorial (see Fig. 40). Nichol went to the 6-inch. Noble set up under a small bell tent near the altazimuth hut. Each observer was accompanied by one of the three lieutenants who were to count the time aloud. Meanwhile, Ramsden, with the three sappers, stood guard at the photoheliograph where a 3-inch telescope[5] had been mounted on a stout post close to the door of the photo hut and with which he could judge when to begin photographing with the Janssen.

Inside their quiet sanctuary, the four astronomers were now well equipped, well prepared, well protected, and, importantly, well distanced from one another—a distance that was wisely maintained for some time after the transit by Tupman who, by forbidding conversation among the observers until after they had completed their notes, also obviated any contamination of the raw data by untimely fraternizing.

The British *Nautical Almanac* for 1874 predicted internal contact at Honolulu to take place at exactly 3:33 local mean time, the sun then being about 21 degrees above the horizon and sinking in the southwest as it approached the winter solstice. As Venus would make external contact with the sun almost 28 minutes earlier (at 3:05.3), the observers would be alerted well in advance of the critical moment.[6]

External contact, descried by both Tupman and Noble at about 3:07, passed.[7] When Tupman was satisfied that external contact had occurred, he and Nichol changed places, accompanied by their respective time counters. Now at the 6-inch spyglass—Venus half on the sun and his fellow-astronomers immersed in a hush as drenching as the now-forgotten November rains—Tupman scrutinized the two celestial spheres that looked back at him from the other side of the glass, first using his double-image micrometer[8] to measure cusps, then carefully inserting his eyepiece. But the

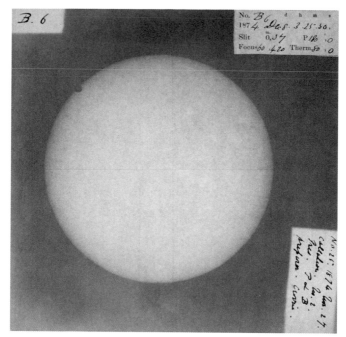

Fig. 54. Photograph of the 1874 transit of Venus taken at Honolulu shortly
after external and shortly before internal contact at ingress

Fig. 55. Photograph of the 1874 transit of Venus taken at Honolulu shortly
after internal contact

114

notorious black drop, the cause of so much preparatory anxiety, proved but an invisible bugbear: Venus, completely visible as it gradually moved onto the solar disc, remained perfectly circular and uniformly black. At last the critical moment, internal contact, came; and although it eluded Nichol, it was recorded by both Tupman and Noble at—mirabile dictu!—precisely the same instant: 3h 35m 54s Honolulu mean time (Figs. 54 and 55).[9]

At the photoheliograph, gratification was not as immediate as at the telescope. Ramsden, who had seen everything arranged in the darkroom—and who even had the boxes containing the photographic plates opened early in order to permit them to acquire the ambient temperature[10]—had practiced repeatedly with the Janssen on the transit of Venus model with good results;[11] so similar results should have been his on December 8 as he exposed the Janssen slides right on time: thirty seconds before external and thirty seconds before internal contact. But the photoheliograph, alas, was misaimed, leaving half of Venus out of the picture. And even though other photographs were pronounced "more or less good," this could only have been a preliminary judgment.[12]

But the carpe diem excitement of transit day had hit Honolulu with full force. It had radiated across the observatory grounds, through the gates braced against the curious throngs, beyond the wondering eyes that peered down from the trees and into the enclosure,[13] past the children with their smoked glass, and even onto the *Scout* where Captain Cator had observed the event.[14] At Waikīkī, David Flitner, along with Captain Daniel Smith and Mr. F. S. Pratt, had all observed internal contact to within less than five seconds of the time recorded by Tupman and Noble. Contact had even been observed at the Survey Office by C. J. Lyons, W. D. Alexander's assistant.[15]

Still, Tupman was skeptical of the observations and was quick to express his concerns:

> The important phase of the phenomenon [viz.] internal contact presented wholly unexpected appearances totally unlike anything we had been led to anticipate. For many minutes before contact a faint light was seen behind Venus beyond the Suns limb rendering the complete circle of her disc visible. From that time until the establishment of complete contact no sudden or definite phase could be seized upon such as the practice with the working model induced us to watch for.
>
> The eye observations of contact therefore do not present results of extreme value.[16]

Mindful that the astronomers (from practice on the model) were expected to obtain the time of internal contact to within a second or so of the truth, Tupman found disconcerting the gradual (rather than instantaneous) submergence of Venus into the sun, with "nothing sudden to note." But he was more optimistic about the photographic observations, at least initially. Of the Janssens taken at quick intervals at both external and internal contact and of the several dozen additional plates taken both before and after internal contact, only some appeared to have been tarnished by defective pointing of the photoheliograph. And even if these—the sixty Janssen exposures at internal contact—were the most critical, the others were not without value—or so it was hoped.[17]

December 8 came and went with lingering uncertainty. At approximately 5:18 P.M., the sun dropped into the sea while the transit was still in progress.

27

· · · · ·

A Memorial in Westminster Abbey

As the sun set in Honolulu on the eve of December 8, the black blemish of Venus still upon its face, it was already the morning of December 9 in England, almost 160° of longitude and an ocean and a half away. The transit, invisible at Greenwich, had gone unobserved—but not unheeded. A short distance down the Thames from the Greenwich Observatory, at another edifice brimming with British history, behind the tall stained glass through which the dim London sunlight fell lugubriously upon the crowd of effigies and timeworn inscriptions—there, at Westminster Abbey, the day would be etched in stone and stamped indelibly into the collective British memory.

Earlier in the year, the president of the Royal Astronomical Society, John C. Adams, had called to the attention of the Society a petition that was about to be presented to the dean of the abbey, requesting therein the placement of a memorial. The petition read:

> Reverend Sir,
> It appears to us that the approaching transit of Venus offers a fitting occasion for the erection of a memorial to Jeremiah Horrocks, curate of Hoole, in Lancashire, to whom the science of astronomy is indebted for the earliest observation of Venus upon the sun's disc. He predicted, by his own calculations, the transit of the year 1639, which he and his friend Crabtree had the exclusive privilege of witnessing. The labours of Horrocks in connection with this memorable occurrence, as well as the originality of his views on other astronomical subjects, have, by the unanimous consent of scientific men, assigned to him a high place in the roll of illustrious astronomers who adorned Europe in the seventeenth century.
> We therefore venture to request your permission to place in Westminster Abbey a tablet or some other memorial to Jeremiah Horrocks.[1]

The petition, which was signed by both Airy and Adams as well as by a number of the more distinguished fellows of the Society, was not in vain.

A memorial tablet to the clergyman-astronomer Horrocks, with an inscription by the abbey's dean, Arthur Penrhyn Stanley, was placed in the

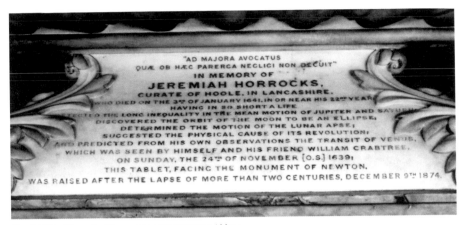

Fig. 56. The Horrocks Memorial in Westminster Abbey

nave of the church, near the West Door.[2] Facing the memorial of his most illustrious legatee, Isaac Newton—who in his *Principia* had paid posthumous tribute to his perspicacious predecessor[3]—the marble scroll (Fig. 56) began with Horrocks' own words, in Latin, regarding his alleged ecclesiastical duties on that memorable day. But it ended with a certifiably woeful truth on the proportions of English negligence: Worse than the case of Captain Cook's much-delayed but ultimately large and impressive monument at faraway Kealakekua, the raising in the middle of London of a tiny tablet in honor of "the pride and boast of British astronomy" had required more than two centuries.[4]

28

· · · · ·

To the Top of the Mountain

J ust as the work of the expedition had begun upon its arrival in Honolulu nearly three months before the day of the transit, so too was the work to continue for as many months thereafter.

On December 9, Tupman wrote a thankful letter to Captain Cator remarking that the success of the previous afternoon's observations at 'Āpua had been "in no small degree due to the able assistance rendered by yourself and the Officers of HMS 'Scout'." He also suggested to Cator that if the transit had been successfully observed at either or both of the auxiliary stations, the required chronometer runs to those stations for the purpose of connecting their longitudes to Honolulu's could soon be launched.[1]

Before the day ended, the man-of-war *Reindeer,* carrying the man-of-god Dunn, returned from Waimea with news of Johnson's success. After the *Tenedos* followed on December 10 with a qualified report of Forbes' achievements,[2] arrangements were made that the *Tenedos* should execute all the chronometer runs (there would be a total of six), and on December 13 all the available chronometers—twenty of them—were placed aboard the ship.[3] Set in boxes in a specially prepared berth near the mainmast and surrounded by about 8 inches of horsehair padding to absorb the vibrations of the screw propeller,[4] this collective concentration of clockwork conveyed a strong sense of seriousness to the otherwise delicate longitude work.

On December 15 the *Tenedos* returned to Kailua-Kona, this time fully loaded with Captain Tupman and the ticktocking cargo. Forbes and Tupman dutifully compared chronometers and observed, that very evening, several clock stars.[5] But there was time for a bit of recreation too, and the following afternoon the *Tenedos* took the two on a leisurely excursion down the coast to Kealakekua Bay, Henry Barnacle tagging along.[6]

It had been nearly one hundred years since the *Resolution* and

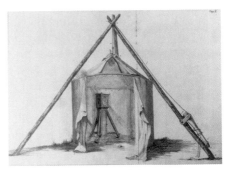

Fig. 57. Portable astronomical observatory designed by William Bayly. Observatories of this kind were carried aboard the *Resolution* and the *Discovery* and were erected in 1779 at Kealakekua Bay where they were protected by native *kapu* (taboos).

the *Discovery* had, in these very waters, firmly anchored Captain Cook and his crew to the ambiguities of the Pacific. Both forbidding and inviting, both morbid and vivacious, simultaneously both full of life and full of death, Kealakekua Bay had also been, a century earlier, a place where Hawai'i's first astronomical observatories (Fig. 57) required the protection of native taboos.[7]

But this was 1874, and the scene had been transformed. Forbes reflected:

> I had already seen the North side [of the bay] where the village of Kawalua [Ka'awaloa] is situated, but today I crossed over to the other side, & had much pleasure in recognizing many of the spots mentioned in Capt. Cook's voyages, & even figured in his chart of the bay. The form of the coast which he gives, with the sandy beach on the Kealakakoa [*sic*] side, is, so far as I could judge, quite correct. The fish-pond marked on his plan, is still there, but it is now cut with square sides so as to form an oblong. The <u>morai</u> [*heiau*] or sacrificial edifice still remains, in the form of a stone platform raised about 7 feet above the ground, and covering a space of some 30 x 40 yards. These measurements I judged by the eye. In Capt. Cook's Voyages (Oct° edition vol 3 p 132) I find it stated that its length was 40 yards, its breadth 20 yards, & its height fourteen (yards?). This is the Morai on which, at the request of Tereeoboo [Kalani'ōpu'u] (the King of that district at the time), the remains of William Watman, a seaman of the gunner's crew, & the faithful follower of Capt. Cook, were deposited in the year 1779.
>
> I also saw the other division of the Morai described in Capt. Cook's voyages where it is said "a space, of about 12 feet square, was sunk about three feet below the level of the area". On this square building there is now no roof & it is now difficult to say whether the opening on the west side was intended for a window or a door. It was in this enclosure that Captain Cook was placed between the two idols when the curious ceremony was performed by the priests to honour "Orono" [Lono] as Captain Cook was called by the natives, a name for one of their oldest & most honoured gods.
>
> I have identified the places above mentioned solely by the aid of the chart & descriptions in Captain Cook's voyages. The natives seem to be quite ignorant of the history. The great point of discrepancy between this bay as it now is, & the bay described by Captain Cook, lies in the very small number of houses that there are. These are all in ruins. One of the inhabitants, about 80 years old, says that in his youth there were 1200 houses on the north side of the bay. There are now hardly a

dozen. The same fact applies to the whole coast. At Kailua there are hundreds of ruined houses. Everything bears witness to the depopulation of the islands.[8]

The depopulation that Forbes was now recording had been widely noticed and was widely lamented. In fact, King Kalākaua, who was in Washington at the very moment that Forbes was pondering the issue,[9] had just pledged the previous February that he would devote his reign to its remedy: to "the increase of the people."[10] Others—Leonard Darwin's father among them—may have wondered whether there was any remedy at all.[11]

But, disturbing as they may have been, Hawai'i's demographic trends were not as quickening to Tupman as Forbes' recent but not altogether novel complaint that Barnacle could leave "so soon as is desired as he is no use in the astronomical department."[12] And before the *Tenedos* returned to Honolulu,[13] the captain conveyed his decision to the unsuspecting astronomer:

> Dear Sir,
>   There seems to be no longer any reason to detain you in the Sandwich Islands as part of the Transit of Venus Expedition. I request therefore that you will return to England, leaving Honolulu on or about January 10 in the Australian Steamer.
>   2. I shall advise the Accountant General of the Navy by letter of the date of your departure. Under the Regulations of your engagement you are entitled to your salary until your arrival in England by the shortest route.
>   3. Should you think proper to delay on the journey it cannot be at the expense of H. M.'s Government.
>   4. I will make the arrangements for your departure in Honolulu—in the mean time you are at liberty to spend your time in any way you may think proper.[14]

Barnacle received Tupman's orders on December 17 and made his last journal entry the same day. He left Kailua-Kona on January 2 and was finally banished from Honolulu on January 11, by which time Tupman had secretly elaborated to Airy on the incorrigible behavior of the "mad" scientist:

> I regret to say that M[r] Barnacle has been a great nuisance to us and worse than useless as regards taking part in the observations. In fact he is not in his right mind. I shall send him home by the next steamer instead of keeping him here at considerable expense to the country. . . . He is either mad or the greatest impostor that ever lived. He ought to be made to refund the whole of his salary, for I have been unable to get him to do any work whatever, and Professor Forbes found he could not

entrust him with anything as he never tells the truth even by accident. It is a great misfortune that he came with us—no person in his right mind could conduct himself as he does—In short he has brought nothing but discredit on the expedition.[15]

But with or without Henry Barnacle, George Forbes had work to do; and from the day immediately following the transit, he had dutifully continued the germane and often routine astronomical labors. These now went on well into January,[16] as they did for Richard Johnson on Kaua'i.[17]

By January 21, Forbes' astronomical duties had been essentially completed. The Hodgson telescope, the transit instrument, and the clock had all been dismounted; the hut had been taken down; all the instruments had been packed, so far as was possible, in the same way as when they had left Greenwich; and Noble, who had come to Kailua-Kona to serve as Barnacle's replacement, was en route to Honolulu aboard the schooner *Prince*.

But to the east, and still looming over him, was the mighty Mauna Loa—the largest single mountain on Earth[18] and one that, Forbes knew, was volcanically explosive. Her summit caldera, Moku'āweoweo, was especially prone to fiery fulminations, and one particularly prolonged outbreak—beginning in April 1873 and lasting 547 days until October 1874—had been witnessed by Isabella Bird and only narrowly missed by Forbes.

In November, when Forbes landed with Barnacle at Kailua-Kona, the mountain had been quiet. The astronomers had been permitted to do their work and to observe the appointed celestial luminaries in December without the distractions of terrestrial fires. The transit had come. Mauna Loa had been at peace. Pele had slept.

The peace was shattered on January 10, 1875. With an outbreak that was to last a month on the summit, Pele, who had rumbled but gently in late December, now poured forth her molten fury. Two weeks later, on Sunday, January 24, George Forbes made what proved to be his last journal entry: "I have been waiting here since the packing was done until a man-of-war should be sent to take us to Honolulu. I have occupied the time in various computations & arranging my papers.—Today I have a letter saying that I shall be relieved about the 1st [of] February. Accordingly I shall start immediately to visit the crater."[19]

29

· · · · ·

More Attention from the King

By mid-January, the six chronometer runs connecting Honolulu with the two auxiliary stations were complete, and Captain Tupman sent a letter of gratitude to Captain Van der Meulen of the *Tenedos* informing him that those operations appeared "exceedingly satisfactory."[1] It was now time to tidy up and return to England.

But the tidying up, scientific and otherwise, was a time-consuming affair and continued into February. David Flitner's contributions to the transit enterprise, for one thing, called for reciprocation.[2] And whether called for or not, more heed would be given to the meridian mark—a wispy wooden upright that, in early November, had been erected more than 4 miles away in the mountains above Honolulu.[3]

But Honolulu's transit frenzy had clearly ebbed, even if her petty annoyances did not. As before, these continued to spill from two sources: nature and society. Nature, which had on December 28 served up the surprising—an earthquake[4]—now served up the unsurprising: more rain. Society did the same.

The January casting-out to San Francisco of madman Barnacle had relieved Tupman of a major source of exasperation, but it alone was not a palliative for all the social ills that continued to plague the expedition. The flood of intrusive guests continued into January and then into February, by which time Tupman was counting them not only "numerous" but positively "inconsiderate."[5]

Then there were those whose ill manners were prompted by evil spirits: those at whose hands a dozen "spirits" disappeared from the expedition's stock, and those (two marines from the *Reindeer*) who became "drunken rascals who stole our wines & beer to supply their shipmates & for 3 days gave us much trouble." When on February 9 all the required astronomical observations were at last concluded, the conclusion, such as it was, must have come none too soon for the beleaguered Tupman, who that very day again had cause to snarl into his journal: "One of our Servants drunk on stolen liquor."[6]

Mercifully, not all of Hawai'i's people, native or foreign, were as dissolute or as unsavory. And although some members of the expedition—Forbes and Johnson among them—had already departed from Hawai'i by early February,[7] others who remained behind found themselves hobnobbing with high society. They dined with the French commissioner Theodore

Ballieu and his wife and with the "High Chiefess" Bernice Pauahi Bishop. They visited and were visited by Princess Ruth. And when King Kalākaua—who had called upon them within a week after his return from the United States on February 15—gave a state ball soon thereafter, they were in attendance.[8]

Finally, on March 10, the expedition broke up the establishment at 'Āpua. Three days later—in accordance with the economic wisdom dictated in Airy's instructions—a sale was conducted, a sale that attracted much attention and realized several hundred British pounds.[9]

> Mar. 13. The sale. Our household goods sold well, many friends desiring to obtain a memento of our visit. The long shed, Cook house, walls of huts, transit hut complete, water pipes & taps, 6-foot fencing and a large pile of lumber were knocked down to His Majesty the King for a very small sum, as no one would bid against him. We were not altogether sorry for this as His Majesty has given us the land rent free & had aided us in many ways tending to save expense to the British Government.[10]

After spending more than six months in Hawai'i, the last of the transit of Venus party would be conveyed from Honolulu to Mare Island—the headquarters of the U.S. Coast Survey near San Francisco—aboard HMS *Reindeer.* Her departure was fixed for March 20.[11]

On Tuesday, March 16, the end in sight, Tupman, undeterred by "very wet weather," attended a magnificent farewell dinner at the palace.[12] Given by King Kalākaua to Tupman and to the captain and officers of the *Reindeer,* the dinner's lavish menu included mock turtle soup, stuffed *uhu,* and roast goose; shrimp curry; chicken, duck, and plover; pastries and fruit; a Roman punch; strawberries and cream; and more. The bill of fare, printed on white satin ribbon and enclosed in a bouquet of artificial flowers, was placed on each plate. This epicurean delight, a triumph of both taste and art, was said to have been far superior to anything of its kind before attempted in Honolulu.[13]

Still more delights awaited at Waikīkī where, two days later, Tupman attended a festive gathering of an estimated two hundred persons. The afternoon affair, a Hawaiian-style picnic that included music and croquet and was honored by the presence of the king and queen, was held at the residence of Princess Miriam Likelike and her Scottish husband the Honorable Archibald Cleghorn.[14]

Other post-transit events, already on Honolulu's horizon in March of 1875, were not as playful. The last of the British expedition was now ready to depart, and away would go the last British man-of-war, leaving Hawaiian waters empty of the Union Jack. British influence in the Islands—precariously propped up, with Captain Cook's ghost, on a slender 24-foot concrete post at Kealakekua Bay—was being reduced to symbolism and sentiment, and British commissioner Wodehouse, aware that King Kalākaua had recently returned from Washington, was already wailing: "Great efforts are being made to establish a paramount American influence in this group, and I fear that unless the English Naval Flag is constantly displayed, they will be successful."[15]

But the *Reindeer* was waiting to go—and would go. And on March 19, just ten days after Wodehouse's lament, Tupman's sojourn in Hawai'i drew to a close with his last journal entry:

> Continuous heavy rain. . . . Paid numerous farewell visits. Busy packing & preparing for final departure . . . arranged . . . the shipment of the Instruments Etc for Europe (in all 73 Cases). Ramsden, Noble & Nichol went to farewell State breakfast at the Palace. Tupman paid farewell visits to the British & French Commissioners; turned over the Observatory Grounds (Apua) to Major Boyd, His Majesty's Chamberlain; settled all accounts & gave to the French Commissioner a letter concerning the site of Lieutenant Fleuriais' pier.[16]

Tupman would not soon forget his brief encounter with the people of Honolulu. Although secret irritations had riddled his private journal, his published statement on behalf of the O'ahu contingent would reveal no acrimony, nor would it contain even a hint of bitter memories: "The reminiscences of our six months' sojourn on that far distant island will ever be of the most agreeable."[17]

The fullness of life among the "savages," if not entirely forgotten, had been selectively burked by that subtle form of duplicity called good manners. And by polite diplomacy, if not genuine sentiment, Tupman was particularly grateful to King Kalākaua, telling Airy at Greenwich: "Up to the last moment of leaving Honolulu we received the same courteous hospitality from His Majesty & the principal officers of State & residents as greeted our arrival, and it seems to me that the British Government should tender its thanks to His Majesty for our kind reception."[18]

30

· · · · ·

Homeward Bound

U pon the completion of their duties in Hawai'i, members of the expedition could—and did—take separate ways home to England. Barnacle was the first to go in January and reached England the following month. Johnson, who followed as far as San Francisco in early February, lingered in Canada and would not see home until the fall.[1] In the meantime, Tupman and Noble, who were among the last to depart in March, reached the Mare Island Navy Yard in early April[2] and, after a delay of nearly three weeks, proceeded homeward across North America by train.[3]

But Tupman and Noble were not the only Englishmen on the eastbound train. Nor were they the only men who had observed the recent transit from the Pacific. From San Francisco to Chicago they were joined by a familiar-looking shape that had appeared at Greenwich many months previous: a witty and self-deprecating man who, though now sporting "a scrubby beard 3.1415962 inches long or thereabouts," was leisurely making his own way home after his somewhat disappointing efforts to observe the transit from New Zealand. The man was Leonard Darwin.[4]

For Darwin, transit day—December 9, New Zealand time—had been gloomy. Of the half-dozen English observing stations (including his own at Burnham, about 18 miles from Christchurch) that extended over a distance of a thousand miles, "not one of them saw anything of value." When the rains came, he and his colleagues had forsaken their work and had gone out riding. A "wonderful bit of bad luck," he later would call it, as the next day was "glorious," and he could then take many good photographs of the sun with the unused plates![5]

His disappointment sharpened into levity, Leonard Darwin proceeded to Wellington and from there to Melbourne where a congress of transit of Venus observers was scheduled for February and where he was to have the honor of representing the British expedition. Then it was on to Sydney to catch "the San Francisco Mail."[6]

Now bound for North America, Leonard Darwin's pass through Hawai'i was brief. Had circumstances postponed the late March departure of the Sandwich Island transit men just a fortnight longer, he might have rendezvoused with them at Honolulu. As it was, Darwin did not reach the Islands until early April, about two weeks after the sailing of the *Reindeer* carrying Tupman and Noble to California. And even though his father's good reputation had preceded him, his visit to Hawai'i was not all that he would have desired.

Before Darwin's ship, the *Mikado,* could reach Hawai'i, an outbreak of measles was detected among the passengers. A double discomfort was the immediate result: the sickness itself, and the quarantine—or at least the prospects of one—that awaited the ship as the luscious Hawaiian Islands drew near. Native Hawaiians, having already seen foreign diseases—including this very one—ravage their numbers, were no friends to the insidious contagion. And as the *Mikado* approached Hawai'i, Leonard speculated that the dreaded disease might realize its worst harm upon himself and his fellow passengers by keeping them from landing in the Islands altogether. On April 5, he was at last forced to concede his lamentable state:

> The measles have done us what harm they could; we were not allowed to land at Honolulu and had to loaf about the deck for 8 hours within a stone['s] throw of an island, which I do not suppose I shall ever see again. As far as we could see the island was very picturesque, and we heard that the most beautiful place—a cliff where the last king threw a whole army over—was within an hours ride of the town. Every one grumbled, but I think they did perfectly right, as the measles is a very fatal disease to the natives, and there had been no cases for some years. Dr. Harkness [Fig. 58] came on board at Honolulu and he told me that the King—a native—was a great admirer of fathers works, and that if I had landed he should have taken me to pay my respect[s]. It would have been rather good fun seeing how he managed things, but I expect he is quite European in his manners.[7]

Fig. 58. William Harkness

Thus being denied even the slightest mischance of transmitting the deadly disease to King Kalākaua, Leonard Darwin proceeded to California, arriving at San Francisco on Sunday, April 11. Then, after spending several days in the Yosemite wilderness, he boarded the train eastward.

The train carrying the three astronomers reached Chicago on May 6. There the two transit men from Hawai'i split up. Noble went on to New York. Tupman, taken ill, stayed behind in Chicago. And Darwin, after writing his mother a partial account of his American experiences,[8] proceeded on to Washington to encounter still more:

127

From Chicago I went on to Washington and stopped there about 3 days. I had a card [of] introduction from an American transit of Venus man to one of the Astronomers at the Observatory, which opened the doors of that institution to me, and every one was wonderfully civil to me. One of the "professors" there had been in the American Engineers . . . and we struck up a sort of friendship. He took me to look through the great telescope there, the biggest of its kind in the world, and I saw the moons of Uranus, at least every one else saw them and I said I did. The systems on which this observatory and the Greenwich one are worked are entirely different; at Greenwich every thing goes on like clock work and no one is expected to use his brains at all except the Astronomer Royal. Here all the assistants are highly educated men, all of them gentlemen; but the head of the institution is an old admiral who does not know much about it. The result is that with better material they do not turn out such good work, and there is not such good discipline.[9]

After some further sightseeing in America, including visits to Boston[10] and Niagara Falls, Leonard Darwin crossed the Atlantic from New York and was back in England on June 19. Ten days later, George Tupman reported his own return to the Astronomer Royal.[11] Though the two men were perhaps already looking ahead to the 1882 transit—when they would both once again contribute to the British observational efforts—it was now only the summer of 1875, and the 1874 transit work was nowhere near its completion.

31

· · · · ·

Some Challenging Correspondence

hough the British 1874 transit of Venus enterprise was made difficult by both the complexity and the delicacy of the task, the matter was frustrated even further by the ineptitude and the irresponsibility of the participants. Both Henry Barnacle and Richard Johnson contributed to that frustration.

Johnson's leisurely journey home via Canada did not pass unnoticed. News of his return to Britain did not reach Greenwich until October 1875—and even then it was a return not to England, but to Ireland![1] More exasperating still was the questionable whereabouts of Johnson's work, let alone his person. A concerned Captain Tupman made an inquiry,[2] and Airy, thoroughly miffed by the Irishman's disregard of his very specific instructions, was soon chiding:

> I have repeatedly inquired from Captain Tupman with much anxiety about the transmission to this place of copies of the whole of your Transit-of-Venus observations: and I believe that he has always conveyed my inquiries to you, and the answers have not been satisfactory to me. . . . Pray let me call your attention to the Instructions, Chapter (II), Article 1, that all observations are to be delivered up "not later than the day of landing in England" which of course means "in Britain". And then Article 2 "As a general rule, observations and calculations are to be written out in duplicate, for transmission of copies to England by different channels." The obvious purposes of these provisions were, that security should be given to the deposit of the observations here, and that they should be brought under my cognizance as soon as possible.
>
> Pray let me beg you to give your immediate and best attention to these objects [emphasis in original].[3]

Though Johnson was quick to reply and quick to apologize,[4] his response would not be satisfactory for another year and a half. Not until April of 1877—and only after several more letters from Airy—did he at last surrender all the documents requested weeks (if not years) earlier.[5]

Henry Barnacle's post-transit behavior proved equally annoying to the Astronomer Royal—but more from the correspondence he sent than from what he failed to send.

Having arrived in England much before any of his fellows, Barnacle promptly wrote to Airy announcing his safe return.[6] Though this effectively closed his connection with the transit of Venus expedition,[7] an astronomer once "mad" had now grown indignant and was determined that Airy should know the reason—and know it several times over.

By early March, and even as the last of the transit of Venus party lingered in Honolulu, the first salvos were being launched from Barnacle's pen when, in a letter to Airy, he let it be known that it was not until a few hours before his final departure from Honolulu that he had been explicitly made aware, in a conversation with Tupman, of Forbes' low estimation of his astronomical abilities, saying, and not entirely without justification: "If I was incapable of doing my work I think I should have been informed of it previously."[8] Rising to his own defense, Barnacle soon sent Airy a detailed account of some of the work that he had done, or attempted to do—adding as evidence his official journal, a notebook containing the original observations he had made at Honolulu, and a meteorological report he had voluntarily kept at Kailua-Kona. These documents argued on behalf of Barnacle's dedication to his work and against accusations of incompetence, which Barnacle averred were both unwarranted in their substance and untimely in their revelation. Seeking to implicate Forbes and to vindicate himself, he told Airy: "I think you will see, that whilst at Honolulu when I was allowed to do work I did it, and it seems to me a very childish and unwarrantable accusation on the part of Forbes, and contrary to positive facts to say that I was incapable."[9]

Barnacle argued to Airy that he had "just cause" for complaining about not being allowed to share fully in work that would have been "a pleasure" to him. He argued, with curious "proof," that the treatment he had received "throughout" from Forbes had been "almost insulting." He argued, and he would argue again, that he had been treated unfairly. But he failed to argue convincingly.

Henry Barnacle's desire to exonerate himself was not altogether unpredictable. The termination of his affiliation with the expedition also meant the end of his employment by the government. But it was a situation that he hoped would be short lived, and in May 1875 he sought Airy's help:

> I am . . . about to write to several friends of high position and influence, to ask them to mention me for some post in any Government Scientific department, but before doing so I shall be obliged if you will kindly favour me with a few lines stating what you can in my favour, as to steadiness of character & c. and I trust you will also allow me to refer to you if I should find it necessary to do so.
>
> If you will kindly use your influence in mentioning me for any post in the meteorological, or any other scientific department, I shall be very thankful.[10]

130

Airy's response to this plea was daunting: "There is no admission now to any scientific department under the Government except under the competitive examination of the Commissioners of Civil Service"—to which he added the disappointing note: "Nothing that I could do would be of the smallest use."[11] But Barnacle, incredulous, would not be stilled. Six months later, in November 1875, he again wrote to Airy, not to report how he had fared on the Civil Service examination (or even to say whether or not he had bothered to take it), but rather to accuse Forbes of libel and to reiterate his request for a testimonial. His letter crescendoed with the lament: "It has hurt me very much indeed this ending of the Expedition for I gave all my soul, and energy to the work, first because I knew the great value of it, and secondly [because of] the love I have for the science of Astronomy."[12]

Airy patiently replied that he could not possibly furnish the requested testimonial, explaining that he had never had any direct role in the practical part of Barnacle's preparations (at Greenwich) for the transit, nor could he attest to his performance in the Sandwich Islands, where his immediate commanders had been Tupman and Forbes.[13] Still, Barnacle would not be placated and responded with a letter from Chigwell, where he now held the post of assistant master of the Chigwell School, Essex:

> M^r. Forbes by stating what he has, has deliberately taken my character away by libel, it is so utterly untrue that I cannot allow it to drop, to allow it is to admit its truth, it places me in a most awkward position, for when applying for a post of course a testimonial with regard to the Expedition is required. . . . I should be much obliged if you would ask Cap^{tn} Tupman for one as I was always treated by him with the utmost consideration, and in the most gentlemanly manner, I cannot ask M^r. Forbes for one, for tho' he knows most about me, (Cap^{tn} Tupman having his time so occupied) and had my work, which he used, and said was all right, yet of course he would say things to shield himself.[14]

Lack of a testimonial letter had already produced adverse effects, Barnacle claimed. It had already kept him from a post that could have doubled and nearly tripled his annual income—"a matter of no small importance" about which he thought Airy would sympathize.

But if he wanted more than pity, he did not get it. In early 1876—and now desirous of the head mastership of the Chigwell School—he again wrote to Airy, insisting that Forbes' accusations (that he had "been of no use on the Transit of Venus Expedition . . . [and] neither could nor would do the work") were utterly false and needed to be refuted. The documentary evidence—including the daily work that Barnacle reported having handed to Forbes and that (Barnacle proposed) Forbes now should be required to produce—would help to disprove the case against him. Barnacle then stated three requirements: first, that Forbes write a retraction of his accusations; second, that Tupman apologize for making a "random statement" to Airy of Forbes' accusations without giving him (Barnacle) an opportunity to refute them "on the spot" at Honolulu; and third, that failing one or both of these first two requirements, Airy should write for him a testimonial. From want of such a testimonial, Barnacle reminded Airy, he had already "suffered much" and could, as he had been told by a lawyer, "claim much as reparation."[15]

Airy parried the threat simply by telling Barnacle that there must have been some mistake: He had never told Barnacle that Tupman had informed him that Forbes had reported Barnacle as having been "of no use" on the expedition. And with regard to a testimonial, Airy could not from his own knowledge provide one but needed to defer to Captain Tupman, from whom he now had a report, and not a very flattering one.[16]

But Airy's response to Barnacle's complaints were disingenuous. Some of the testy post-transit correspondence between Barnacle and Airy had, in fact, been shown to Tupman, and Tupman had replied privately to the Astronomer Royal by giving a less-restrained evaluation of the mad stargazer than Airy was inclined to reveal:

> I have said elsewhere that Mr Barnacle was not in his right mind, or, if he were, his mind was of a very abnormal order. He brought great discredit on the Expedition & thoroughly disgusted all the other members.
>
> It is a matter of very great regret to me that I formed my opinion of him, previous to our departure, too much from his own account of himself.
>
> You will remember that I had no one with whom to replace him.[17]

But even more damaging to Barnacle's post-transit aspirations would have been Tupman's more robustly expressed opinion of his teaching qualifications—an opinion that Airy had concealed from Barnacle by abridging the painful truth: "Mr Barnacle complains that among his numerous testimonials there is a blank for the time he was attached to my party for observing the Transit of Venus. I cannot conscientiously express a favourable opinion on his qualifications for teaching anything, particularly mathematics. . . . He was prevented by cloudy weather from observing the Transit of Venus, a great misfortune—to him."[18]

Tupman's merciless critique, softened by Airy into a coup de grace, effectively snuffed Barnacle's aspirations to launch a career by leaning on either his transit of Venus experience or on the man at Greenwich who had put him in the way of that experience. A failed astronomer, Henry Barnacle now advanced toward an ecclesiastical career by default. In 1877, the year following Airy's crushing letter, he was ordained a deacon.[19]

32

· · · · ·

Reducing the Data

The 1874 chase after the astronomical unit, punctuated as it was by per-
sonalities and peradventure, refused an abrupt and singular climax
and instead faded as slowly as the evening twilight on a midsum-
mer's day at Greenwich. There, the gargantuan amount of data generated
by the transit observations—in Hawai'i and elsewhere—was collected, and
Tupman was put in charge of the reductions. Then, upon completing their
share of the work, the last of the observers—all of whom, happily, returned
from their various stations without death or accident[1]—were finally discharged. But Tupman and the work lingered, and in 1876 Airy wrote of the
ongoing besiegement: "In the astronomical part of the reductions, there has
been great labour and difficulty in the determination of local sidereal times;
some books of observations required extensive transcription; some instrumental errors are still uncertain; [and] the latter determinations have per-
plexed us so much that we are inclined to believe that, in spite of the great
facilities of reduction given by the transit instrument, it would be better to
rely on the altazimuth for time-determinations."[2]

As the work dragged on over the next several years, the additional
computing staff hired to labor with the wearisome data would make slow
progress, and Tupman, who gave himself liberally to the task, would often
be taken ill.[3] But the reductions could be excruciating: Just to calculate the
longitudes of two stations (Honolulu and Rodriguez) necessitated the use
of three million figures, and this was but a fraction of the work required.[4]

Airy, it seems, had attempted to ease the burden by producing a set of
reduction formulae that introduced, at least to the initiated, "no mathematical novelty."[5] The initiated in this case were, however, not solely British but
a larger international scientific community; and because Airy understood
that different nations, different observers, different theoretical views, and
different classes of instruments had been involved in the transit chase, he
also understood that the British observations begged for treatment as part
of a larger whole. Still, of the more than fifty stations around the world
where the transit had been more or less successfully observed, the largest
fraction of those by far had been within the British Empire;[6] so the British,
with Airy at the helm, could not properly abandon their post. It was a formidable and daunting task. And it required patience—something of which
Her Majesty's Government had a limited supply.

By April of 1877, that patience was all but exhausted. In the House of

Commons, pressure was mounting to have the results of the government-supported transit observations laid before Parliament.[7] And although it had already become evident that several different stages of the phenomenon at both ingress and egress needed to be discriminated, and that special care was required (as Stone had earlier argued with respect to the 1769 transit) in the interpretation of the language employed in the reports of the various observers, Tupman and Airy capitulated: Their report—preliminary though it was—was ready for printing by mid-July.[8]

Because in New Zealand (as on the island of Hawai'i) the transit observations had suffered from bad weather, meaningful data had been collected, prima facie, from only four stations and their subdivisions: Egypt (Mokattam Hill [above Cairo], Thebes, and Suez); Rodriguez (Point Venus, the Hermitage, and Point Coton); Kerguelen's Land (Observatory Bay, Supply Bay, and Thumb Peak); and the Sandwich Islands (O'ahu and Kaua'i).[9] But there was ample data in hand with which to work; and so, after approximately two years' efforts at reducing that data, Tupman and Airy prepared to reveal for public scrutiny a new number for solar parallax, using every available combination of ingress and egress and several "phases" of each of these.[10]

Although this method at first threw up a dizzy range of values—from 8".407 to 8".933 (Table 5)—the vertigo could easily be mitigated by a bit of mathematical manipulation: The ingress observations alone, when all the combinations were considered inter se, could be made to yield, by assigning various "weights" to the various phases, a mean solar parallax of 8".739, while a similar combination for egress observations inter se gave 8".847. And if there were any residual compunctions resulting from the spread between the two of a mere million miles (or 0".108), such bedeviling inner voices could be quietly suppressed with another bit of legerdemain: by giving a greater weight (10.46) to the result of all the combinations for ingress and a lesser weight (2.53) to the combinations for egress.[11] This mathematical hocus-pocus yielded, as a general value, a solar parallax of 8".760, corresponding to a mean solar distance of 93,300,000 miles, and these were the numbers sallied forth in the 1877 House Report.[12] Although the report readily admitted that the "weights" assigned to the various observations would always remain open to criticism, the resulting figures were publicly palatable. The AU had been extracted from the numbers by massaging them into compliance.

Still, such an ad hoc determination of the solar parallax was ill seeming, and Airy was quick to mention this caveat:

> The Report on the observations of the Transit of Venus, which I have the honour to submit . . . applies only to the telescopic observations made at different stations of the expedition undertaken by the British Government, and to the conclusions deduced from these observations. It will probably be their

Table 5. Resulting values of mean solar parallax from various combinations of ingress and egress, as presented in the 1877 House Report. For an explanation of the various phases—marked α, β, γ, δ, ε, ζ—see note 10.

INGRESS

	Phase	Parallax	Weight
Combination of Ingress Accelerated at the Sandwich Islands with Ingress Retarded at Rodriguez—Resulting Value of Mean Solar Parallax from 3 Different Phases of Observation	α β γ	8.683 8.758 8.782	1.5 4.5 1.5
Combination of Ingress Accelerated at the Sandwich Islands with Ingress Retarded at Kerguelen's—Resulting Value of Mean Solar Parallax from 3 Different Phases of Observation	α β γ	8.735 8.727 8.736	1.5 4.5 1.5
Mean		8.739	

EGRESS

	Phase	Parallax	Weight
Combination of Egress Retarded at Mokattam and Suez with Egress Retarded at Rodriguez—Resulting Value of Mean Solar Parallax from 2 Different Phases of Observation	δ ζ	8.837 8.888	1 3
Combination of Egress Retarded at Mokattam and Suez with Egress Accelerated at Thumb Peak and Observatory Bay, Kerguelen's—Resulting Value of Mean Solar Parallax from 2 Different Phases of Observation	δ ζ	8.793 8.883	1 1
Combination of Egress Retarded at Thebes with Egress Retarded at Rodriguez—Resulting Value of Mean Solar Parallax from 3 Different Phases of Observation	δ ε ζ	8.407 8.684 8.933	1 1 3
Combination of Egress Retarded at Thebes with Egress Accelerated at Thumb Peak and Observatory Bay, Kerguelen's—Resulting Value of Mean Solar Parallax from 3 Different Phases of Observation	δ ε ζ	8.550 8.875 8.908	1 1 1
Mean		8.847	

Lordships' wish that, as soon as the photographs of the Transit of Venus which have been taken shall be completely measured, a further Report, based upon those records, and, if possible, upon the combination of all, with the similar observations taken under the authority of foreign Governments, should be prepared for submission to their Lordships.[13]

Though the ambitious scope of Airy's "further Report" would never be fully realized, Tupman labored indefatigably on—even when, in November of 1877, it had become clear that the government would refuse to sanction his stipend beyond the end of the following March. "I cannot allow a mere pecuniary consideration to prevent me finishing off properly the work I have had so much to do with," he wrote to Airy. "The Lords of the Admiralty will allow me to remain under you as long as you please, although they cannot grant special salaries. Perhaps things will be nearly completed by the end of March 1878."[14]

But when March of 1878 came, so too did the gauntlet, thrown down by E. J. Stone. Stone, now Her Majesty's Astronomer at the Cape of Good Hope, had received for himself a copy of the Parliamentary Report of the previous year, and he was aghast! Having meticulously examined the details of that document, he proceeded to conjure an independent number for solar parallax that differed considerably from the value given in the official report; and he felt duty-bound to wave his views before other astronomers. His ruminations were published in the March 1878 issue of the *Monthly Notices of the Royal Astronomical Society*.[15] There Stone maintained that the whole strength of the transit of Venus method for the determination of solar parallax rested upon the assumption that there were phases of contact of the limbs of Venus and the sun that could be recognized by observers as distinctive. The two phases of greatest value, he wrote, were the so-called *apparent* and *real* contacts. But at one of the principal stations, the Sandwich Islands, apparent contacts had been missed, Stone judged, leaving but four meaningful observations of real contacts there: those of Tupman, Noble, Johnson, and Cator.[16] Combining, then, those useful observations made at the Sandwich Islands with others made at Rodriguez, Kerguelen, and Burnham (New Zealand), Stone proceeded to obtain as a general result from the ingress observations a solar parallax of 8".86. The egress observations, also reassessed by Stone, yielded 8".98. The two numbers combined gave 8".88 for the mean solar parallax—a number that compared favorably with Stone's earlier determinations by a variety of methods, including his reassessment of the 1769 transit observations. And this, when considered alongside results obtained elsewhere by others, seemed to point to a value of 8".89, corresponding to an AU of 91,940,000 miles.

Tupman was not caught entirely off guard. Even before seeing Stone's work, he had formed his own opinion that the treatment of the ingress, as exhibited in the Parliamentary Report, was unsatisfactory. He was now prepared to emend his numbers: A mean solar parallax of 8".857, he now thought, was proper for the ingress observations. For the egress observations, however, Tupman summoned new witnesses: Stone had not yet seen the mass of Australian, Indian, and other data from the 1874 transit now lodged at the Royal Observatory at Greenwich; and, upon examining these, Tupman found that they yielded a parallax of 8".792. A general solution to the whole gave 8".813, and Tupman thought it impossible to deduce from the observations a parallax much larger than this.[17] This was tantamount to a polite concession to—but an ultimate dismissal of—Stone's data juggling.

Still Tupman was unfinished, and in June of 1878 he collectively published a series of extracts from numerous transit of Venus reports received at the Royal Observatory.[18] Superseding the 1877 Parliamentary Report, Tupman was now able to reveal and to include in his reductions some forty-eight separate observations of internal contact at egress and thirty-one at ingress—including, among the latter, David Flitner's observations at Waikīkī. But not all these observations were, he thought, equally worthwhile. Of the ingress observations, for example, Tupman rejected eleven outright, including two made in Hawai'i: Captain Cator's were dismissed because he had used a telescope of very low power, gave no description of the phenomena observed, and made his sketches afterward from memory; Dunn's observations were discarded because his telescope was small and much shaken by the wind, but also because he was some twenty seconds behind several other observers near him in recording the moment of contact. To such marginal observations Tupman assigned a "weight" of zero. Still, there were twenty respectable observations of ingress: eight of these were given double "weight" (including those of Tupman and Johnson) and the remaining dozen a "weight" of one. The resulting value for solar parallax was 8".845. Similar surgery was performed on the forty-eight observations of internal contact at egress: fourteen were given a "weight" of two; twenty-seven a "weight" of one; and seven a "weight" of zero. The resulting parallax figure was 8".846. This brought the ingress and the egress observations close to happy uniformity—or so it would seem. Still Tupman was unsatisfied, saying, "Although the . . . results of Ingress and Egress present such an unexpected agreement, it cannot be said that the mean 8".8455 is entitled to much confidence, since all the observations would be fairly well satisfied by any mean solar parallax between 8".82 and 8".88."

As to the value of the 1877 Parliamentary Report, Tupman admitted that it had been produced somewhat hurriedly and under pressure. But he was defensive of that earlier work in which he had played such a major role and thought that the calculation of the solar parallax contained therein was a "perfectly legitimate deduction"—and this even though suspicions of "doctoring" the calculations had now crept into the discussion.

In 1879, Tupman was still voluntarily devoting his time to the completion of the transit work, laboring every day at the observatory with (Airy reported) the same "regularity and vigour" as one of the assistants. The hasty call from the legislature in 1877 had left much work undone; and considerable labor was necessary to put reports and calculations in a shape adapted to the eventual printing of the account of the whole enterprise.[19] In September, Airy received (through the Admiralty) a notification from the Treasury saying that a sum that appeared sufficient would be allowed for the continuation of the transit of Venus calculations, and that Tupman (now a major) would be permitted to devote his time to that object until the end of June 1880.[20]

In the autumn of 1880, the transit of 1874 now almost six years past and that of 1882 fast approaching, Tupman concluded his Home Journal[21] and presented Airy with the calculations and other documents. Airy was probably little surprised to find that some of the work was presented in great detail, especially for District B, the Sandwich Islands; and, grateful to Tupman for bringing the work to that point, regarded his efforts as "heroic."[22]

Still, the work was yet undone; and it was now Airy's task to see it through to completion.

33

· · · · ·

Publishing and Retiring

A s the 1880s began to overtake the 1870s, the 1874 transit of Venus, now receding further and further into the past, became but a fading memory to the aging Astronomer Royal. The seven Sandwich Island astronomers, once bound together by Airy's commanding persona on a far-away Polynesian archipelago and for a lofty purpose, now went to their separate destinies. Richard Johnson and George Forbes—both of whom remained lifelong bachelors—returned to academic life, the one to Ireland, the other to Scotland. Henry Glanville Barnacle beat his testimonial-seeking sword of post-transit vituperation into a religious plowshare that planted him in Australia. George Lyon Tupman bore down at Greenwich on the 1874 data, then bore away to New Zealand for the 1882 transit. E. J. W. Noble, who soon after his return to England was summoned by the Admiralty to return to his headquarters at Portsmouth,[1] and Francis E. Ramsden, who, even after his aim at the photoheliograph had gone astray on transit day, had seen to it that the precious photographic plates had been "most carefully packed" for their passage to England[2]—these two quietly faded into oblivion. John Walter Nichol, the energetic and promising young astronomer from Edinburgh, having successfully seen one transit of Venus, would not live to witness another; after his post-transit work in England on the reductions of the astronomical observations made at Honolulu, followed by two brief years of astronomical work and study in Germany, he died suddenly and prematurely in November 1878 from a "pulmonary affection."[3] Meanwhile, at Greenwich, George Biddell Airy, the consummate utilitarian, suffered perhaps the worst fate of all: being compelled by retirement to outlive his own usefulness.

Paradoxically, Airy was busied and bothered by the aftershocks of 1874 because he was too good for his own good. From his instructions—conscientiously calling for the return to England of every instrument and even some of the prefabricated huts—he got more than he anticipated. But because the transit had not been seen at home, and because the five expeditions to distant lands had been funded by the public purse, it was not unreasonable to expect that some public interest would follow the 1874 transit, and it did. By April of 1876, and with Airy's permission, the South Kensington Museum in London had erected, for public education and as part of a larger scientific exhibition, some of the instruments used at the five British stations,[4] among them: an equatorial telescope (and hut), an altazimuth (and hut), a transit instrument (and hut), a transit of Venus model, and several clocks. Also included was the Honolulu photoheliograph.[5] On May 13, Queen Victoria was at South Kensington, and Airy, the good public servant, went to explain the astronomical instruments and even showed Her Majesty one of the transit of Venus photographs.[6]

It was, in fact, the transit photographs rather than the instruments used to make them that were of more than ceremonious concern to Airy. Because the telescopic observations had not been uniformly successful, Airy, for a while, held out hope for the photographs. Having been brought to Greenwich along with the written accounts of the telescopic observations, the photographs from all five British stations had been placed in the hands of Tupman and his assistant C. E. Burton for examination and measurement.[7] Each photograph had been measured six times by Burton and six times by Tupman. In the end, however, came bitter disappointment: "As soon as Tupman and Burton began to take measurements from the photographs, difficulties ensued. The 3.9 inch image of the sun had to be enlarged in order to yield a sufficiently precise number, but on enlargement the limb of both the Sun and of Venus proved indistinct, the silver faded off to nothing and the measurement became, as Tupman termed it, 'guesswork'. In addition, the size of the sun and of Venus varied from photograph to photograph, owing, Airy concluded, to photographic irradiation."[8]

The photographic measurements were hopelessly varied and inconsistent; and although Tupman worked on them until 1878, he concluded that the defects in the photographic images were of such magnitude as to forbid their employment in the determination of solar parallax—adding somewhat cynically that they did not even give a sufficiently accurate diameter of the sun.[9] It came, then, as no surprise when Airy, in publishing the overall results of the 1874 transit enterprise, thought it best "to abstain from publishing the results of the photographic measures as comparable with those deduced from telescopic view."[10] This was just as well, for two independent assessments of the photographic results were both disastrous, producing the grossly skewed values of 8".08 (Tupman) and 8".17 (Burton) for the solar parallax,[11] Airy himself saying: "The results from photography have disappointed me much. The failure has arisen, perhaps sometimes from irregularity of limb, or from atmospheric distortion, but more frequently from faintness and from want of clear definition. Many photographs, which to the eye appeared good, lost all strength and sharpness when placed under the measuring microscope. It was once remarked to me 'You might as well try to measure the zodiacal light.'"[12]

Such a brazen—and expensive—disappointment may have been the single greatest reason why photography would not be officially employed by any nation for observations of the 1882 transit,[13] Airy himself stating, as the general opinion, that it would be "useless" to repeat photographic observations.[14]

The 1874 transit of Venus and its lingering labors effectively chased Airy from Greenwich and closed his days as Astronomer Royal. Seven long years passed between the well-timed celestial appearance of 1874 and the much-delayed terrestrial appearance of the official published results; and some of the work required in preparing those results for the press, Airy complained, "occupied all the hours, not engaged on routine business, on which I could usually have reckoned for other matters of science."[15] By 1879, the great mass of reductions and manuscripts related to the transit had grown to an estimated equivalent of two hundred bound volumes.[16]

In July of 1881, Airy would observe his eightieth birthday. He was now ready for a quieter life and would later tell David Gill: "It had been my wish to retire from the Observatory in the summer of 1880, but the old Transit of Venus was still hanging over me. My part was cleared off in the summer of 1881, and then I took my opportunity."[17]

The *Account of Observations of the Transit of Venus, 1874, December 8, Made under the Authority of the British Government: And of the Reduction of the Observations,* edited by Airy, was finally published, fittingly, in the year of his retirement, 1881. Supplemented by an introduction and an appendix, Airy's *Account* was divided into five parts, one for each of the five British stations, and ran to more than five hundred pages in total length, fully half of which was devoted to the expedition to the Hawaiian Islands. Still, this weighty tome was but an abridgment of the bulk of the matter originally intended for publication[18]—and there were two items conspicuously absent from the document: the name of Henry Glanville Barnacle and a new value for the astronomical unit.

But a new number for the AU was out of place in such a document, Airy thought. In fact, it was only after the publication of his *Account* that such a number might properly appear; then the British observations could be brought together with those of all other participating nations and the subject treated as a whole and in the manner Airy himself had, by early 1875, already prescribed.[19]

Even so, the Astronomer Royal could not resist the temptation to pry open the cosmic lid, and in November 1877—long after the transit itself but just four short months after his report to Parliament—Airy had published separately his own computed results for the British telescopic observations of the transit.[20] Although his numbers were not beyond dispute, he and his transit of Venus men had come very close to realizing Halley's eighteenth-century dream: They had gotten the sun's distance right to within one-half of one percent; and Airy's figure—a solar parallax of 8".754 (and a corresponding solar distance of 93,375,000 miles)—had come within 0".04 of the modern value.[21]

The 1882 transit came the year following Airy's retirement; and even as it approached, and even as Richard Proctor published his quibbles with Airy's numbers,[22] the author of *Transits of Venus* had already written, in 1874, these hopeful words:

We cannot doubt that when the transits of 2004 and 2012 are approaching, astronomers will look back with interest on the operations conducted during the present [nineteenth-century] 'transit-season;' and although in those times in all probability the determination of the sun's distance by other methods . . . will far surpass in accuracy those now obtained by such methods, yet . . . I think the astronomers of the first years of the twenty-first century, looking back over the long transitless period which will then have passed, will understand the anxiety of astronomers in our own time to utilise to the full whatever opportunities the coming transits [of 1874 and 1882] may afford; and I venture to hope that . . . they will not be disposed to judge overharshly what some in our own day may have regarded as an excess of zeal.[23]

But whatever may have been the excesses or the shortcomings of nineteenth-century astronomy, the importance with which the Hawaiian Islands were regarded in the British 1874 transit of Venus enterprise had been clearly indicated in Airy's decision to send the largest of his five contingents—seven astronomers—and his top man, George Tupman, to Honolulu. This was exactly as it should have been. For Airy had already surmised, many years before the momentous event, that the "Owhyhee" site would be, in a word, "indispensable."[24]

34

. . . . .

Reaffirmations

Romance, both real and imagined, is an inextricable part of Hawai'i's ethos, and it didn't take long to romanticize the transit of Venus. In Washington, headquarters of the American 1874 transit efforts, composer John Philip Sousa produced both a transit of Venus march and a transit of Venus novel.[1] Hawai'i produced a transit of Venus lei: "[a] white paper star lei that was in vogue . . . in the '70's, commemorating the Transit of Venus of 1874. They were appropriately called Hoku (star), and were made of stiff, white paper, forming many points, to convey the idea of scintillation. They were fashionable for some time, for head or hat decoration, and were known to foreigners as Venus leis."[2]

If this was evidence that an earlier nineteenth-century European romanticism had, after more than a half-century lag, at last reached full flower in the Pacific, the post-transit 1870s would prove not only a time of floral festooning in Hawai'i but a time of Carlylean genuflecting as well. The posthumous apotheosis of national heroes—surely no less a hallmark of British romanticism than the bookish constructions of Thomas Carlyle or the lyrical flourishes of Keats and Wordsworth—had, by 1874, already enshrined one such hero at Kealakekua Bay. Then, in 1877—and almost as if the sentiments of the time demanded it—Princess Miriam Likelike, wife to the British-born Archibald Cleghorn, deeded to British commissioner Wodehouse a piece of newly hallowed ground "to keep and maintain . . . a monument in memory of Captain Cook." One could almost hear the clanging of the church bells at Great Saint Andrew's in Cambridge proclaiming the Cook family hagiography to the larger world as the dead captain now became as broadly embraced by his motherland—or nearly so—as ritual and symbolism would allow.[3]

King Kalākaua personally visited the Cook Memorial in the aftermath of the 1874 transit[4] and, the following decade, paid a visit to Cook's mother country during his historic trip around the world. It was a trip that would twice recall the 1874 transit.

In January of 1881, aboard the *City of Sydney* and en route to San Francisco on the first leg of his journey, King Kalākaua met an English astronomer. Homeward bound from Australia, the man was, so it happened, somewhat of an authority on transits of Venus. But he was also a fervent exponent, and one of the nineteenth-century's foremost popularizers, of the belief in the possible existence of extraterrestrial life. He had, in fact, already published a book on the subject—*Other Worlds than Ours*—that would (by 1900) go through at least twenty-nine printings, making it by one reckoning one of the most widely read books in the entire extraterrestrial life debate. The man must have spoken, then, with at least some authority when, before the *Sydney* reached the Golden Gate, he showed Kalākaua "remote suns," "discoursed" with him and other passengers on the possible existence of extraterrestrial intelligence, and even discussed the "astral" theories of the Polynesians. Whether or not the king or the astronomer fully realized the other's credentials is not known, for Hawai'i's Merrie Monarch, it is said, liked to travel incognito. The astronomer was—incredibly—Richard Proctor.[5] (See Fig. 12.)

Several months after this unlikely encounter, King Kalākaua would again be bound for California, where he would pursue his astronomical interests more actively. After a transatlantic voyage from Liverpool to New York followed by a transcontinental train trip to San Francisco, he would climax his round-the-world jaunt with a visit to the nascent Lick Observatory on Mount Hamilton. Still under construction in 1881, the Lick Observatory would soon be home to the world's largest telescope, a new 36-inch instrument by the celebrated Alvan Clark and Sons. But the Clarks, no strangers to the American 1874 transit of Venus proceedings (Fig. 59),

had already furnished the Lick Observatory with one telescope: an instrument that soon would be specially mounted for Hawai'i's king. Kalākaua would be, for his own part, well prepared for the occasion. He had personally met the observatory's now-deceased benefactor James Lick while on his 1874–1875 Reciprocity Treaty trip to Washington and had already written longingly of the Lick Observatory that something of its kind was needed in Hawai'i. When, on the night of October 19, he at last peered through the Clark 12-inch, he would become "almost the first" man to do so from Mount Hamilton. Less than fourteen months later, the same telescope would be used to observe the 1882 transit of Venus.[6]

Fig. 59. Telescope by Alvan Clark and Sons used by the U.S. observing team at Vladivostok for the 1874 transit of Venus

144

Following the excitement of 1874, the 1882 visitation of Venus against the sun was predictably anticlimactic.[7] Between the two transits there had been, for one thing, a tactical alteration in the pursuit of the AU that would soon sound triumphant in the work of men such as Sir David Gill (see Fig. 17). Gill's work on minor planets—specifically Iris, Victoria, and Sappho—would eventually permit him to deduce a solar parallax of 8".80, or an Earth-sun distance of 92.9 million miles, a number so accurate that it would still be in use well into the twentieth century.[8]

Still, Venus would not be denied. The year following the conclusion of King Kalākaua's astronomically informed odyssey, on the morning of December 6, 1882 (Hawaiian time), Hōkūloa again slithered across the sun. Although the simple-minded passion for spectacle may have been, in the public eye, surfeited and dulled by the 1874 transit, professional interest in such matters was not so easily turned aside, and Assistant Surveyor General C. J. Lyons of Honolulu observed the event from the Survey Office on King Street, very near the site of the once-vital but now-vanished 'Āpua observatory. Meanwhile, the British, though conspicuously absent from Hawai'i, were again active elsewhere in the Pacific.

Leonard Darwin, now thirty-two years of age and newly married, returned—this time to Australia, where he readied himself for the 1882 transit in the company of his wife Elizabeth. But as in 1874, the weather once more thwarted his efforts. Writing back to England from his station near Brisbane, he told his mother that although the mornings immediately before transit day had been bright and promising, and although Elizabeth, having practiced "for many days counting aloud from the chronometer," stood ready to assist him at the critical moment, the weather simply did not cooperate at the critical time, the clouds being "as thick as ever." In the end, he could only describe himself as probably one of the very few people who had been "twice round the world to see a thing without seeing it."[9]

George Tupman, too, returned to the Pacific, though perhaps with some reluctance. Following his 1874 transit work, his astronomical prowess had not gone unnoticed, and in 1878 he had been a candidate for the position of Radcliffe Observer at Oxford University.[10] But although his candidacy failed in a predictable manner—he was not, after all, a man with Oxbridge credentials—he was able in a fashion to recover his reputation in Polynesia. Having rediscovered the observatories left in New Zealand by Leonard Darwin and his comrades eight years before, he observed the transit from Burnham[11] and soon after was back in Hawai'i. On February 12, 1883, he and his wife, en route to San Francisco after the transit, arrived in Honolulu aboard the *Zealandia*. They were just in time to witness, on the grounds of the new 'Iolani Palace, King Kalākaua's much-belated coronation, the ritual public crowning having been delayed precisely nine years. Although nearly a decade had intervened between Venusian transits, the king had not forgotten; and when he was afterward called upon by

Fig. 60. Order of Kalākaua

Tupman, the Merrie Monarch honored the English astronomer by investing him with the Order of Kalākaua.[12] (Fig. 60).

REAFFIRMATION 3: LONGITUDE

Ten years after the 1874 transit of Venus—and more than two hundred years after the founding of the Royal Observatory at Greenwich—astronomers had not yet been shorn of the politics of longitude. In the United States, during the years and decades immediately following the Civil War, questions about longitude could be especially unsettling. The system of American railroads that had permitted both Leonard Darwin (in 1875) and David Kalākaua (in 1881) to make transcontinental journeys was at the heart of the problem, and railroad companies and their passengers felt it acutely.

From Atlantic to Pacific, the United States now had a longitudinal extension of more than 50°, and various towns and cities within its borders had local times that differed by up to more than two hundred minutes. A traveler bound for California from New York and journeying under a succession of meridians progressively farther and farther to the west was required—if anxious to maintain correct local time—to adjust his watch as rapidly as he advanced his longitude. After the end of the Civil War, burgeoning railway companies only aggravated the problem by keeping their own time, as did many towns and cities along the railway routes, to the considerable inconvenience of passengers.[13] Even in Hawai'i the situation, though not as extreme, was similar: As the nineteenth century drew to a close, the *Hawaiian Almanac and Annual* was still printing a table permitting readers across the island chain—from Ni'ihau to Hilo—to obtain local time by applying the appropriate correction to standard time.[14]

The regional, national, and global anxieties engendered by problems of time and longitude prompted the United States, in December of 1883, to send invitations to all nations with which it had diplomatic relations. The following autumn, in answer to those invitations, a group of delegates assembled in Washington at a gathering that brought together in one place more than forty men renowned in both diplomacy and science. From France and Russia, from Sweden and Venezuela, from Germany and Turkey, from Liberia and Japan—from twenty-five countries around the world they came, with one principal aim: "For the purpose of fixing upon a meridian proper to be employed as a common zero of longitude and standard of time-reckoning throughout the world." The director of the Physical Observatory at Paris, Professor Janssen (whose photographic apparatus had been used in

146

Honolulu ten years before to capture images of Venus in transit across the sun), would be there, as would the American astronomer Asaph Hall, together with the superintendents of both the U.S. *Nautical Almanac* (Simon Newcomb) and the U.S. Coast and Geodetic Survey (Professor Hilgard). Indeed, the purpose of the conference was so lofty and its tone so earnest that the distinguished British physicist Sir William Thomson (Lord Kelvin) would eventually receive a special invitation from the conferees to attend the meeting.

Among the nations represented at the conference was the island nation of Hawai'i, and King Kalākaua commissioned two representatives: Privy Counselor Luther Aholo and Surveyor General W. D. Alexander.[15] Great Britain sent four delegates—one of whom was so influential that Alexander would later describe him as "probably the most distinguished member of the Conference, and the one who exerted the greatest influence in the discussions."[16] The man was John Couch Adams (Fig. 61), director of the Cambridge Observatory.[17]

Adams exerted a formidable influence upon his fellow conferees, even more than he himself expected;[18] and the truth of Alexander's flattering assessment of the man can easily be gauged by examining the *Protocols of the Proceedings,* a document of more than two hundred pages that records the proposals, discussions, and resolutions of the conference, along with the attendance and voting record of each delegation.[19]

The 1884 International Meridian Conference met on eight separate occasions, and Adams' voice was heard from the very first. His speech in favor of counting longitude in two directions (from 0° to +180° to the east and from 0° to –180° to the west) was "very effective," thought Alexander; and his defense of the adoption of the *civil* day (beginning and ending at the instant of mean midnight on the prime meridian) rather than the *astronomical* day (beginning and ending at noon) as the Universal Day was "clear and forcible."[20]

Fig. 61. John Couch Adams and his Cambridge gravesite

Before adjourning, the conferees passed seven resolutions. The first—which expressed the desirability for "a single prime meridian for all nations, in place of the multiplicity of initial meridians which now exist"— met no opposition, and not a single nation voted against it. Then the Hawai'i delegation joined Adams and his British colleagues and, with the majority, voted in favor of Resolution II: "That the Conference proposes to the Governments here represented the adoption of the meridian passing through the centre of the transit instrument at the Observatory of Greenwich as the initial meridian for longitude."

It was with this vote that the Hawai'i delegation reaffirmed what Captain Cook and his astronomer William Bayly had first set forth more than a century earlier: The Hawaiian Islands had a definite location. Their place on the map, refined by the work of 1874 transit of Venus expedition, would henceforth be permanently fixed to the Greenwich Meridian (Fig. 62). The transit instrument there—Airy's transit circle— would be the defining tool for longitude the whole world over. Time and place, the warp and woof of both science and society, would be made tractable by consensus. And Hawai'i would again do as the world would do: It would, in effect, arrange itself around England.[21]

Fig. 62. The Prime Meridian of the World at Greenwich

35

· · · · ·

A Meeting in Siberia

The 1884 International Meridian Conference was held during the month of October. Nearly simultaneously with its proceedings and just a short journey by rail to the north, George Forbes was in Philadelphia. There, under the auspices of the Franklin Institute, an International Electrical Exhibition had opened on September 2, and two weeks later, on Tuesday, September 16, Forbes delivered a lecture on "Dynamo-Electric Machinery."[1] The exhibition closed in October.

Forbes now had time to scurry southward to Washington, where he could lend his support to the British delegation and learn firsthand of Greenwich's triumph. But whether or not he did so is of little moment, for even if he did, it is unlikely that so short a journey could have been filled with as much adventure—or misadventure—as were the days and weeks immediately following his departure from Honolulu almost a decade earlier.

George Forbes survived his encounter with Madame Pele atop Mauna Loa and left Honolulu on February 6, 1875.[2] Bound for San Francisco, he allowed the *Tenedos* to carry him more than 2,000 miles to the east, but then he would go no farther. For long before this—as long ago as May of 1874, in fact—Forbes had suggested to Airy, just prior to his departure from England, that it might be possible for him to return home by going west, through Siberia.[3] By linking up with some of the Russian observers of the transit—and there had been several Russian teams scattered across Asia[4]—he might be able to avail himself, he believed, of an opportunity not likely to pass his way again.

Airy himself had been skeptical. And although he had cooperated by providing the address of Otto Struve of the Pulkowa Observatory, he had attempted to discourage Forbes from such a journey: The distance ("measured by thousands of miles"), the climate ("the most severe upon earth"), and the season ("the coldest month of the year") all counseled against such a scheme.[5] Still, the plucky young Forbes would not be dissuaded; and when the time came, he launched his plan, unaware of the challenge that awaited him:

> I was meditating about my journey home by India or North America when I was told that perhaps I might be able to go by Siberia from Pekin [Beijing]. I happened, at that time, to be unhampered by considerations of time and money, and as I

149

should have less chance afterwards of travelling by this route than by the others I determined to try it, and my ignorance of the countries and their languages made me the more anxious to do so, for the greatest pleasure in a man's life is the overcoming of difficulties as I have perceived in my travels and in the laboratory and in carrying out engineering works; and I had often wondered how travellers in Africa or in Central Asia with neither languages nor banks could proceed, and I hoped by making this journey to be taught this lesson.[6]

Having been told by a Siberian-born resident of Honolulu, Alatau Atkinson,[7] that he might be able to get through Siberia, Forbes recrossed the Pacific to Japan, where he hoped to learn something about the way to and through Siberia. To his great good fortune (for no one else in Japan could tell him anything), the Russian ambassador there was Otto Struve's half-brother. From him Forbes obtained letters to people in China, and he was soon bound for the Asian mainland.

After visiting the coastal cities of Shanghai and Tientsin (Tianjin) and procuring, from the Russian Consul, letters to people in Siberia, he began to prepare for his journey inland. Anticipating a month or more within the trackless confines of the Gobi Desert, he bought provisions for six weeks. He also carried as much money as he deemed necessary, some in silver dollars; and he cautiously supplied himself with a shotgun, a rifle, and a revolver.

Two days' journey by horse brought him to Pekin, where just a few months earlier the Americans had stationed a transit team. But European travelers in that part of the world, if allowed at all, were—like transits of Venus—rare sights, and the British Embassy in Pekin offered Forbes only discouragement. Fortunately, the Russian ambassador M. de Butzow and his associates were more than helpful. They lent Forbes books, taught him Russian phrases, and sent

Fig. 63. Chinese astronomical instruments photographed by George Forbes in 1875 at Peking (Beijing)

150

word to the Russian postmaster, five days' journey ahead, to prepare camels for his use. Before leaving Pekin, Forbes gained access to places where no European had ever been—and even had the opportunity to photograph them.[8] (Fig. 63).

When the time came, Forbes left Pekin on a litter between two mules. After five days' journey, punctuated by stops at the ruined Summer Palace and the Sepulchre of the Ming Emperors, the seemingly misplaced astronomer, now alone among thousands of Chinese and feeling ill at ease, safely reached the city of Kalgan (Zhangjiakou), where the Great Wall separates China from Mongolia. From here the journey across the desert was 800 miles and—at 25 miles per day—would take about a month.

Forbes now surrendered £5 apiece for baggage camels, each of which carried 400 pounds, and £15 for a two-wheeled camel cart that was covered and lined and inside of which he spread a mattress. Heading northwest and into the setting sun, each step bringing him closer to home, Forbes now walked, slept in the cart, and attempted along the way to shoot wild game as mirages played with his aim.

Halfway across the desert there was trouble. His camel driver said that the camels could go no farther. When the driver began to unpack the animals, Forbes told him that he would not let him unload the camel that bore his provisions, and he showed his revolver as an argument. Though it was a convincing argument, Forbes was in a frightful predicament, and rescue seemed inconceivable until it rose out of the hot sand in the form of a passing caravan headed for the town of Urga (Ulaanbaatar)—whereupon Forbes, with equal miraculousness, produced out of his own pocket a letter of introduction to the caravan's leader. Soon supplied with fresh camels, he was able to join the procession and to continue his journey among the wayward scenes and the unfamiliar faces.

It was now the month of May, and daytime temperatures approached a hundred degrees in the shade. Strange sights and strange events awaited him still: a ruined building, like a church—possibly, he thought, the grave of Ghenghis Khan; lamas dressed in bright-colored robes and riding on horseback; many great temples built of wood; and more.

After lodging with the Russian Consul at Urga, Forbes moved on to Kiachta with the caravan, a journey of seven days. It was here that Forbes' homeward adventure began to climax. It was here that Kathleen Campbell entered his life:

> If I were to begin my history of Miss Campbell at the point where I can speak from my own knowledge, I would tell you that I came to know her in Kiachta, a town on the frontier which bounds Mongolia from Siberia. But when I say this I know that you will wish to ask me how it came about that . . . a young lady, of an old Scottish family, could be found by me in so distant and inhospitable a country, so far away from all her people. For at

that time Siberia was unknown to any English people excepting two or three, for there were no railways, and it led to no place whither people wished to go, and the Russians did not care to have strangers in the place where they kept their convicts and political exiles. For which reasons, at the time when these things happened Siberia was not known to Englishmen.

. . . The father of Miss Campbell was a lieutenant in the British Navy. He married young and died early. . . . Miss Campbell not wishing to be a burden to her mother, and having a good education, sought for a position as Companion to some lady. A Russian lady Mrs Grant, the wife of an Englishman of great energy who set up the rapid Chinese post over the Desert of Gobi . . . asked her to go to Riga where she intended wintering. Riga is on the German Frontier of Russia. So they went, but at Riga Mrs Grant said "I have changed my plans and I shall not stay here. I go to the East of Siberia and you must come with me." So this girl of barely 17 years, who had never been away from home, who understood none of the language & less of the customs of the Russians, was carried off to that terrible country in mid-winter. . . . Such a journey [in open sleighs] covering thousands of miles brought discomforts and dangers and home-sickness. There was nothing to remind her of the home she had left. All was so different. The Sun & Moon & Stars alone were common to both countries and she told me that it pleased her to look at them and to feel that her own people might also see them. They were the only bond between her old & her new world.

By the time Forbes arrived at Kiachta in mid-1875, Miss Campbell had made friends among some of the town's principal merchants. One of these, a Mr. Tokmakoff, had learned the tea trade among the English in China and spoke English well; and it was with Tokmakoff and his wife that Miss Campbell eventually went to live to help educate their two little girls; and it was with them, rather than with Mrs. Grant, that she was residing when the caravan carrying Forbes rode into town.

At first, Forbes had no plans for a lingering layover. But then he met, at the dinner table of his Russian host Sokoloff, the prima donna Madame Leonova of Petersburg who, with her manager, was on a professional tour through Siberia. The result was most unexpected.

For the journey ahead, Forbes had already purchased from M. Pfaffius, the commissary of the Frontier, a large covered traveling carriage called a *tarantass;* had ordered for placement therein a very large pillow stuffed with eiderdown; had had some of his traveling clothes repaired; and had received a permit for getting horses at post stations along the Russian post roads—when a performance by Madame Leonova altered his plans:

I might then have started on my homeward journey without ever knowing that there was in the same town a countrywoman of my own—and as I discovered years afterwards a connection by marriage—had I not attended the concert given by Madame Leonova. For there I was presented by Tokmakoff to Miss Campbell who lived in the house. Imagine our delight to hear again our own language from native lips. So we talked about the events which led up to her being settled in this outlandish place & she told [me] about . . . her desire if possible to go to Europe before the next winter should set in. So I went from her full of sorrow, and wondering much whether her wish could by any chance be fulfilled. And I could see but little hope for her. Then in a moment it came upon me that my coming to Kiachta at this time was a fortunate thing and that I must be the means of rescuing her from Siberia and protecting her on the way.

Forbes now sought Kathleen Campbell out, telling her that he could think of no other way by which she might reach Europe except by trusting herself to him and taking passage in his *tarantass*. After some trusted friends, including the Tokmakoffs, advised her to accept this chance if she desired ever to get back to Europe, she began her preparations, while George Forbes waited, passing his time among foreigners, seeing great stores of tea, dining with the Chinese governor, and playing cards. Finally, all was ready:

When at last the day came for us to start I packed my own luggage in the tarantass, and then drove to fetch my "popuschik" as your travelling companion is called in that country. Now a tarantass has four wheels and no springs, but the two axles are joined by poles on which the body of the carriage rests. There are no seats except the one raised in front for the driver or "yemschik." The rest of it reminded me of a broad flat bottomed boat like the ferry boat at Portnacraig. In this you pack your luggage and fill up the corners with hay and put your large pillows in place and then you sit or lie on the top. . . .

When all the luggage was put in place and my popuschik had said farewell to all the people who came to see her start, we jumped in, and the yemschik with a call to his horses and a crack of his whip drove ahead. "Now you fools get on, there my dove, look to the road" he sang out to his team and away we flew. Thus we started upon our long journey, and soon the first milestone told us that we had 5278 versts [about 3,500 miles][9] to travel together before reaching railways, and I think that then for the first time I knew what a responsibility was involved in accepting the guardianship of this girl.

Now the thumping *tarantass* tumbled into the wilderness and the westward-slipping sun quietly set. But before it rose the next morning, Forbes would have his newly assumed responsibility—and his judgment—put to a severe test. For he was now in the midst of a great wood where wolves and more might lurk:

> In the middle of the first night we were driving down a hill when we heard a creaking and groaning & the carriage stopped and settled slowly to the ground, for the two front wheels were broken to splinters. We abused Pfaffius in our hearts for having sold me so rotten a machine and after a time sent the yemschik back to the post-station to borrow a fresh pair of wheels, and he went. We slept a little. Hours passed and he came not back. And at last a traveller came bye in his tarantass, and he had heard of our plight at the post-station, and he told us that our man was not intending to come. Then he drove on quickly, for in Siberia when you see an accident you look the other way for fear of being called as a witness to the magistrate and this might delay your journey many months. Now we found ourselves in a difficult case for it was clear that one must go back while the other must be guard over our goods. For the road here lay in a great wood, and the woods in these parts were often infested with bandits who were escaped convicts, and would think little of murdering a traveller for the sake of the food or clothing which he might find. Now I knew that Miss Campbell could argue better with the postmaster because she knew the language, and I have often observed that in case of danger or alarm a woman prefers action to inaction; so I put my revolver into Miss Campbell's hand, and bade her return for wheels horses & a driver, and a hard time she had for the distance was over six miles, and then the postmaster would not give the horses, but she threatened to write it in the book so in the end she got the horses and after many hours she returned sitting with the yemschik on the axle of the fresh wheels; and she has never forgiven me for having sent her on this errand the more so, and I cannot blame her, because on her return exhausted and in pain, she found me sleeping peacefully in the tarantass.

Still many miles and many days ahead, the town of Irkutsk was not reached until approximately a week after leaving Kiachta. Here Forbes stayed at an inn, while Miss Campbell went to another lodging that had been prepared for her. But whom did Miss Campbell know in Irkutsk who would proffer such a courtesy?

His name was Josef Szlenker, a Polish political exile whom Miss Campbell had met on her way out to Kiachta in the company of Mrs. Grant, and who since that time had made Miss Campbell's better acquaintance. The two were, in fact, engaged to be married.

If this was not enough to astonish George Forbes, there was more. Kathleen Campbell, having been told that her fiancé was to be given his liberty, had wished to go back to Europe to wait for him. But this, she now learned, was not true: There was no hope that he would ever obtain his freedom. What was the couple to do?

Josef Szlenker, as with a last gasp, made a desperate proposal. He asked Kathleen to marry him and live in Irkutsk. She consented. And George Forbes withdrew into contemplation: "Now when I took it upon myself to take Miss Campbell from her friends in Kiachta I had not reckoned on having to deal with matters of this kind and I felt myself somewhat in a difficulty. It would be very easy to do nothing, but this seemed barely honourable after I had taken her under my charge, for I could never forgive myself if any harm should come to her. So in the end I resolved to make enquiries about Mr Szlenker."

What Forbes discovered was both disturbing and inspiring. Szlenker's father, of a good and wealthy family, had been one of the leaders in the Polish revolution of 1863. When he died in exile, his son—now Kathleen Campbell's fiancé—was but a minor and would have gotten his liberty but for the attempts he had made to escape. He was now a prosperous merchant in Irkutsk and, even though his house was searched by the police while Forbes was still in the town, he did enjoy some limited freedom there.

When Forbes learned all these things and more, he did not try to dissuade Miss Campbell from marrying the man. And before leaving Irkutsk, he saw them joined in the Roman Catholic church there. Still, his mind would not rest:

> After the marriage had taken place I wondered a great deal whether I had done rightly, for these matters were foreign to my usual occupations. Here was I, a youngster of twenty six years, but only a boy in knowledge of the world, whose sole interest in the world had till now been the study of the laws of science, here was I first carrying off this girl of eighteen from those under whose protection she was, and then giving her in marriage to an exile. But placed as I was I could not see how I could honourably have done less or done differently. Yet I was much concerned about my rashness, and all the more so when I now received a new proof of the devotion and unselfishness of [this] woman. For I found that the Russian officials had refused to allow the marriage to take place until Miss Campbell had signed a document saying that she would remain an exile in Siberia for the rest of her life and would not make any attempt to escape. And she signed it.

George Forbes left Irkutsk in his *tarantass,* somber and alone. Now preying on his mind was not the fate of one friend but of two. He headed away for England much preoccupied: "I had only one thought and this was to mix myself up still further—as if I had not already gone far enough—in the affairs of my two exiles. For I resolved that by one means or another, & by fair means or foul, I should deliver them from exile."

Before reaching Europe, Forbes would see other exiles, some on the march, others in cages, still others pressing upon him letters to friends that they could not trust to the post. Still, Mr. and Mrs. Szlenker were not forgotten.

Four months out of Pekin, Forbes at last reached Moscow and then St. Petersburg, some 3,000 miles from Irkutsk. From Moscow he wrote to Airy, saying that his return from the Sandwich Islands had been much slower than he had anticipated (it was now September 1875), that he hoped to be in London in a week or ten days, and that he would call on the Astronomer Royal on his way home to Scotland. Nowhere in the letter did he mention the Szlenkers nor even hint of his Siberian travails.[10]

But good fortune again smiled on George Forbes, this time in the person of the Duke of Edinburgh, who was presently in Moscow and who had lately married the only daughter of the tsar. Cleverly arranging a personal audience with the duke, Forbes spoke to him, politely and with circumspection, about his travels—but this he followed up with a letter telling him about the Szlenkers. Hoping that the duke's own marriage to a Russian lady might interest him in a similar marriage between a Russian subject and a British subject, Forbes climaxed his letter by saying that after having seen so much of Siberia, it would be a pleasant thing to conclude his travels by recording an act of clemency by the tsar—namely, the release of the Szlenkers.

After personally delivering his letter to the apartment of the duke, Forbes took the train to England and soon settled back into his laboratory and his more predictable work at Glasgow. Three months later he received the news: Josef and Kathleen Szlenker were being freed. Going straight to the telegraph office in Glasgow—"walking on air," he wrote—he sent a message to Irkutsk bearing the jubilant tidings. Josef Szlenker replied: "The news of our deliverance brought by your telegramm . . . was a great & unexpected event for me. Your generous act gave me my liberty which for 12 years I had in vain hoped for, & more especially since I have joined my lot with my dearest Kathleen's life,—Accept many warm thanks, I hope soon to be able to see you & press your hand & thank you personally."[11]

This time, Josef's hopes would be quickly realized. Within a year, the Szlenkers would pay a visit to their hero's residence at Pitlochrie, Scotland. "Never did the highlands seem so happy and free," Forbes would later reminisce, as at that moment.

Though an aging George Forbes would, in his Pitlochrie shed, one day surround himself with books (see Fig. 17), he would also claim long before this that he had never done anything worthy of being put down in one. Yet his transit of Venus adventures had taken him around the world. Repeatedly challenging his mettle, they had begun with high ambition and mighty purpose.

And they had ended like a fairy tale.

Appendix A. Measuring the Earth

. . . . .

From 'Upolu Point, at the northern edge of the island of Hawai'i, the North Pole of the sky, near which the North Star (Polaris) stands, is more than 20 degrees above the northern horizon. On the same island, at Ka Lae (South Point), the North Star is better than a full degree—twice the diameter of the full moon—closer to the horizon, a notable and significant difference. But further still, if a man were to navigate across all the major inhabited islands of the Hawaiian archipelago, from Ka Lae at 18° 56' north to the northern shore of Kaua'i at 22° 14' north, he would traverse not 1 but more than 3 degrees of latitude, and the shifting celestial scene would be proportionally magnified.

Though ancient Hawaiian astronomers probably observed and understood, in an elementary way, the changing appearance of the sky consequent upon such changes in latitude, they were not students of "degrees" nor of their astronomical or terrestrial subdivisions. They did not measure location in terms of latitude and apparently had no notion of how to calculate the larger geometric consequences: that, for example, the Earth's circumference is approximately 360 times as great as the distance that separates 'Upolu Point from Ka Lae or 120 times the north-south distance from Ka Lae to Kaua'i. But students of "degrees" did exist elsewhere; and they realized that geometrically precise astronomical observations (similar to those theoretically available in Hawai'i) not only provided palpable evidence of the spherical shape of the Earth, they also provided the data necessary to calculate its size.

The mathematical foundations for such insights were developed not in the Pacific but in the Mediterranean, where by the first century B.C.E. the Greek astronomer Posidonius (ca. 135–51 B.C.E.) provided a geometric demonstration of how the size of the Earth could be determined. Such a demonstration proceeds as follows.[1]

Suppose that Rhodes and Alexandria lie on the same meridian and that the distance between the two cities is 5,000 stades. The star Canopus is seen to graze the southern horizon from Rhodes when it transits the meridian; but at Alexandria, Canopus crosses the meridian at a height above the horizon that is equivalent to "one forty-eighth of the zodiac circle" (i.e., 360/48 = 7.5 degrees). It follows that the segment of the meridian circle separating Rhodes from Alexandria is also one forty-eighth part of a circle (i.e., their latitudes differ by 7.5 degrees). Thus, a complete (meridian) circle circumscribing the Earth must be forty-eight times greater than the distance separating Rhodes from Alexandria, or 240,000 stades.[2]

Though Posidonius' estimate for the Earth's circumference was remarkably accurate for its time, his efforts had been essentially duplicated if not surpassed by those of Eratosthenes (ca. 276–196 B.C.E.), who used a similar technique (Fig. A.1). Supposing that Syene (in Upper Egypt) and

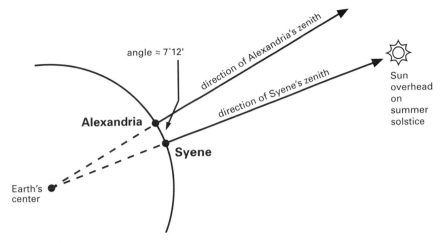

A.1. The geometry of a shadowless noon according to Eratosthenes. Although shadowless noons occur twice annually on all the major Hawaiian Islands (just before and just after the summer solstice), are celebrated in Island mythology, and are as observable in Hawai'i as in Egypt, the procedure of using a shadowless noon to attempt to determine the size of the Earth was apparently unknown in ancient Hawai'i.

Alexandria lie on the same meridian and that the distance between them is 5,000 stades: "Now Eratosthenes asserts, and it is the fact, that Syene lies under the summer tropic. Whenever, therefore, the sun, being in [Cancer] the Crab at the summer solstice, is exactly in the middle of the heaven, the gnomons (pointers) of sundials necessarily throw no shadows, the position of the sun above them being exactly vertical. . . . But in Alexandria, at the same hour, the pointers of sundials throw shadows, because Alexandria lies further to the north than Syene."[3]

Assuming that the lines traversed by all rays of sunlight that reach the Earth at whatever location are essentially parallel, the gnomon's shadow at Alexandria permitted Eratosthenes to indirectly measure the noonday sun's angular distance south of that city's zenith on the summer solstice, an angle that he estimated to be about 7 degrees, or one-fiftieth of a circle. He inferred that Syene (modern Aswan) and Alexandria were separated on the Earth along a meridian circle by the same ratio—that is, one-fiftieth of the Earth's circumference. If the distance from Syene to Alexandria was 5,000 stades, then the Earth's circumference was 50 x 5,000, or 250,000 stades.[4]

Given the simple elegance of the methods of both Posidonius and Eratosthenes, the fact that similar inferences were not made elsewhere is remarkable, even though the requisite astronomical observations were probably commonplace. Hawai'i's skies, for example, not only permit the sort of stellar observations made by Posidonius, they also allow solar observations similar to those of Eratosthenes. Because the Hawaiian archipelago lies within the tropics, zenith suns—and their consequent "shadowless noons"—are regular occurrences on all the major populated islands,[5] just as they were at Syene on the summer solstice. They are even commemorated in Island mythology.[6]

159

Appendix B. Relative Distances—Sun, Venus, and Earth—According to Copernicus

· · · · ·

For obtaining a set of relative distances among Venus, Earth, and the sun, Copernicus' method can be summarized as follows.

From the Earth, the planet Venus appears alternately in the morning sky (before sunrise) and in the evening sky (after sunset), but it is never seen more than approximately 47 degrees from the sun. When it occupies this extreme position—called its maximum elongation—the observed Venus-Earth-sun angle is about 47 degrees, and the inferred Earth-Venus-sun angle is 90 degrees. The Venus-sun-Earth angle can then be deduced (180 − [47 + 90]), and a triangle in space can be constructed. From the values of the angles, the relative lengths of all the sides of the triangle can be calculated. Thus the relative distances separating the Earth from Venus, Venus from the sun, and the Earth from the sun can be gotten (Fig. B.1).

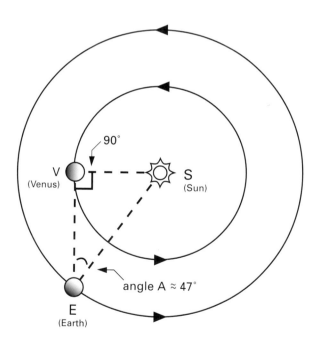

B.1. Distance to Venus in AUs. At maximum elongation, when Venus is seen from Earth along line EV, angle A is approximately 47° and EV, which is tangent to Venus' orbit, is perpendicular to VS, the radius of Venus' orbit. The Venus-sun distance, VS, can now be computed relative to the Earth-sun distance, ES, using the following trigonometric formula: VS/ES = sin A. The distance ES in the Copernican system is the Astronomical Unit (AU) of heliocentric astronomy. If ES is assigned the unit value of 1, then VS = sin A x 1, and thus the Venus-sun distance can be given as some multiple of this unit.

Appendix C. The Circumstances of a Transit of Venus

• • • • •

As Venus travels around the sun inside the Earth's orbit, it regularly reaches a position called *inferior conjunction* (Fig. C.1), and it is at such a time that transits of Venus can occur. But because the orbital paths of Venus and the Earth are not coplanar, and because Venus must therefore cross the Earth-sun plane (the *ecliptic*) twice as it swings around the sun—once as it moves northward through its *ascending node* and again as it moves southward through its *descending node*—it is only if an inferior conjunction occurs when the Earth, Venus, and the sun are simultaneously on or near the *line of nodes* (Fig. C.2) that Venus can be seen from the Earth to move in front of the sun. It will then appear as a dark, moving spot silhouetted against the sun's bright surface and will trace out a path like those illustrated in Figure C.3.

The interval between two consecutive inferior conjunctions is, for Venus, approximately 584 days. This is called its *synodic period*. Because the ratio of Venus' orbital period to that of the Earth is 0.6152 : 1—that is, because eight orbits of the Earth are nearly equal to thirteen orbits (or five synodic periods) of Venus—it is only after an interval of approximately eight years (i.e., eight Earth orbits) that the same two planets will return to nearly the same positions they occupied, relative to the sun and each other, eight years earlier. Then and only then can a second transit of Venus follow as soon as eight years after the first.

It is, furthermore, only if a transit of Venus occurs when the planet is near but not precisely on one of its nodes that a second transit can be seen after an eight-year interval. The two transits will then trace against the sun's disc a pair of parallel lines about 20 to 24 arc minutes apart, the second transit nearly replicating the first. The transit paths of 1631/1639, 1761/1769, and 1874/1882 illustrated this well (Fig. C.3). The seventeenth- and nineteenth-century pairs occurred late in the year (early December) as Venus was moving northward across the ecliptic near its ascending node. Each member of the eighteenth-century pair occurred in midyear (early June) as Venus crossed the ecliptic moving southward near its descending node—a circumstance that will again be obtained during the next transit pair of 2004/2012.

After the second transit of such a pair, a long series of inferior conjunctions will occur during which Venus will pass either above or below the sun's disc rather than across it, and more than a century must lapse before the next transit.

Although *transit seasons* can include both single transits as well as the double transits illustrated in Figure C.3, we now live in a period of double transits, the circumstances of which repeat themselves every 243 years.[1]

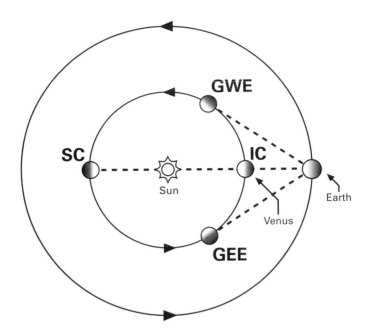

C.1. Four special configurations of Venus relative to Earth. In chronological (counterclockwise) order they are: inferior conjunction (IC), greatest western elongation (GWE), superior conjunction (SC), and greatest eastern elongation (GEE).

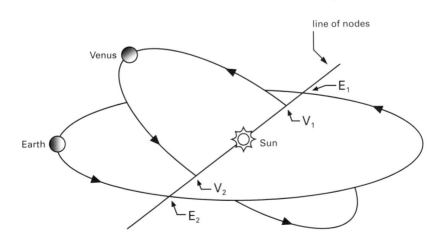

C.2. An illustration of the orbits of Earth and Venus and the line of nodes where their orbital planes intersect. The December transits of 1631/1639 and 1874/1882 (illustrated in Fig. C.3) occurred when the Earth was near E_1 and Venus near V_1 (its ascending node). The June transits of 1761/1769 occurred (as will those of 2004/2012) when the Earth was near E_2 and Venus near V_2 (its descending node). The inclination of Venus' orbit relative to Earth's ($\approx 3^{1}/_{2}°$) is exaggerated here for purposes of illustration.

162

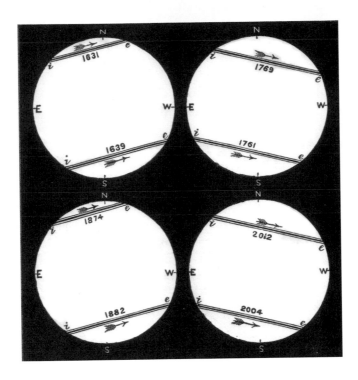

C.3. Eight transit of Venus paths, in four pairs, between the years 1631 and 2012. In all cases, the most northerly, the central, and the most southerly transit paths are depicted, as are the places of ingress *(i)* and egress *(e)*. Note that Venus always enters the solar disc from the east (left), that the paths of transit pairs (one to the north of the sun's center, the other to the south of it) are sensibly parallel, and that their angular separation must be less than the angular diameter of the sun. Note also that for the December transit pairs (1631/1639 and 1874/1882), the second transit is more southerly and that for the June transit pairs (1761/1769 and 2004/2012) it is more northerly than the first transit.

    If, in each of the four images, a horizontal line is drawn through the center of the sun from east to west, such a line being made to extend for some distance in both directions beyond the sun's disc, and if each transit path is then similarly extended until intersecting with that line, then the points of intersection would mark Venus' nodes, and it would be readily apparent that at the time of the first transit of each pair (viz., the transits of 1631, 1761, 1874, and 2004), Venus has just passed one of its nodes, whereas at the time of the second transit of each pair (viz., those of 1639, 1769, 1882, and 2012), Venus is approaching a node.

    For a mathematical treatment of the other noticeable feature of this figure—viz., that a greater distance separates the paths of the December transit pairs (of 1631/1639 and 1874/1882) than the June pairs (of 1761/1769 and 2004/2012)—see the extended note in the book from which the illustration has been taken: Proctor, *Transits of Venus*, 111n.

Appendix D. Geometry and the Astronomical Unit

· · · · ·

The parallactic method of surveying space—and thereby obtaining, for example, the absolute distances to Venus and the sun—is based upon the familiar method of triangulation: finding all the properties of a triangle given some of those properties.

Six quantities describe a triangle: the lengths of its three sides and the values of its three angles. Given any three of these quantities in succession around the perimeter of a triangle (e.g., two angles and the included side), the remaining quantities can be determined unambiguously by calculation.

Suppose, now, that Venus could be detached from its orbit and placed high in the sky at midnight so that its apparent position against the background stars could be precisely measured by two Earthbound observers (A and B in Fig. D.1) at widely spaced terrestrial locations. If the distance (say, in miles) between the observers is known and the parallactic displacement of Venus relative to the more distant celestial bodies is carefully measured, angles a and b can be gotten. These angles, together with the baseline AB, give us the three quantities needed to solve the triangle and to thereby derive the distance (in miles) from Earth to Venus. Using the already known planetary distance ratios (see Table 1) and assuming the derived distance to Venus in miles to be equal to 1.000 – 0.723 = 0.277 AUs, we can now calculate the AU in miles.

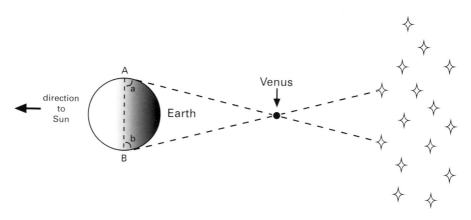

D.1. An imaginary triangulation of space: finding the distance to Venus by placing it high in the sky at midnight

But unlike the *superior planets* (Mars, for example) whose orbits lie outside the Earth's, Venus never reaches the sort of position illustrated in Figure D.1; its angular separation from the sun is, in fact, never greater than

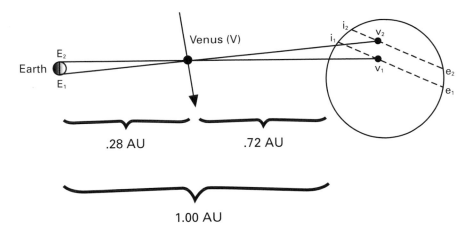

D.2. Deriving the AU from a transit of Venus

about 47 degrees. But rather than attempting to measure Venus' parallactic displacement against a dark night sky, such measurements can be made during a transit when the planet is darkly silhouetted against the bright solar disc. Hence the utility of the transit phenomenon in finding the AU.

The general circumstances of a transit of Venus that permit the AU to be inferred directly are sketched, in simplified form, in Figure D.2.[1]

At the moment indicated in the figure, Venus, moving in the direction shown by the arrow, is seen by a northern observer at station E_2 to be projected on the sun's face at v_1, while by a southern observer at E_1 Venus is seen at v_2. From a knowledge of relative distances in the solar system, if the Earth-sun distance (AU) is expressed as a unit value (1.00), then the Venus-sun and the Earth-Venus distances have the values 0.72 and 0.28, respectively. This proportion, 72 to 28 (or 18 to 7), also describes the proportional sizes of lines (distances) E_2E_1 and v_2v_1: as the triangles E_2VE_1 and v_2Vv_1 are similar, their parts must also be similar—that is, proportional. Thus, if stations E_2 and E_1 are 7,000 miles apart, then the distance v_2 to v_1 is 18,000 miles. Further, supposing that v_2 and v_1 have been accurately determined with respect to their positions on the sun's disc, then the proportion that v_2v_1 bears to the sun's disc—that is, to the sun's diameter—is readily gotten: Thus, for instance, if v_2v_1 is one-forty-ninth the solar diameter, that diameter is 49 x 18,000 = 882,000 miles.

The distance to the sun—the astronomical unit—can now be gotten by comparing the sun's apparent size with its real size. Let E (in Fig. D.3) be the Earth. Let S be the sun. Let the large circle represent the celestial sphere, the unshaded half being the hemisphere visible to an Earthbound observer when the sun is above the observer's horizon (represented by the broken line).

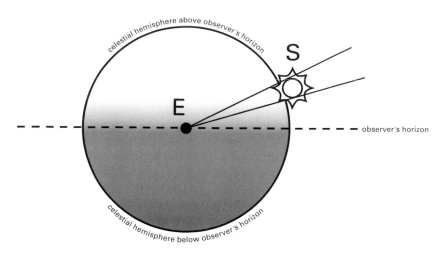

D.3. The relation between the sun's distance and its apparent angular size

Now, because S subtends an angle of approximately 32.5 arc minutes as seen from E, the circumference of the large circle, which contains 360 x 60 = 21,600 arc minutes, is equivalent to 21,600 ÷ 32.5 ≈ 665 solar diameters. Once the circumference of the circle is known in solar diameters, the radius ES can be calculated in similar units: if 2π (ES) = 665, then ES = 665 ÷ 2π ≈ 106.

The sun's distance (the astronomical unit), which is equivalent to ES, will therefore be about 106 times as large as the sun's diameter. Using the figure 882,000 miles for the solar diameter, the AU would be an estimated 106 x 882,000 ≈ 93,500,000 miles.

Delisle's method may be described as follows: A northern observer (such as E_2 in Figure D.2) sees the transit begin earlier than a southern observer, as Venus contacts the sun at i_1 earlier than at i_2. If each observer notes the exact moment of ingress in local time and, by knowing his precise longitude, converts his local time into Greenwich Time, the difference (in Greenwich Time) between the observed moments of ingress at i_1 and i_2 will yield a measure of the planet's orbital speed, whence, by Kepler's Third Law, its distance can be deduced. Similar remarks apply, mutatis mutandis, to the observations of egress (at e_1 and e_2).[2]

It may be wondered why, historically, the AU was not found by observing directly the parallax of the sun. One difficulty is that the maximum parallactic displacement of the sun as seen from opposite sides of the Earth is less than 18 arc seconds (the solar parallax doubled ≈ 17".59), a very small angle that is difficult to measure accurately. This, together with the sun's large angular size and its overpowering radiance, militates against the determination of its exact direction among the much fainter background stars.

166

Stories Behind the Figures
• • • • •

Note: This section contains background details relating to some of the figures that appear throughout the text. It is intended to supply additional information for those who may be interested in greater detail than is provided in the captions.

Fig. 5. Frequently recognized as the champion of modern science in England, Francis Bacon (1561–1626) was also an intellectual inspiration to the Royal Society of London. Granted its royal charter in 1662, the Royal Society epitomized the new "experimental philosophy" of nature—an alternative to the Scholastic philosophy taught at the universities and criticized at length by Bacon.[1] By the time of the 1874 transit of Venus, the Royal Society had long been at the leading edge of scientific advance in England.

In 1665, following Bacon's call for educational reform,[2] the *Philosophical Transactions* began to appear under Society auspices.[3] It was there, in the pages of the *Transactions*, that Society fellow Edmond Halley drew attention to transit phenomena—first in 1691[4] and again in 1716[5]—especially extolling the rare transits of Venus as celestial aids in helping astronomers measure the much-sought-after solar parallax and thus determine the Earth's true distance from the sun.

But the Royal Society did more during the first century of its existence than merely publish scientific papers or abstruse tomes.[6] It was directly involved with the invention and development of several of the instruments of navigation and astronomy of which Captain Cook was an early beneficiary.[7] The reflecting telescope, the quadrant, and the chronometer all received the scrutiny of the Society; and onto the ingenious men responsible for their advent—Newton, Hadley, and Harrison—the Society bestowed both recognition and reward. The Copley Medal—the Society's highest honor, first conferred in 1731 and given annually thereafter—found many worthy recipients, including, in 1776, James Cook.[8]

But among the many hallmarks of seventeenth-century British science, the establishment in 1675 of the Royal Greenwich Observatory was an event whose eventual impact upon Hawaiian history remains unparalleled. It was in March of that year that Royal Society founder and patron King Charles II signed a royal warrant appointing twenty-eight-year-old John Flamsteed as his "astronomical observator," setting before him the task of "perfecting the art of navigation."[9] In 1710, Queen Anne appointed a Board of Visitors to direct the observatory's affairs, a board to consist of the president and other members of the Council of the Royal Society; and four years later, she gave her royal assent to the Longitude Act.[10]

It was John Harrison's quest after the longitude prize, pursuant to the Longitude Act of 1714, that resulted in the creation of his celebrated timepieces, a replica of one of which (by Larcum Kendall) was to sail to Hawai'i with Captain Cook.

Fig. 6. The 1874 *Nautical Almanac* gave this explanation regarding the use of lunar distances:

Lunar Distances.—These pages contain, for every third hour of Greenwich mean time, the angular distances between the apparent *centres* of the Moon and certain heavenly bodies, such as they would appear to an observer at the centre of the Earth. When a Lunar Distance has been observed on the surface of the Earth, and reduced to the centre, by clearing it of the effects of parallax and refraction, the numbers in these pages enable us to ascertain the exact Greenwich mean time at which the objects would have the same distance. They are arranged, from *west* to *east*, commencing each day with the object which is at the greatest distance *westward* of the Moon, in the precise order in which they appear in the heavens; W. indicating that the object is west, and E. east of the Moon. Thus we have at one view, by a simple reference to the date, all the lunar distances which are available for the determination of the Longitude.[11]

Figs. 7 and 8. Hawai'i, located near the upper right in Figure 7, was an excellent station for observing the beginning of the transit under Delisle's method; but it was not a suitable site for the employment of Halley's method because the Earth's rotation would carry the Islands to the dark side of the planet before the end of the transit, at which time the side of the Earth depicted in Figure 8 would be turned sunward.

Fig. 9. After entering the navy as a midshipman in 1828 at the age of seventeen, Benjamin F. Sands (1811–1883) rose to the rank of lieutenant in 1840 and subsequently had a long and active officer's career. Following the Civil War, he was appointed superintendent of the U.S. Naval Observatory at Washington in 1867 and was commissioned rear admiral in 1871.

In 1872 and 1873, Sands sent letters to British Astronomer Royal George Airy expressing the American interest in observing the 1874 transit of Venus from Hawai'i and underscoring the favorable meteorological and astronomical situation of Hawai'i as well as its accessibility from the west coast of the United States. Less than ten months before transit day, Sands was placed on the retired list.[12]

Fig. 12. An alumnus of Cambridge University (St. John's College, 1860), Richard Anthony Proctor (1837–1888) was elected a fellow of the Royal Astronomical Society in 1866 and served as RAS secretary from 1872 to 1874. In his role as Airy's critic, it was posthumously written of him that "his profound study of the circumstances under which the transits of 1874 and 1882 would occur enabled him definitely to correct the mistakes into which the (then) astronomer royal

had inadvertently fallen with reference to the localities whence, and the modes in which, those phenomena would be most advantageously observable."

Fig. 17. It was in this book-lined abode built by Forbes and described by him as "a hermit's library in a pleasant grove" that Sir David Gill (inset) labored during the last three years of his life on his monumental *History and Description of the Cape Observatory.* Like Forbes, Gill (1843–1914) was born in Scotland. In 1872 he accepted an offer to work at Lord Lindsay's private observatory at Dun Echt near Aberdeen, and he was with Lindsay on Mauritius to observe the 1874 transit of Venus. From 1879 to 1907, Gill served as the director of the Cape of Good Hope Observatory, and it was during this period that George Forbes, by his own account, twice had the happiness of going to South Africa and seeing his friend at work. In 1916, two years after Gill's death, Forbes' biography, *David Gill, Man and Astronomer,* was published in London.[13]

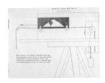

Fig. 20. Because the eighteenth century observations of Venus' contact with the sun had been vitiated by the black-drop effect, and because the precise observation of contact was critical to the success of the transit of Venus method for determining the AU, substantial efforts were marshaled against the threat that a black-drop, or kindred hazards, would reappear in 1874, and several nations— France, Germany, Russia, America, and England—produced artificial transits for the practice of observers.[14] It was hoped that practice with a model would bring observers close to uniformity in their descriptions and timings of the various transit phenomena and that nearly uniform observational reports would result on transit day.

Describing Airy's transit of Venus model, George Forbes wrote:

The arrangement adopted by the Astronomer Royal consists essentially of a metal disc with two arcs of circles drawn upon it to represent the sun's edge with the metal between them cut away. Behind these there passes a glass plate with a circle of metal to represent Venus let into it flush with its surface. The glass plate is moved by clock-work so that the different phenomena are observed in succession exactly as they will be seen in the true transit. As the artificial planet passes in succession the two arcs representing the sun's edge, the phenomena of ingress and egress are successively observed. Before contact takes place, the sun has two cusps at the point of contact where Venus is touching the edge of the sun. The distance between the points of these cusps rapidly diminishes, the space between them being intensely black. They suddenly meet. But between the planet and the sun's edge a light shade is still seen which lasts several seconds before the planet appears completely detached. If instead of watching the meeting of the cusps, the part between them be studied, a sudden diminution of intensity of the

169

blackness is seen about a second before the meeting of the cusps. The diminution of brightness is very sudden, and this is the phenomenon to be chiefly attended to in the actual observation. It occurs almost exactly at the moment of true contact, though the "black drop" does not disappear until some seconds later. It is of the utmost importance that the nature of these different phenomena should be carefully studied by all the observers.[15]

Fig. 21. Pierre Jules Cesar Janssen (1824–1907) conceived his novel device in 1873, and by its use a rapid series of photographs was made possible. His apparatus consisted of three circular discs with the same axis: The first, pierced by twelve slits, served as the shutter; the second contained a window; a circular photographic plate (such as the one shown here) was fixed to the third. By synchronizing the movement of the first two discs, a series of separate images could be obtained on the glass plate. Photographic prints could then be made in quantity, and a post-transit scrutiny of the successive positions of Venus in relation to the solar limb could ensue. And because the device provided a tool for the analysis of motion on the basis of its elements, Janssen had here realized one of the operations necessary for the invention twenty years later of cinematography.[16]

Fig. 26. Built and opened in the early 1870s and described by Isabella Bird in 1873 as "a long, stone, two-storied house with two deep verandahs festooned with clematis and passion flowers, and a shady lawn in front," the Hawaiian Hotel was, wrote Ms. Bird, the "perfection" of a hotel.[17]

Fig. 29. The work of the transit of Venus party in establishing their location was painstaking and precise. The latitude was obtained by meticulously observing with the altazimuth the zenith distances of carefully selected stars. From the mean of the resulting colatitudes (68° 42' 3".14), its complement was derived, giving 21° 17' 56".9 (north) as the adopted latitude of the altazimuth pier. The longitude was pursued with equal diligence by combining observations of meridional transits of the moon, zenith distances of the moon's upper and lower limbs, and occultations of stars by the moon. These observations, when combined with those made by Fleuriais in 1868, gave the Honolulu station a longitude of 10h 31m 26.3s (± 2s)—or 157° 51' 34".5 (± 30")—west of Greenwich.[18]

In addition, but no less importantly, the relative positions of the instruments within the observatory were determined; and from a precisely defined point within the grounds (14.75 feet due south of the center of the transit pier), distances and bearings were taken to several external points for the expressed purpose of connecting the transit of Venus station with the Hawai'i Government Survey. These points included the spire of Kawaiaha'o Church, 1,040 feet away, and the survey station on Punchbowl, 5,104 feet distant,[19] as well as points on both Tantalus and Diamond Head.

Fig. 35. The transit instrument and its companion clock are shown here inside a 13-foot-square, prefabricated wooden shelter, the separate pieces of which were stenciled with numbers indicating a convenient order for setting it up.[20] The companion clock is the Dent No. 1916.

The transit instrument used in Honolulu was one of five, precisely similar in all respects, constructed for the five British stations by Messrs. Troughton and Simms. Having an 18-inch axis consisting of a central 6-inch cube and two projecting cones, the 44-pound instrument boasted a focal length of 40 inches and an aperture of 3, and yet was perfectly balanced on its pivots. At the eye end, the observer could view clock stars[21] through a system of webs, or wires, five vertical and two horizontal, mounted on a plate driven by a micrometer screw. Because the transit instrument was commonly used after sunset, the wires were illuminated by artificial lamplight passing through either the eastern or western pivot, onto a reflector, and down to the eyepiece.

Assuming that adequate practice at the transit of Venus model would serve to minimize discordance among observers noting different phenomena at the time of contact, it remained to determine accurately the times of those observations. The transit instrument was critical in such determinations, being used to obtain local time from observations of clock stars as they transited the meridian.

The utmost importance of the transit instrument and the observations derived therefrom was matched by the careful labor displayed in properly mounting it in the meridian. After digging a pit through the Honolulu topsoil to the level of the coral beneath, a solid pier of brick and cement was built up to about the surface of the ground. On this foundation was laid, leveled, oriented, and cemented a 1,500-pound stone, 6 feet by 3 feet and 6 inches thick. Then, two upright stone piers—4 feet 11 inches high, 24 x 21 inches at the base and 11 x 11 inches at the top, and weighing nearly 1,400 pounds each—were set up on the stone slab, leaving ample room for an observer to sit between them. These three stone giants, sent out from England with the expedition, provided a solid mounting for the transit instrument, whose reliability was ensured by being systematically monitored for perceptible deviations in level, collimation, and azimuth.[22]

Fig. 36. Among the new manufactures ordered in 1870 for the transit of Venus expeditions were a dozen identical clocks from Messrs. E. Dent and Co., of London, three of which were sent to Hawai'i. The most important of these, numbered 1916 and seen in Figure 35, was used hand-in-hand with the transit instrument.[23] The other two were secondary clocks, numbered 2012 and 2013. Dent 2012, pictured here, was used in conjunction with Nichol and Tupman's observations at the 6-inch telescope seen in Figure 39.[24]

Fig. 37. For lunar observations intended to yield Honolulu's longitude, an altazimuth similar to the one shown here was provided. A telescope with a 2-inch objective and a 20-inch focal length was carried on a horizontal axis to which were attached two vertical circles, each 14 inches in diameter. One circle could be read, to seconds of arc, by micrometer microscopes.

The altazimuth was protected by a wooden hexagonal hut about 8 feet in diameter, complete with a revolving roof, slit, and shutter (see Fig. 31). It was accompanied by a pendulum clock by E. Dent and Co. that was intended to be compared with the transit clock (Dent No. 1916) before and after every observation, such comparison being made by chronometer.[25]

Fig. 38. The photoheliograph used in Honolulu (and pictured here) was one of five—one for each of the British stations—executed by the celebrated optician John Henry Dallmeyer. Mounted equatorially and furnished with driving clocks, they were crafted of brass tubing 5 inches in diameter for a length of 6 feet, from which they opened out into a cone of about 2 feet, for a total length of approximately 8 feet. They were sufficiently large at one extremity to receive sensitized photographic plates. They had objective lenses measuring about 4 inches in diameter and produced in the focal plane an image of the sun of about half an inch. This image was then magnified to about 4 inches on the photographic plates, which measured 6 inches square and were supplied for the five British stations by the highly respected glassworks company, the Chance Brothers, of Birmingham.

Fig. 39. In Honolulu on transit day, George Tupman would observe internal contact with this telescope, the largest at the Honolulu site. Having a focal length of 7 feet 5 inches and equatorially mounted, it had been purchased by the government from the executors of B. D. Naylor. It was sheltered by a wooden hut, the roof of which could be removed in pieces.

Fig. 40. The 6-inch Cooke telescope shown in Figure 39 was supplemented by the smaller instrument pictured here: a 4.5-inch refractor, also by T. Cooke and Sons. The personal property of Captain Tupman, it was equipped with an observing seat adjustable to different heights. Attached to the seat was a movable bar that enabled the observer to steady his hands while pointing the instrument.[26] The 4.5-inch Cooke was protected by a small hut of wood and canvas that was removed entirely when the instrument was in use.[27]

 **Fig. 45.** By 1874, Chester Smith Lyman (1814–1890) had become a professor of physics and astronomy at Yale, but in earlier life, after graduating from the Yale Divinity School in 1842 and holding a pastorate over the First Congregational Church in New Britain, Connecticut, he was obliged to travel for his health. After spending more than seven months at sea, he reached the Sandwich Islands via Cape Horn in May 1846. He was to remain in Hawai'i little more than a year, and during his stay in Honolulu he was to teach briefly at the Royal School, where among the royal pupils was the young David Kalākaua. Seventeen letters written to him by Hawaiian royal children between the years 1847 and 1849 are still preserved among his papers.[28]

At Yale, Lyman, who considered teaching as his major lifework, used his own private observatory for training students and even made equipment for teaching demonstrations. His inventiveness—coupled with his interest in practical horology, once evidenced in his construction of a Hawaiian sundial[29]—led to his devising improvements in escapements and compensation pendulums for observatory clocks.

After 1866, Lyman regularly observed sunspots from Yale's Sheffield Observatory using a 9-inch Clark telescope. On December 8, 1874, using a smaller instrument by the same maker, he carefully observed Venus just hours before the commencement of the transit—an event that would occur after sunset and be unobservable from his location.

 **Fig. 46.** The temporary quarters of astronomers George Forbes and Henry Barnacle, Hulihe'e Palace was built in 1838 by John Adams Kuakini using local materials: lava rock, coral mortar, and the native woods '*ōhi'a* and *koa*. Upon Kuakini's death in 1844, the Hulihe'e property passed to his adopted son William Pitt Leleiohoku, the husband of Princess Ruth Ke'elikōlani, and eventually to the princess herself. After Ruth's death it was acquired in 1884 by King Kalākaua, who modernized it and made it his summer residence. The photograph shown here was taken sometime before 1884.

 **Fig. 48.** Built in 1929 by Charles L. Murray of the Hawai'i Territory Survey, this 4 x 4-foot concrete slab is imbedded with flat, beach-worn pebbles in the form a double circle. Inside the circle is a bronze button centered over the original transit of Venus station mark, described as "a drill hole in a 2' x 2' x 1' thick brick pier." This was probably the pier that supported the transit instrument marked "A" in Figure 47.[30]

 Fig. 49. The inscription for the Cook Memorial (inset) was composed by British commissioner James H. Wodehouse.[31]

Fig. 50. The telescope used by George Forbes at Kailua-Kona, comparable to the Lee and purchased by the government from Richard Hodgson, was described by Hodgson as an equatorial refractor with an object glass measuring 6 "French Inches" and a focal length of 7 feet 3 inches. It was mounted on a mahogany polar axis 12 feet 3 inches in length, 10.5 inches square at the middle, and tapering to 8 inches square at the ends, came with declination and hour circles 25 inches in diameter, was fitted with clockwork motion, and possessed powers of resolution described by Forbes as admirable.[32]

Fig. 52. Marking the position of his observatory on the hillside above Waimea with "three arrows cut on rocks,"[33] Richard Johnson established his site so unforgettably well that it continued to be a prominent feature on Waimea survey and tax maps right into the twentieth century.[34]

Fig. 53. On transit day, a detachment of marines was posted around the enclosure at the 'Āpua site in order to prevent any disturbance. Similar military guards were provided at both Kailua-Kona and Waimea. Of the five principal British stations scattered around the world for the 1874 event, Honolulu was designated as Station B—hence the appearance of the letter B on the flag, together with the date and the astronomical symbol for Venus.

Fig. 55. The British *Nautical Almanac and Astronomical Ephemeris* for 1874 gave Venus and the sun semidiameters of 32".1 and 16'16".2, respectively, for December 8, and predicted a time of approximately 3:33 for internal contact at Honolulu, the sun then being about 21 degrees above the horizon and sinking in the southwest. This photograph was taken approximately 7 minutes later, at 3:40 (±40 seconds).[35]

Fig. 58. Born in Scotland and educated in America, William Harkness (1837–1903) was appointed professor of mathematics at the U.S. Naval Observatory in 1863 and later served as the observatory's civilian astronomical director as well as the director of the *American Ephemeris and Nautical Almanac.* He was the head of the U.S. 1874 transit of Venus team at Hobart Town (Tasmania), devised a measuring machine (the spherometer caliper) to determine accurately the positions of Venus and the sun in photographs, and was in charge of the reduction of all American transit observations.[36]

Fig. 59. Now kept at the U.S. Naval Observatory in Washington, this telescope (a 5-inch refractor) is one of eight identical instruments furnished by Alvan Clark and Sons for the American 1874 transit of Venus observations. An instrument considerably larger than this—a Clark 12-inch—was used by King Kalākaua during his visit to the Lick Observatory in 1881.

Fig. 60. To commemorate his election to the throne, King Kalākaua created the Order of Kalākaua in September 1875. Awarded for distinguished service rendered to the state or sovereign, the Order of Kalākaua was divided into four classes. In 1882, George Tupman was admitted into the class of Knights Commander.

The insignia of Knights Commander (shown here) consisted of a cross in gold with blue and white enamel. Supported by the arms of the cross was a wreath of gold leaves. A *pūlo'ulo'u*—a staff tipped with a ball to designate the presence of royalty—was fixed to the leaves between each arm, and a *kāhili*—another symbol of royalty—was centered upon a blue and white cross-borne shield, around the edge of which were impressed the words "Kalakaua February 12th 1874." A crown surmounted the whole; when worn, the medal was suspended from the neck with a ribbon of alternate blue and white stripes.[37]

Fig. 61. Adams was born on June 5, 1819, at Lidcot in Cornwall. The son of a poor tenant farmer, he was admitted to St. John's College, Cambridge, in 1839 as a sizar and in 1843 graduated at the top of his class as senior wrangler, outperforming his nearest rival by a better than two-to-one margin. Generally credited as the codiscoverer (with Leverrier) of the planet Neptune while yet in his twenties, he went on to become professor of mathematics at St. Andrew's University in 1858, Lowndean Professor of Astronomy and Geometry at Cambridge in 1859, and director of the Cambridge Observatory in 1861—a position he held for the rest of his life. A man of exceptional mathematical talent, he was a fellow of the Royal Society and recipient of the Copley Medal; and he served as president of the Royal Astronomical Society from 1851 to 1853 and again from 1874 to 1876. Described as a "man of learning as well as of science," he collected eight hundred volumes of early printed works that he subsequently bequeathed to the Cambridge University Library; and many of his personal papers still survive. Despite his many honors and achievements, Adams was humble and self-effacing, refusing knighthood and declining the office of Astronomer Royal in 1881 upon Airy's retirement. He died at the Cambridge Observatory on January 21, 1892, and was buried in a quiet corner of a small graveyard nearby (see the inset).

 **Fig. 62.** Although the status of the RGO as a producer of accurate positional data on a continuing basis was already acknowledged worldwide by the time George Airy retired, major changes in the institution's focus on *positional astronomy* accelerated as Airy's successor, William Christie, began to oversee the RGO's transformation into an institution where *physical astronomy* (astrophysics) also had a place. Yet Airy's reputation and the continuation of his legacy into the twentieth century had already been assured as early as 1851. It was in that year that the best-known of the instruments designed by him for the reequipping of the observatory—the Airy Transit Circle— came into service. Like the portable transit instrument used in Honolulu in 1874, the Airy Transit Circle was intended to carry out accurate positional measurements in accordance with the traditional aims of the RGO. The high regard in which the Transit Circle was held was perhaps best indicated in 1884, three years after Airy's departure from Greenwich, when the International Meridian Conference in Washington proposed that the Prime Meridian of the world pass directly through the center of Airy's transit instrument. Though the Airy Transit Circle was retired from service in 1954—by which time it had been used for more than 750,000 observations—the prime meridian remained, as it still remains, fixed at this historic place.[38]

 Fig. 63. Regarding the Chinese instruments, Forbes writes:

The French Jesuits at Peking, in the seventeenth century, helped the Chinese in their astronomy. In 1875 the writer saw and photographed, on that part of the wall of Peking used by the Mandarins as an observatory, the six instruments handsomely designed by Father Verbiest, copied from the instruments of Tycho Brahe, and embellished with Chinese dragons and emblems cast on the supports. He also saw there two old instruments (which he was told were Arabic) of date 1279, by Ko Show-King, astronomer to Koblai [Kublai] Khan, the grandson of Chenghis [Genghis] Khan. One of these last is nearly identical with the armillae of Tycho; and the other with his "armillae aequatoriae maximae," with which he observed the comet of 1585, besides fixed stars and planets.

The single caption written by Forbes for the two photographs reproduced here reads: "Ancient Chinese Instruments, Including quadrant, celestial globe, and two armillae, in the Observatory at Peking. Photographed in Peking by the author in 1875, and stolen by the Germans when the Embassies were relieved by the allies in 1900." George Forbes, *History of Astronomy*, 75–77.

Abbreviations

• • • • •

AC	*Alumni Cantabrigienses*
AH	State Archives of Hawai'i
BDAS	*Biographical Dictionary of American Science*
BJ	Henry Barnacle's Transit of Venus Journal (RGO 59/67)
DNB	*Dictionary of National Biography*
DSB	*Dictionary of Scientific Biography*
FJ	George Forbes' Transit of Venus Journal (RGO 59/69)
HAA	*Hawaiian Almanac and Annual* (also known as *Thrum's Annual*)
HG	*Hawaiian Gazette*
HMCS	Hawaiian Mission Children's Society
JJ	Richard Johnson's Transit of Venus Journal (RGO 59/74)
MNRAS	*Monthly Notices of the Royal Astronomical Society*
NAAE	*Nautical Almanac and Astronomical Ephemeris*
PCA	*Pacific Commercial Advertiser*
PPSG	*Proceedings of the Philosophical Society of Glasgow*
PRO	British Public Record Office
RGO	Archives of the Royal Greenwich Observatory (Cambridge University Library)
RJ	Francis Ramsden's Transit of Venus Journal (RGO 59/68)
THJ	George Tupman's Home Journal (RGO 59/56)
TJ	George Tupman's Transit of Venus Journal (RGO 59/70)

Notes

· · · · ·

2. Location

1. Allen writes: "Arcturus has been an object of the highest interest and admiration to all observant mankind from the earliest times, and doubtless was one of the first stars to be named; for from Hesiod's day to the present it thus appears throughout all literature." Although Hesiod's reference in his *Works and Days* to the heliacal rising of Arcturus is regarded as fixing his own date in history at about 800 B.C.E., Arcturus must have had a place outside of or even prior to such literatures—in, for example, the Egyptian astronomical calendar, which antedated Hesiod by several centuries. Allen, *Star Names*, 98, 99n, 100.

2. Taylor, *The Haven-Finding Art*, 40–41. That the Mediterranean Sea formed the proverbial cradle of Western civilization was, to Adam Smith, not a mystery, nor were the navigational skills developed there inexplicable accidents. In his celebrated work on *The Wealth of Nations* (1776), Smith observes:

> The nations that, according to the best authenticated history, appear to have been first civilised, were those that dwelt round the coast of the Mediterranean Sea. That sea, by far the greatest inlet that is known in the world, having no tides, nor consequently any waves except such as are caused by the wind only, was, by the smoothness of its surface, as well as by the multitude of its islands, and the proximity of its neighbouring shores, extremely favourable to the infant navigation of the world; when, from their ignorance of the compass, men were afraid to quit the view of the coast, and from the imperfection of the art of ship-building, to abandon themselves to the boisterous waves of the ocean. To pass beyond the pillars of Hercules, that is, to sail out of the Straits of Gibraltar, was, in the ancient world, long considered as a most wonderful and dangerous exploit of navigation. It was late before even the Phoenicians and Carthaginians, the most skillful navigators and ship-builders of those old times, attempted it, and they were for a long time the only nations that did attempt it. (*The Wealth of Nations,* bk. 1, chap. 3)

3. See Lee Motteler, "Hawai'i's First Chart? A Recent Rediscovery" (1980). Motteler reviews the various claims to European discovery predating Cook's, concluding that the earliest verifiable cartographic representation of the Hawaiian Islands is the 1778 chart of Kaua'i and Ni'ihau drawn by Thomas Edgar, master of HMS *Discovery,* on Cook's fateful third voyage.

4. Cook's interest in the origins and migrations of the early Hawaiian people is clearly evidenced in his own writing. In January 1778, shortly after his discovery of the Hawaiian Islands, he entered these reflections in his journal: "I have already observed that these people are of the same nation as the people of Otaheite and many others of the South sea islands. . . . How shall we account for this Nation

spreading it self so far over this Vast ocean? We find them from New Zealand to the South, to these islands to the North and from Easter Island to the Hebrides; an extent of 60° of latitude or twelve hundred leagues north and south and 83° of longitude or sixteen hundred and sixty leagues east and west, how much farther is not known." Price, *The Explorations of Captain James Cook*, 222.

5. "Hawaii-nui [Hawai'i-loa] is a fisherman from lands adjoining Kahiki-honua-kele. He knows the sea called 'Sea where the fish run' (O-kai-holo-a-ka-i'a) which used to lie where these islands now lie. He sailed from Kahiki-honua-kele and discovered these islands, first Kauai, then Oahu, then the Maui group, then Hawaii, which he named after himself. The other islands he named after his children, and various land divisions after his eight navigators who sailed with him, of whom Makali'i was chief. To return to Kahiki [Tahiti] they sailed west guided by the star Hoku-loa." Beckwith, *Hawaiian Mythology*, 364. Some of the navigational elements of this story eventually became preserved among the stars, as Makali'i became the Hawaiian eponym for the Pleiades, a star cluster that now passes near the zenith of Kaua'i. It was "zenith stars" such as the Pleiades and Arcturus that were (or may have been) used to help guide legendary Polynesian navigators (such as Hawai'i-loa) to island destinations at the northern edge of the tropics. About the additional importance of the Pleiades in marking the New Year in the ancient Hawaiian calendar, see Kyselka, "On the Rising of the Pleiades." As Kyselka notes, the process of precession gradually repositions the Pleiades on the celestial sphere: 1,500 years ago they passed directly over Ka Lae (South Point) on the island of Hawai'i.

6. Johnson and Mahelona, *Na Inoa Hoku*, 5, 16.

7. A brief account of the astronomical traditions of prehistoric Hawai'i can be found in Chauvin, "Useful and Conceptual Astronomy in Ancient Hawaii."

8. Because Eratosthenes and Posidonius measured the value of meridian (north-south) arcs, the inferences made therefrom were of the Earth's *polar* rather than its *equatorial* circumference. It is now known that, due to the Earth's oblate shape, the length of a degree of latitude varies from about 110.6 km at the equator to 111.7 km at the poles and the Earth's polar circumference is about 135 km less than its equatorial circumference.

9. In the seventeenth century, the work of Richard Norwood in England and Jean Picard in France produced a value of about 69 miles for one degree of latitude; the inferred value for the Earth's (polar) radius was just shy of 4,000 miles. Sellers, *The Transit of Venus*, 113–115.

10. The adoption, by the international community of scientists, of the meter (metre) as the fundamental unit of distance in the metric system is historically based upon a knowledge of the Earth's figure (its size and shape). During the closing decade of the eighteenth century, the French, in formulating for the civilized world a system of metric units of measure, defined the meter as one ten-millionth of the distance between the equator and the North Pole along the meridian of Paris, the relevant astronomical work being undertaken by Delambre and Mechain and completed by 1799. See Mason (1962) and Warren (1979).

3. The Astronomical Unit

1. Van Helden, *Measuring the Universe*, 4. Copernicus himself continued to find the ER a useful unit and used it, for example, to express the distance to the moon. See his *De Revolutionibus Orbium Celestium*, bk. 4, pt. 17.

2. Hoyle, *Astronomy*, 155.

3. Van Helden, *Measuring the Universe*, 47. A historically illuminating list of measured and accepted values for the AU—nearly eighty values in all, extending from the time of Aristarchus into the twentieth century—can be found in David W. Hughes, "Six Stages in the History of the Astronomical Unit" (2001).

4. This figure assumes, for the equatorial radius of the Earth, the modern value of 6,378.140 km (3,963.1433 miles) and adopts Aristarchus' measure of the Earth-sun distance as 180 times the Earth's mean diameter, or 360 ER, the figure given by Woolf (citing Heath's *Aristarchus of Samos*) on page 7 of his *Transits of Venus*. Alternatively, Van Helden (*Measuring the Universe*, 8) speculatively gives, for Aristarchus' measure, both a figure close to this (380 ER) and one four times as large (1,520 ER).

5. Van Helden, *Measuring the Universe*, 27. The sun is, in truth, about four hundred times farther from the Earth than is the moon.

6. Van Helden, *Measuring the Universe*, 155.

7. Van Helden, *Measuring the Universe*, 129, 154. Because the orbit of Mars brings that planet closer to Earth than any other except Venus, the parallax of Mars when at opposition is easier to measure than that of most other solar system objects. This is especially true if Mars is at perihelion and the Earth at aphelion when opposition occurs, for then the planet can be as little as 56 million kilometers (about 35 million miles) away from Earth. Such close approaches occur at intervals of fifteen to seventeen years.

Although Venus comes closer to Earth than does Mars (as close as 0.27 AU, or about 25 million miles), it reaches its nearest-to-Earth position when at inferior conjunction, at which time it is usually difficult if not impossible to observe.

8. An authoritative nineteenth-century discussion of parallax—and of the attempt to derive the solar parallax from transits of Venus—can be found in Newcomb, *Popular Astronomy*, chap. 3.

The solar parallax, defined as the angle subtended by the Earth's equatorial radius at the sun's mean distance, is an exceedingly small angle: about 8.8 arc seconds. The human eye cannot perceive such a tiny angle unaided. The cause of this is twofold: the wavelength of the light entering the pupil of the eye and the diameter of the pupil when the light enters it. Because both these quantities—the wavelength of light and the diameter of the pupil—vary, the eye's power of resolution has a limited range of values: from about 30 to about 60 arc seconds. The sun's parallax is, therefore, several times smaller than what the naked eye can detect, even under the best conditions.

9. Van Helden, *Measuring the Universe*, 115.

10. Van Helden, *Measuring the Universe,* chap. 12 and p. 146. The planet observed by Flamsteed and Cassini was Mars, from whose parallax the parallax (and distance) of the sun was derived.

11. Van Helden, *Measuring the Universe,* 151–152.

12. Newton's values varied from 10″ to 13″. See Van Helden, *Measuring the Universe,* 154–155.

13. Van Helden, *Measuring the Universe,* 155–156.

4. From Toxteth to Tahiti

1. Carlyle, *On Heroes,* xxxiii–xxxiv.

2. Carlyle, *On Heroes,* 23.

3. The word "telescope" was not coined until 1611. Drake, *Galileo,* 27n.

4. Transits of Venus, much like the more commonplace sunspots, are visible without telescopic assistance. Maskelyne, for example, in anticipation of the 1769 transit, wrote this: "The Planet Venus, intirely divested of her Radiancy, will traverse the Sun's Face from East to West on the 3d of June 1769, in the Form of a round black Spot, and will be seen, if the Weather be clear at the Time, to all Places of the Earth where the Sun is up. She will be visible to sharp Eyes without a Telescope, only defended by the Interposition of a dark Glass; but will appear much more beautiful, and may be observed to much more Advantage, with the Help of a Telescope." Maskelyne, "Instructions."

When Venus transits the sun in 2004, it will subtend an angle of 61 arc seconds and will be visible to the naked eye using suitable filtration. Bishop, ed., *Observer's Handbook 1993,* 106. For a more inclusive treatment of transits of Venus, see Meeus, "The Transits of Venus."

About the alleged discovery of sunspots, historian of astronomy Stillman Drake writes that

> great bitterness arose between [Christopher] Scheiner [a Jesuit professor at the University of Ingolstadt] and Galileo concerning the question of priority in the discovery of sunspots, and this dispute appears to have had a great deal to do with Galileo's ultimate trouble with the church. Even apart from this it is most unfortunate that such a debate should have arisen, as neither man was first to observe sunspots—a phenomenon that was certainly mentioned in the time of Charlemagne, and possibly was referred to by Virgil—or even first to publish on the subject. That honor belongs to Johann Fabricius of Wittenberg, whose booklet printed in the summer of 1611 seems to have escaped their attention. (Drake, *Galileo,* 82)

5. Koestler, *The Sleepwalkers,* 406–411.

6. Van Helden, *Measuring the Universe,* 20, 47.

7. Van Helden, *Measuring the Universe*, 96–97, 105; George Forbes, "The Coming Transit of Venus," *Nature*, April 9, 1874, 448. A retrospective and somewhat modified view of the alleged unobservability of the 1631 transit was offered by Proctor in 1874: "I do not know where any calculation of the circumstances of the [1631] transit can be found; but an investigation of my own (sufficiently accurate for a past and unseen phenomenon) shows that in the Southeastern parts of Europe the egress might have been observed . . . after sunrise on the morning of December 7." Proctor, *Transits of Venus* (1st ed., 1874), 11–12. (Unless otherwise noted, all subsequent references to Proctor's *Transits of Venus* are to this edition.)

8. Biographical information on Horrocks can be found in Whatton, *Memoir of Jeremiah Horrox*. Whatton, who prefers "Horrox" to "Horrocks," gives 1619 as the year of Jeremiah's birth, even though this would have meant that his entrance to Emmanuel College, Cambridge, on May 18, 1632, preceded his fourteenth birthday. Alternatively, the Savilian Professor of Astronomy at Oxford had earlier suggested that Horrocks made his transit observations at the age of twenty-four, thereby implying 1615 as the year of his birth. Hornsby, "Discourse." See also "Jeremiah Horrox," *Nature*, June 12, 1873, 117–118, and June 19, 1873, 137–138; and DNB, vol. 9, 1,267–1,269.

9. A sizar was "a student originally financing his studies by undertaking more or less menial tasks within his college and, as time went on, increasingly likely to receive small grants from the college without being 'on the foundation'." Leedham-Green, *History of the University of Cambridge*, 245–246.

10. Van Helden, *Measuring the Universe*, 106.

11. Van Helden, *Measuring the Universe*, 105–106. Woolf writes (*The Transits of Venus*, 12) that although Horrocks was engaged in the double process of emending Kepler's tables and refuting those of Lansberg, it was while reconsidering the more basic errors of the latter that he made the important discovery missed by Kepler: Whereas Kepler's tables led to the prediction that the next transit after 1631 would not occur until 1761, the tables of Lansberg, Woolf notes, predicted that Venus would transit the northern tip of the sun in 1639. Horrocks' own account of his indebtedness to Lansberg is reproduced in Proctor, *Transits of Venus*, 13–14.

12. New Style designates a date reckoned in accordance with the Gregorian calendar. This would have been November 24 (Old Style [O.S.]). The Gregorian calendar was not adopted in England until 1752.

13. Although he had little time to notify other "votaries of astronomy," Horrocks did alert a younger brother at Liverpool, but overcast weather there on the day of the transit thwarted the desired observations. He did not inform other friends, saying that "most of them care little for trifles of this kind, preferring rather their hawks and hounds, to say no worse." Whatton, *Memoir of Jeremiah Horrox*, 130–131.

14. On December 10, 1872, J. R. Hind wrote for Astronomer Royal George Airy the following retrospective account: "[Regarding] Horrock's observation of first internal contact of Venus on 1639 Dec. 4 . . . I find the mean time at Hoole (2° 49′ W) of first internal contact comes out 3^h 14^m 26^s. . . . Horrock's says the limbs were in contact at 3^h15^m. . . . The sun's altitude at the time was less than 3°, so narrowly did the first observation of Venus upon the Sun escape being deferred for more than 120 years." RGO 6/269, file 15, leaf 378.

15. Whatton, *Memoir of Jeremiah Horrox,* 123. Proctor (*Transits of Venus,* chap. 1) borrows heavily from Whatton in retelling Horrocks' first-person account verbatim.

16. Among the accomplishments of Horrocks, Whatton gives the following: He was the first to predict and observe a transit of Venus; to provide a value for the sun's parallax near to one that it was subsequently thought to have; to discover that the orbit of the moon about the Earth is an ellipse with the center in the lower focus; to explain the causes of orbital motion; to devise an experiment using a pendulum for illustrating the action of a central force; and to commence a regular series of tidal observations for the purpose of philosophical inquiry. In addition, he improved astronomical tables; recommended the adoption of decimal notation; detected the inequality in the mean motion of Jupiter and Saturn; and wrote his opinions on the nature and motion of comets. "That so much should have been achieved," Whatton continues, "by so young a man, notwithstanding many disadvantages, may seem almost incredible." It is perhaps no wonder that John Herschel called him "the pride and boast of British astronomy." Whatton, *Memoir of Jeremiah Horrox,* 91–92, 95.

17. The legend of Horrocks' religious compunctions on the day of the 1639 transit has been challenged by Chapman in his "Jeremiah Horrocks."

18. "Transit of Venus: Historical Events," *PCA,* December 19, 1874. Horrocks then beheld, he tells us, "a most agreeable spectacle, the object of my sanguine wishes," while his friend Crabtree, some miles distant, observed Venus upon the sun's disc with less emotional restraint:

> Rapt in contemplation, he [Crabtree] stood for some time motionless, scarcely trusting his own senses, through excess of joy; for we astronomers have as it were a womanish disposition, and are over-joyed with trifles and such small matters as scarcely make an impression upon others; a susceptibility which those who will may deride with impunity, even in my own presence, and, if it gratify them, I too will join in the merriment. One thing I request: let no severe Cato be seriously offended with our follies; for, to speak poetically, what young man on earth would not, like ourselves, fondly admire Venus in conjunction with the Sun, 'pulchritudinem divitiis conjunctam'? (Whatton, *Memoir of Jeremiah Horrox,* 124, 129)

19. Van Helden, *Measuring the Universe,* 152; Halley, "De Visibili."

20. Van Helden, *Measuring the Universe,* 144–145, 152, 155. Woolf (*The Transits of Venus,* 16) writes: "If it is at all necessary . . . to select any single factor as the major stimulant in bringing about the enormous enterprise associated with the eighteenth-century transits of Venus, it was certainly Halley's paper of 1716."

21. George Forbes regarded Halley's method as a *particular case* of the method of durations because, strictly speaking, it required observations to be made from a station where the transit commenced just before sunset and ended just after sunrise. George Forbes, "The Coming Transit of Venus," *Nature,* May 28, 1874, 66. Elsewhere, Forbes wrote that: "Halley's method is called that of durations. It has been applied by choosing stations on a principle differing slightly from that indicated by Halley. The method proposed by him can only be applied when Venus passes near to the Sun's centre. For if it do not, the transit will last so short a time that it will be impossible to find an accessible station when the commencement takes place just before sunset and the end just after sunrise." George Forbes, "The

Transit of Venus in 1874," PPSG 1872–1873, 378. Halley's method is thoroughly described in "Edmond Halley's Famous Exhortation of 1716, With explanatory footnotes by James Ferguson, FRS," in Sellers, *The Transit of Venus*, 204–217.

22. Howse, *Nevil Maskelyne*, 20; George Forbes, "The Coming Transit of Venus," *Nature*, April 23, 1874, and May 7, 1874, 489 and 12–14. The calculation is: $1.5 \div 60 = 0.025$.

23. Proctor, *Transits of Venus*, 45–46.

24. There were likely many more if unreported observations by interested amateurs are included. Woolf, *The Transits of Venus*, 21, 134 ff. Proctor (*Transits of Venus*, 51) reports that the 1761 transit was observed by at least 176 persons at no fewer than 117 stations.

25. The 1761 observations by Maskelyne and by the Mason-Dixon team were published in the Royal Society's *Philosophical Transactions* 52: 196–201 and 378–394. Mason and Dixon were originally dispatched to Bencoolen, but misfortune placed them at the Cape. Their story, given in some detail by Woolf (*The Transits of Venus*), has been recently retold by Sellers, *The Transit of Venus*, 122–127.

26. Maskelyne, in his "Instructions" (see note 4), wrote as follows:

> The Theory of the Motions of Venus being not known sufficiently in Dr. Halley's Time, it turned out that Venus in the last Transit passed over the Sun's Disk at a much greater Distance from his Centre than he had supposed she would, which very much altered the Circumstances of the Phaenomenon, and rendered it much less advantageous for determining the Sun's Parallax than he had hoped for. Moreover, unfortunately, the Astronomers who were sent out by the English and French Nations to make the proper Observations were not all able, through unavoidable Accidents, to reach the intended Places most suitable for drawing the greatest Use from the Observations, or were hindered from making them by bad Weather. Therefore, though considerable Advantages were derived to Astronomy from the Observations of the last Transit made by Astronomers in various Places, yet we are still to expect to receive the full Benefit which this Phaenomenon is capable of affording us, from the ensuing Transit, which will happen on the 3d of June 1769; which is as well circumstanced for the Purpose as we can well desire, and indeed more favourably than the last Transit was expected by Dr. Halley to be.

Thomas Hornsby had, by 1763, already expounded on Halley's mistake in the *Philosophical Transactions* (see note 8).

27. Woolf, *The Transits of Venus*, 148, 192.

28. At the invitation of King Christian VII of Denmark and Norway, the 1769 transit was observed by the Jesuit astronomer Maximilian Hell (1720–1792) from Vardø. Just above the Arctic Circle, at a latitude of more than 70° north, this was not an altogether unfavorable observing site; for although the transit was in progress at midnight, the sun was above the horizon for its entire duration, from 9:30 P.M. to 3:30 A.M. Hell, who had been appointed the first director of the Vienna observatory in 1756, who had observed the 1761 transit of Venus in Vienna, and who was a man of experience and reputation, witnessed contact at both ingress and egress—or did he?

His own written report of his transit observations raised doubts—and eventually provoked the suspicion that he had fallen asleep during the transit and had missed the critical moments of egress entirely! By the 1860s, George Airy himself had fallen victim to such doubts and wrote: "To these [observations] great suspicion has attached, [and] many astronomers, without hesitation, designated them as forgeries." Hell's exculpation didn't come until 1883 when the American astronomer Simon Newcomb, while on a visit to Vienna, discovered that the fabrications were not Hell's but his critics'. See: Ashbrook, "The Reputation of Father Hell;" Sarton, "Vindication of Father Hell;" Newcomb, *Side-Lights on Astronomy,* chap. 15; Airy, *Popular Astronomy,* 145–146; Gould, *Captain Cook,* 55; Woolf, *The Transits of Venus,* 117, 137, 143, 176–179. A nearby but even more northerly station than Hell's was occupied by William Bayly (1737–1810), who observed the 1769 transit from Cape North (latitude: 71° 15′). Sent there by the Royal Society, Bayly's observations were published in its *Philosophical Transactions.* Bayly later served as astronomer on Captain Cook's second and third Pacific voyages. See note 34.

29. Beaglehole gives the following coordinates for what Gould calls "Maskelyne's Limits": The latitude limits were 5° and 35° S, and the longitude limits stretched from 172° E to 124° W along the northernmost boundary (at 5° S) and from 172° W to 139° W along the southernmost boundary (at 35° S). Beaglehole, *Captain Cook,* 103. Hornsby's coordinates, between the latitudes of 4° and 21° S and the longitudes of 130° and 190° W (from Greenwich), were similar. Woolf, *The Transits of Venus,* 162. Regarding the French (Pingre's) desire to observe the 1769 transit from the South Pacific, see Woolf, 152–153, 157.

30. Beaglehole, *Captain Cook,* 132.

31. Beaglehole, *Captain Cook,* 148–149.

32. Maskelyne, "Instructions" (see note 4).

33. Green had been the assistant to Nathaniel Bliss, the fourth Astronomer Royal at Greenwich and Maskelyne's immediate predecessor, and had continued to work at the Royal Observatory after Bliss' death. He had also accompanied Maskelyne to Barbados in 1763 for the second sea test of John Harrison's fourth marine chronometer, a replica of which, made by Larcum Kendall, was to travel with Captain Cook as a longitude watch on his last two voyages of exploration and was with Cook when he was in Hawai'i in 1778–1779. During the three-year voyage of the *Endeavour* (1768–1771) to Tahiti and back, with the newborn *Nautical Almanac* in hand and navigating by the method of lunar distances (rather than by the chronometer), Cook and Green set an altogether new standard of observation and accuracy in fixing the latitude and the longitude of the places that they visited. Eric G. Forbes, "The Greenwich Observatory," 590; Chauvin, "Lunars and Automatons."

34. Lownes, "The 1769 Transit of Venus." The Royal Society alone sponsored three transit of Venus expeditions for that year: one to the North Cape of Norway, one to Hudson Bay, and one to Tahiti. Observing the transit from Hudson Bay was William Wales, and from the North Cape, William Bayly—both of whom were to sail with Cook as astronomers on his second Pacific voyage (1772–1775), and one of whom (Bayly) was to return with Cook on his third (1776–1780). See note 28.

35. Gould, *Captain Cook,* 53.

36. Maskelyne, who joined with the Royal Society and the directors of the East India

Company in encouraging the observations of the transit of Venus and thus in the "promoting [of] Astronomy and Geography, on which Navigation so greatly depends," had explicitly written in his 1769 transit "Instructions" that "Observations of the Transit of Venus made in various Places, together with the other [astronomical] Observations made there in Consequence of it, will have another great Use in settling the Latitudes and Longitudes of the Places."

37. Beaglehole, *Captain Cook,* 182.

38. Cook and Green, "Observations." The citation given here is found on pp. 410–411.

39. Woolf, *The Transits of Venus,* 148–149.

40. Clerke more fully describes and explains the black drop as:

> substituting adhesion for contact, the limbs of the sun and planet, instead of meeting and parting with the desirable clean definiteness, *clinging* together as if made of some glutinous material, and prolonging their connection by means of a dark band or dark threads stretched between them. Some astronomers ascribed this baffling appearance entirely to instrumental imperfections; others to atmospheric agitation; others again to the optical encroachment of light upon darkness known as 'irradiation.' It is probable that all these causes conspired, in various measure, to produce it. (Clerke, *History of Astronomy,* 235)

A more recent attempt to explain the black drop as the effect of the "smearing" of the ideal image by atmospheric "seeing" and other causes, and to debunk several alternatives (diffraction of light around Venus, refraction of light by Venus' atmosphere, optical illusion), has been made by Bradley Schaefer in his "Transit of Venus and the Notorious Black Drop Effect."

41. George Forbes, "The Coming Transit of Venus," *Nature,* May 14, 1874, 28.

42. Halley himself had calculated—erroneously, as events proved—that at Hudson's Bay the beginning of the 1761 transit would be visible just before sunset and its end just after sunrise.

43. Biographical information on Delisle, including a description of his proposed method of observing the transit of Venus, his friendship with Halley, and his historical importance as an unofficial "archivist" of transit matters, can be found in Woolf, *The Transits of Venus,* chap. 2. According to Woolf (p. 89), Scots astronomer James Ferguson had, it seems, independently hit upon Delisle's method.

44. Airy's 1857 alert to the Royal Astronomical Society contained the declaration that the method of durations (Halley's method) possessed a "very important advantage, [namely] that it is entirely independent of the assumed longitude of the place of observation." Airy, "On the Means which will be available for correcting the Measure of the Sun's Distance, in the next twenty-five Years," MNRAS 17 (7): 214 (May 8, 1857). James Short—to give an even earlier example—thought that although the determination of longitude was "absolutely necessary" for the success of Delisle's method, it was not necessary for the method of durations. Short, "The Observations of the internal Contact of Venus with the Sun's Limb," esp. pp. 612 and 618–619. Such assessments were entirely in accord with what Halley himself had written in 1716:

For there is no need that the latitude of the place should be scrupulously observed, *nor that the hours themselves should be accurately determined with respect to the meridian:* it is sufficient that the clocks be regulated according to the motion of the heavens, if the times be well reckoned from the total ingress of Venus into the Sun's disc, to the beginning of her egress from it; that is, when the dark globe of Venus first begins to touch the bright limb of the Sun within; which moments, I know by my own experience, may be observed within a second of time. [Italics added] (Quoted in Sellers, *The Transit of Venus,* 207)

45. Hornsby, having obtained from thirteen separate observations of the 1761 transit a solar parallax of 8".692, wrote: "Such is the result of a comparison of the best observations made in places whose longitudes are as accurately ascertained as the present state of Astronomy will permit." Hornsby, "Discourse," 491.

46. Gould, *Captain Cook,* 55; Proctor, *Transits of Venus,* 85; Woolf, *The Transits of Venus,* 189.

47. Woolf, *The Transits of Venus,* 192.

5. Where the Sun Never Sets

1. The phrase "conspicuous consumption" is taken from Thorstein Veblen's nineteenth-century classic of economic thought, *The Theory of the Leisure Class.*

2. "Jeremiah Horrox," *Nature,* June 12, 1873, 117.

3. Halley (Forbes wrote) had left a "legacy to his successors, who, as Englishmen, might be entitled to be proud of his foresight." George Forbes, "The Coming Transit of Venus," *Nature,* April 23, 1874, 489.

4. The previous century had seen the names of Halley and Horrocks successfully invoked by the Royal Society of London in order to obtain financial support from King George II for the 1761 transit observations, that "most laudable undertaking, in which the Honour of this Nation is thus principally concerned." Howse, *Nevil Maskelyne,* 23.

5. Clerke, *History of Astronomy,* 234.

6. Airy, *Account,* iii. In an address given that year (1857) to the Royal Astronomical Society, Airy spoke at length on the means that would be available during the next quarter of a century for refining the value of the astronomical unit. After suggesting that correct determination of that distance had long been honored as "the noblest problem in astronomy," he went on to discuss alternative methods for measuring it. Because he believed that the transit of Venus method, even if attended "with all possible care," did not eliminate the risk of failure, he favored, as a viable alternative "for obtaining a very good measure," observations in 1860 and 1862 of oppositions of Mars when that planet would approach Earth to within less than 0.4 AU. Such observations, if made morning and evening with the same instrument and by the same observer, could have the distinct advantage of "admitting of almost indefinite repetition, demanding no co-operation of distant observers," and, not insignificant-

ly, costing far less labor and expense than a transit of Venus orchestration. Still, he urged that astronomical appetites would not be satisfied unless all practical use was made of the transits of Venus of 1874 and 1882. Airy, "On the Means."

7. Nor did he fail to recommend, in this context, that one of the observing sites should be "Woahoo [O'ahu], or some other point in the Sandwich Islands"—the very islands whose mathematical location had been preliminarily fixed by Captain Cook almost a century earlier, and the refined determination of whose longitude, it was declared, "may be considered as a duty of the British nation." Airy, "On the Preparatory Arrangements."

8. Woolf, *The Transits of Venus,* 4.

9. This minuscule angle amounts to no more than the width of a human hair as seen 125 feet from the eye. Clerke, *History of Astronomy,* 232; "The Transit of Venus," *HG,* January 28, 1874.

10. Woolf, *The Transits of Venus,* 208.

11. Stone, "A Rediscussion." Stone's essay (dated September 23, 1868) rediscussed the 1769 transit observations made at five stations: Wardhus, Kola, Hudson's Bay, St. Joseph, and Otaheite. After carefully interpreting the troublesome language employed in the reports of the various observers (e.g., with regard to the time of internal contact and the breaking of the black-drop), Stone deduced a solar parallax of 8".91, which he thought was not only entitled to "great weight" but was in addition "in most satisfactory agreement with the values which have lately been otherwise obtained." Stone's article was followed within a year in the same journal by numerous transit of Venus–related articles, including two by Airy, four by Proctor, and four more by Stone himself. Other contributors to the discussion within the pages of the *Monthly Notices* of 1868–1869 included Newcomb, De la Rue, Hind, Richards, Toynbee, Ommanney, Davis, and Tennant.

12. Airy to the secretary of the Admiralty, April 9, 1869, RGO 6/267, file 1.

6. Finding the Longitude

1. On the attempts made by Cassini and Flamsteed in 1672 to observe the parallax of Mars and to deduce therefrom the parallax of the sun, see Van Helden, *Measuring the Universe,* chap. 12. Flamsteed's knowledge of Horrocks' earlier work on solar parallax is noted in this chapter. Tycho Brahe's method of measuring the diurnal parallax of Mars, discussed elsewhere in the book, is also illustrated.

2. A brief summary of some nineteenth-century attempts to find the Earth-sun distance can be found in Berry, *A Short History of Astronomy,* 363–367.

3. Following Clerke's taxonomy, these methods may be classified as the trigonometrical, the gravitational, and the phototachymetrical (the last of these being "an ungainly adjective used to describe the method by the velocity of light"). Clerke, *History of Astronomy,* 240.

4. A duplicate of the data in this table can be found in Forbes' fourth installment of

his series in *Nature*, "The Coming Transit of Venus," Parts 1–7, *Nature*, April 9 to June 4, 1874. In both places, Forbes cites the published papers (frequently the Royal Astronomical Society's *Monthly Notices*) from which he has extracted the tabulated numbers. Elsewhere, Proctor has summarized the attempts of Hansen, Leverrier, Newcomb, Stone, Winnecke, and Foucault to determine the sun's distance in his *Transits of Venus*, 88–89. And Newcomb has given a synopsis of twenty-eight papers on the solar parallax published between the years 1854 and 1877—including papers by Hansen, Leverrier, Foucault, Stone, Newcomb, and Cornu—in his *Popular Astronomy*, 538–541.

5. The essence of utilitarianism as a moral philosophy is in the stress that it lays upon the effects that an action has rather than upon the moral goodness (or badness) of the agent who performs the action: If an action produces more beneficial effects than harmful ones, then it is right. The most famous exponents of utilitarianism were English: Jeremy Bentham (1748–1832) and John Stuart Mill (1806–1873).

6. Eric G. Forbes, *Greenwich Observatory*, 19.

7. Cook, King, and Bayly, *The Original Astronomical Observations*.

8. Eric G. Forbes, "The Greenwich Observatory."

9. When, on June 17, 1835, Airy accepted the office of Astronomer Royal, his letter of acceptance was addressed to the man who had offered the position: First Lord of the Admiralty Lord Auckland. This was an early indication of Airy's acknowledgment that the Admiralty officials were (as his son Wilfrid later put it) "his masters." W. Airy, *Autobiography*, 7, 108.

10. Chronometers, which entered into longitude determinations by the time of Cook's second Pacific voyage, eventually came into the general possession of the British Navy. In 1821, three years after the Admiralty took over responsibility for the Royal Observatory from the Board of Ordnance, the charge of the Royal Navy's chronometers was transferred to Greenwich. To accommodate them, the library was converted into a Chronometer Room. Soon, the Royal Observatory had become heavily involved in the routine checking of marine chronometers used by the Royal Navy. Airy, when he first took office, found this annoying: "In the inferior departments of the Admiralty [he noted], especially in the Hydrographic Office, . . . the Observatory was considered rather as a place for managing Government chronometers than as a place of science." During the tenure of his predecessor (John Pond) at the RGO, this chronometer business, Airy thought, had constituted a form of oppression that had led to a general decline in the observatory's efficiency. Still, in 1840—Airy's fifth year at Greenwich—an estimated one-third of the time of observatory staff was devoted to rating chronometers; and by 1874, the number of chronometers actually on hand in the Chronometer Room at the observatory had risen to nearly two hundred, all of which were being regularly rated at least once a week. In his 1874 "Report of the Astronomer Royal to the Board of Visitors of the Royal Observatory, Greenwich" (pp. 14–15), Airy gives the number as 194, of which 46 would be required, he thought, for the transit of Venus expeditions. Of those 194 timekeepers, 154 were the property of the government and were being rated after repair by their makers preparatory to their issue to ships of the British Navy, while the remaining 40 belonged to chronometer makers who had placed them at the observatory for the annual competitive trial. W. Airy, *Autobiography*, 124, 128; Howse, *Greenwich Observatory*, 9.

11. In his 1874 annual report, Airy wrote of the "considerations which, as I conceive, must guide the conduct of this Observatory. Though the terms of its establishment recognised its scientific character, yet the purpose which led to its foundation was utilitarian." Airy, "Report of the Astronomer Royal to the Board of Visitors of the Royal Observatory, Greenwich," (1874), 20. Similar thoughts were repeated elsewhere: "I am not a mere Superintendent of current observations," he wrote, "but a Trustee for the honour of Greenwich Observatory generally, and for its utility generally to the world." W. Airy, *Autobiography*, 153.

12. Airy, "Report of the Astronomer Royal to the Board of Visitors of the Royal Observatory, Greenwich," (1875), 24.

13. Airy's long involvement with longitude determinations began even before his tenure at Greenwich when, in 1826, he was appointed Lucasian Professor at Cambridge and automatically became a member of the Board of Longitude; and, by 1828, when he became director of the Cambridge Observatory, his attention to longitudinal matters, which would form one of the cornerstones of his modus operandi there, had already been signaled by his determination in that year of the observatory's longitude, a feat that he accomplished by sending a half dozen chronometers backward and forward between Cambridge and Greenwich. Meadows, *Greenwich Observatory*, 59; W. Airy, *Autobiography*, 72, 85; "Observatory," Report of the Observatory Syndicate, June 1835, *Cambridge University Reporter* 29.

14. As early as 1868, Airy had anticipated the desirability—perhaps the necessity—of a cooperative enterprise, in 1874, of scientific and military efforts. How could longitudes within the Hawaiian Islands be ascertained with the desired accuracy? It might be done astronomically, or it might be done chronometrically. But while the former would be time consuming (requiring, Airy estimated, perhaps three months to a year), the latter would be costly: "The expense of sending special steamers with chronometers, even from San Francisco to Woahoo . . . would be very great. Here, I think, we must make use of the motions of the Moon. If a hundred transits of the Moon be taken, . . . the probable error of the resulting longitude will be . . . below 1s of time: this accuracy would suffice. . . . No transmission of chronometers would be required." But whether longitudes were determined by a natural clock (the moon) or a mechanical one (the chronometer), Airy understood that astronomers acting alone would fail without military support. He therefore suggested that: "It would be a question for the Naval Authorities whether the determinations of Absolute Longitude should be preliminary to the observation of the Transits [sic] of *Venus*, or whether they should be made about the same time, requiring only one visit of the observer or observers to the station." It was the latter less taxing alternative that was eventually adopted in Hawai'i, but not before Airy reminded the secretary of the Admiralty that: "The labour which I contemplate as to be employed in determining the local longitudes very far exceeds that for the mere observation of the transit." Airy, "On the Preparatory Arrangements," 41; Airy, "A Letter."

15. George Forbes, "The Transit of Venus in 1874," PPSG 1872–1873, 373–394. Some time after, Forbes authored a series of articles on the same subject for the British journal *Nature*. George Forbes, "The Coming Transit of Venus," Parts 1–7, *Nature*, April 9 to June 4, 1874.

16. George Forbes, "The Transit of Venus in 1874," PPSG 1872–1873, 376. See also George Forbes, "The Coming Transit of Venus," *Nature*, April 23, 1874, 488.

17. When, in 1872, Forbes wrote to Airy on the upcoming transit expressing his preference for a post in the Sandwich Islands, he let it be known that he was likewise desirous of becoming "thoroughly acquainted with the employment of instruments and the calculations made during the compiling of the Nautical Almanack." Forbes to Airy, January 17, 1872, RGO 6/273, leaves 491–492.

18. The lunar distance method of obtaining longitude had been successfully practiced during the voyages of Cook, voyages about which Forbes was not unfamiliar as he had corresponded on the matter with the Astronomer Royal. Evidence that Forbes was at least somewhat familiar with the voyages of Captain Cook can be found in his letters to Airy dated September 4 and 10, 1873, in which he speaks of Captain Cook's mapping of the Crozet Islands during his third voyage (1776–1780), and in which he (Forbes) cites directly, in his letter of September 10, from a four-volume abridged account of that voyage published in 1785. RGO 6/273, leaves 516–517, 519–522. Airy's own familiarity with the practice of observing lunar distances with a sextant can be dated as early as his student days at Cambridge. W. Airy, *Autobiography*, 37.

19. Hansen, "On the Construction of New Lunar Tables." Hansen's communiqué is dated "Gotha, 1854, Nov. 3." See also: George Forbes, "The Transit of Venus in 1874," PPSG 1872–1873, 376.

20. Berry, *History of Astronomy*, 285, 366, 368; Clerke, *History of Astronomy*, 230; Meadows, *Greenwich Observatory*, 44.

21. "If . . . the tables in the *Nautical Almanac* predicting the place of the moon are absolutely correct, an observer by watching the instant at which she seems to come to the position of any star, and knowing from the tables the Greenwich time at which she reaches that position, receives an intimation of the absolute time from this gigantic celestial clock. . . . [but] As a matter of fact the tables of the moon are by no means perfect." George Forbes, "The Coming Transit of Venus," *Nature*, May 21, 1874, 51.

22. George Forbes, "The Coming Transit of Venus," *Nature*, May 21, 1874, 51.

7. Into the Setting Sun

1. Astronomer Royal to the hydrographer of the Admiralty, October 10, 1868, RGO 6/267, file 1.

2. Hydrographer of the Admiralty to the Astronomer Royal, October 13, 1868, RGO 6/267, file 1.

3. Airy to Captain George H. Richards, R.N., November 6, 1868, RGO 6/268, file 1, leaves 10–11. Although Airy later modified his views with respect to the methods of Halley and Delisle, he reaffirmed his advocacy of the latter in 1873, saying:

> At Rodriguez, Christchurch, and Kerguelen's Island, the entire Transit
> will be visible; and therefore the method of utilizing the observations by
> comparing the duration of Transit at a southern station with the dura-

tion as observed in the French, German, and Russian stations on or near the Japanese and Chinese seas [Halley's Method] [*sic*] can be used for these three British Stations; and Kerguelen's Island in particular is very favorably situated for this Method. But it is not probable that this Method will be used, or at least that any importance will be attached to it. It is an essential part of the Astronomer Royal's plan, in which he is expressly followed by the French and Russians, and (it is believed) by the Germans also, that the longitude of every station should be accurately determined; and, when this is done, the method of comparison of the Absolute Greenwich Times at the different stations [DeLisle's Method] [*sic*] is greatly superior to the method of comparison of Durations at different stations [Halley's Method] [*sic*]. (RGO 6/269, file 1, leaves 6–7, no addressee, but signed by Airy, March 23, 1873)

4. Memorandum, addressed to the lords commissioners of the Admiralty by the Astronomer Royal, May 25, 1869, RGO 6/267, file 1.

5. Airy, "On the Preparatory Arrangements," 35; George Forbes, "The Coming Transit of Venus," *Nature*, May 14, 1874, 30. Earlier than this, Forbes had been even more specific, saying: "Where practicable, e.g., in the Sandwich Islands, where there are mountains, and where the weather can, I believe, be depended upon, the observatories should be carried to as high a point as possible." George Forbes, "The Transit of Venus in 1874," PPSG 1872–1873, 393.

6. Proctor pointed out that even if the Sandwich Islands experienced good weather on transit day, bad weather at the other end of the baseline would cause the Delisle method, as applied to observations of ingress, to fail totally. Proctor, *Transits of Venus*, 193–194.

7. The "accelerated" and "retarded" times of Venus' observed contacts with the sun were in fact complicated by the Earth's—and hence the observers'—motion.

8. Some time before his transit of Venus plans were finalized, Airy would come to realize that Kerguelen and Rodriguez had more than a strictly astronomical interest, and before the year 1874 dawned, the geology and the natural history of these islands would attract the eager attention of other British scientists. At a meeting of the Council of the Royal Society held on December 1, 1873, the following memorial would be read—as in the chair, as president, sat George Airy:

> The Council of the Royal Society beg leave to submit the following statement to Her Majesty's Government:
> Her Majesty's Government have determined to send out next spring five Astronomical Expeditions for the observation of the approaching Transit of Venus, in as many parts of the globe. Of these expeditions two are destined to remain some months at two of the least explored and most inaccessible oceanic islands of the Southern hemisphere, namely Rodriguez and Kerguelen's Land.
> Under these circumstances the Council of the Society beg leave most respectfully to represent to Her Majesty's Government the desirability of attaching to these two expeditions some persons competent to investigate the Geology and Natural History of these islands during the stay of the expeditions upon them, and to add the following brief statement in furtherance of this request.

It is an unexplained fact in the physical history of our globe, that all known oceanic archipelagos distant from the great continents, with the sole exceptions of the Seychelles and of a solitary islet of the Mascarene group (which islet is Rodriguez), are of volcanic origin. According to the meagre accounts hitherto published, Rodriguez consists of granite overlaid with limestone and other recent rocks, in the caves of which have been found the remains of recently extinct birds of a very singular structure. These facts, taken together with what is known of the Natural History of the volcanic islets of Mauritius and Bourbon to the west of Rodriguez and of the granitic archipelago of the Seychelles to the north of it, render an investigation of its natural products a matter of exceptional scientific interest, which, if properly carried out, cannot fail to be productive of most important results.

As regards Kerguelen's Land, this large island (100 by 50 miles) was last visited in 1840 by the Antarctic Expedition under Sir James Ross, in mid winter only, when it was found to contain a scanty Flora of flowering plants, some of which belong to entirely new types, and an extraordinary profusion of marine animals and plants of the greatest interest, many of them being representatives of north-temperate and Arctic forms of life.

H.M.S. "Challenger" will no doubt visit Kerguelen's Land, and collect largely; but it is evident that many years would be required to obtain even a fair representation of its marine products; and though we are not prepared to say that the scientific objects to be obtained by a naturalist's visit to Kerguelen's Land are of equal importance to those which Rodriguez will yield, we cannot but regard it as in every respect most desirable that the rare opportunity of sending a collector to Kerguelen's Land should not be lost.

Of Alexandre-Gui Pingre's 1761 transit of Venus work at Rodriguez (Isle Rodrigue), Woolf writes:

> In the days that followed [the transit], Pingre and Thuillier determined the latitude and longitude of their station, and together with the officers of the *Mignonne,* set about to explore Rodrigue and its adjoining islands. They triangulated the high points of the island and those of its neighbors, collected specimens of unusual flora and fauna, and recorded descriptions of a fundamental and primitive biological balance now, alas, forever gone. Here was another demonstration of the eighteenth-century ideal of man in the activities of Alexandre-Gui Pingre. An astronomical expedition was broadened and deepened into a voyage of discovery that somehow related the crabs and turtles of an island, its cartographic image, and the phosphorescence of the sea to the spinning planets and the size of the universe. (Woolf, *The Transits of Venus,* 111–112)

9. "Owhyhee and the neighbouring islands are excellent. The factor of parallax is about 0.92 [the maximum being 1.00], and the Sun is at nearly two hours' elevation." Airy, "On the Preparatory Arrangements," 35. The anticipation was that the same phenomenon, the instant of internal contact at ingress, would be seen earlier in Honolulu than at Kerguelen. The estimated time difference would be about twen-

ty-one minutes. George Forbes, "The Coming Transit of Venus," *Nature,* May 7, 1874, 13.

10. Daws, *Shoal of Time,* 159.

11. HAA for 1875, 6. The 1872 census placed the total population of the Hawaiian Islands at 56,897, of which 51,531 were native Hawaiians (including "half-castes"), 1,938 were Chinese, 889 were Americans, and 619 were Britons. The population figure given here for native Hawaiians is the same as the one used by Charles Darwin in his *Descent of Man.*

12. Airy, "On the Preparatory Arrangements," 35, 36.

13. RGO 6/267, file 3, leaf 130.

14. Bishop's letter, dated October 27, 1873 (Honolulu), read:

> Sir, Your despatch of this date, informing me that it is the intention of Her Majesty's Government to send out a party of Officers to observe the Transit of Venus at Honolulu; that they will arrive about the first of September 1874; and that Earl Granville directs you to request that His Majesty's Government will give the party every facility on its arrival at Honolulu, is received; and in reply, I am happy to assure you, and through you Her Majesty's Government, that His Majesty's Government are pleased to know that these Islands are one point chosen for the observation referred to, and will have great pleasure in affording to the party mentioned every facility within their control. (FO 331/40, folio 206–207, PRO)

A biographer of Charles Reed Bishop has written that "Bishop, in 1873, as Foreign Minister of Hawaii under King Lunalilo, made arrangements for the visit of the . . . astronomers . . . for the scheduled observation of the Transit of Venus. . . . His contact with the British scientists provided an item of experience which he would be reminded of some years later in his founding of the Bishop Museum and in his encouraging the establishment of an astronomical observatory." Kent, *Charles Reed Bishop,* 59–60.

15. "Transit of Venus," *HG,* June 24, 1874.

16. "The Planet Venus," *PCA,* September 19, 1874.

17. That the Earth's dominant life forms "have a simultaneous passion for territoriality and Euclidean geometry" has been illustrated by Sagan, *Pale Blue Dot,* chap. 5.

18. Airy's desire that the Americans station observers (of the accelerated ingress) in the Pacific (particularly at the Marquesas Islands or Otaheite [Tahiti]) can be found expressed in his letters of April 2 and May 6, 1872, to Admiral Sands, RGO 6/271, file 15, leaves 709 and 713–715.

19. Proctor, *Transits of Venus,* 221.

20. Newcomb, *Observations of the Transit of Venus* (1880), 12–14.

21. Airy to Admiral G. H. Richards, May 22, 1873, RGO 6/268, file 2, leaf 128.

22. Richards to Airy, May 22, 1873, RGO 6/268, file 2, leaves 130–131.

23. In June of 1859, the killing of a pig on San Juan Island, off the northwestern coast of the U.S. mainland, brought Great Britain and the United States to the brink of war

over the issue of territorial rights in the Pacific Northwest. The long-standing dispute, which was rooted in the ambiguous wording of an 1846 treaty between the two nations, had been proceeding toward a more amicable solution when the British initiated efforts to survey the waters west of the American mainland at the 49th parallel and when, in 1856, George H. Richards, then a captain in the Royal Navy, was selected as "chief surveyor and astronomer" to further that purpose. Richards' survey report, a highly significant document, was completed by November 1858 and reached the government in January 1859. But the Pig War would not be forestalled, and five months later an American squatter, Lyman Cutler, took aim at a "British" pig ravaging his San Juan potato patch and shot the animal dead. Although both sides maneuvered and postured until a military confrontation seemed imminent, the dispute was settled with no further bloodshed when, in 1872, peaceful arbitration awarded the San Juan Islands to the United States. Murray, *The Pig War,* esp. pp. 30–31 and 48; McCabe, *The San Juan Water Boundary Question,* esp. pp. 20–21 and 30–31. The role of native Hawaiian immigrants ("Kanakas") in the Pig War is told by Michael Vouri, *The Pig War,* pp. 29, 31, 36, 46, 103, and 216-217. As of this writing (2003), the island of San Juan still has both a Kanaka Bay and a Kanaka Bay Road.

24. Airy to Richards, May 23, 1873, RGO 6/268, file 3, leaf 134. Kerguelen Island was a much more "inhospitable rock" than Hawai'i. Described by Beaglehole as "the largest of the scattered spots of land in the Southern Indian Ocean, [an island that] sprawls untidily over the sea . . . a mass of rocky hills, bog and running water, split on its northern and eastern sides into dozens of sounds and inlets and minor bays, fringed with rocks and giant seaweed swaying deceptively round them, the whole frequently enough lost in fog; with limited vegetation, treeless, its animal life confined to sea-birds, penguins, and seals," Kerguelen had been visited in December 1776 by Captain Cook and had been called by him, from its sterility, the Island of Desolation. Airy seems to have taken this into account when suggesting the appointment of Perry and Sidgreaves to the Kerguelen station, saying, "The Jesuits are exactly the men to be sent to the outlandish parts." Airy to Richards, July 25, 1873, RGO 6/268, file 3, leaf 157; Beaglehole, *Captain Cook,* 513–516; Ashbrook, "Father Perry's Expedition."

8. The Prime Mover

1. An extended account of Airy's life is given in the *Autobiography* edited by his son Wilfrid. A more compressed biography can be found in the DNB.

2. W. Airy, *Autobiography,* 11, 16, 17, 64, 76, 367. Airy's early penchant for poetry and the facility with which he committed it to memory was to serve him well in later life. Over a lifetime that spanned more than nine decades, he became well acquainted with the works of major English poets (Milton, Pope, Gray, Swift, Byron), and he personally visited Southey and Wordsworth. He committed large quantities of poetry to memory and frequently referred to it as a most valuable acquisition and an ever-present relief and comfort to his mind. Within a fortnight of his death at age 91, he could still be found "reciting the English poetry with which his memory was stored."

3. Leedham-Green (p. 246) reports that a "wrangler" was "one placed in the first class in the Mathematical Tripos, the Senior Wrangler being the man with the highest marks." The honor of being designated a wrangler seems to have been exclusive to Cambridge.

4. The honor of being first Smith's prizeman was a distinction that became part of the Cambridge academic scene when Robert Smith (1689–1768), master of Trinity College and second Plumian Professor, bequeathed upon his death two annual prizes of £25 to two commencing B.A.'s, the best in mathematics and natural philosophy of their year, since known to the world as "Smith's Prizemen." Airy called Smith's Prize "the highest Mathematical honour in the University." Gunther, *Early Science in Cambridge,* 169; W. Airy, *Autobiography,* 72.

5. About Airy's habits, it is said that: "'The ruling feature of his character was order. From the time he went up to Cambridge to the end of his life his system of order was strictly maintained.' He enforced it upon himself no less rigidly than upon his subordinates, and kept up at the Royal Observatory a cast-iron discipline, which powerfully contributed to the efficiency of his administration. He never destroyed a document, but devised an ingenious plan of easy reference to the huge bulk of his papers." DNB (see note 1).

6. Meadows, *Greenwich Observatory,* 6–7.

7. In fact, the British preparations for the 1874 transit were, by the early 1870s, boasted to be in a more advanced state than those of any other country, a condition that was ascribed to the fact that the preparations were directed not by a committee but rather by a single mind—that of Airy. Carpenter, "British Preparations."

8. Richard Anthony Proctor was born in Chelsea on March 23, 1837, and graduated from St. John's College, Cambridge, in 1860 to become an astronomer of distinction. He was elected a fellow of the Royal Astronomical Society in 1866, and in 1872 he became RAS secretary and editor of the *Monthly Notices.* When, in 1866, the failure of a New Zealand bank in which he was a large shareholder left him entirely dependent on his own earnings, he revitalized himself into an author and lecturer of considerable reputation. He went on lecturing tours to America and the Australian colonies; and, returning from the latter via the United States, he there married, in 1881, the widow of Robert J. Crawley and settled at St. Joseph, Missouri, her home. In 1887 he transferred his household and observatory to Orange Lake, Florida. He died on September 12, 1888, of yellow fever, in a New York hospital while on his way to England. Biographical information on Proctor is found in several places: *Alumni Cantabrigienses; DNB; The Observatory* 141 (October 1888), 366–368; *MNRAS* 49:4, (February 8, 1889), 164–168; *Knowledge* 11:36 (October 1888), 265–266; *New Science Review* (April 1895), 393–397; *The Eagle* 15 (1889), 242–245; and *The Times,* September 14, 1888.

9. Proctor was relentless in his determination that the official British efforts—which, he thought, were carelessly excluding scientifically sound alternatives—required reexamination; and several papers, mostly critical essays by Proctor covering the years 1869 to 1873, were subsequently collected under one cover bearing the title *Studies of Venus Transits.* Among the telling statements made therein by Proctor are these:

> On account of the important bearing of the transits of Venus upon the problem of the Sun's distance, men of science are looking anxiously

forward to the two transits which occur in the present century. . . . Indeed both transits were subjected to examination by the Astronomer Royal so far back as 1857; and since then he has continued to put forward from time to time the considerations which have suggested themselves to him as his examination of the subject proceeded. Early in the inquiry he expressed the opinion that the method founded on the observed differences of the transit's duration, as seen from opposite points of the Earth's surface—which method had been the sole one employed in the treatment of the transit of 1769—is wholly inapplicable to the transit of 1874; and he suggested another method of utilising that transit,—a method less perfect in itself, more difficult (astronomically) to carry out, and involving processes of preparation essentially different from those which would be required under the other method. . . . Having had occasion to examine the reasoning of the Astronomer Royal, and to test the conclusions he had arrived at, I have been led to form a totally different opinion of the value of the transit of 1874, so far as the simpler method of observation is concerned. (p. 233)

• • • • •

As regards the comparison between Delisle's and Halley's method . . . I believe I shall be able to show . . . that there is at least a possibility that Halley's method may be so applied to the transit of 1874 as to give absolutely the best means of determining the Sun's distance available before the transit of 2004. (pp. 248–249)

Regarding the Proctor-Airy controversies, Clerke has written: "The conditions of the transit of December 8, 1874, were sketched out by Sir George Airy, then Astronomer-Royal, in 1857, and formed the subject of eager discussion in this and other countries down to the very eve of the occurrence. In these Mr. Proctor took a leading part; and it was due to his urgent representations that provision was made for the employment of the method identified with the name of Halley, which had been too hastily assumed inapplicable to the first of each transit-pair." Clerke, *History of Astronomy*, 233. A summary of the exchange between Airy and Proctor can be found in Dreyer and Turner, 178–185.

10. Airy, "On the Means."

11. Proctor, *Transits of Venus,* 160–161.

12. Proctor, *Transits of Venus,* 161. The 1868 paper by Airy to which Proctor is referring begins as follows:

On two occasions (*Monthly Notices*, 1857, May 8, and 1864, June 10) I have called the attention of the Society to the Transits of *Venus* across the Sun's disk, which will occur in the years 1874 and 1882; and have pointed out that, for determination of the difference between the Sun's parallax and the parallax of *Venus*, the method by observation of the interval in time between Ingress and Egress at each of two stations at least, on nearly opposite parts of the Earth (on which method, exclusively, reliance was placed in the treatment of the observations of the Transit of *Venus* in 1769), fails totally for the Transit of 1874, and is embarrassed in 1882 with the difficulty of finding a proper station on the almost unknown Southern Continent. (Airy, "On the Preparatory Arrangements," 33)

13. Proctor, *Transits of Venus,* 182.

14. Proctor, *Transits of Venus,* 185.

15. "At the Visitation of the Greenwich Observatory on June 7, 1873, it was proposed by Professor Adams, and carried unanimously, that [the] Government should be applied to for the means of organising parties of observers in the Southern Ocean, with the view of finding additional localities in the sub-Antarctic regions for applying Halley's method to the observation of the transit of 1874." Proctor, *Studies of Venus Transits,* 296. Elsewhere Proctor reports that on June 7, 1873, Adams proposed that Professor Cayley (president of the Royal Astronomical Society and chairman of the Board of Visitors at Greenwich) should apply to the government "for the means of organising parties of observers in the Southern Seas, with the view of finding additional localities in the sub-Antarctic regions for observing durations"—that is, for applying Halley's method; and that Airy—now, by Proctor's account, somewhat of a chameleon-like character—supported Adams' proposal. Proctor, *Transits of Venus,* 196–197. Adams had, in fact, already given Airy this opinion of the matter: "I am strongly of [the] opinion that it is important to observe the duration of the Transit at as many favourably situated stations as possible. The true conclusion to be drawn from the discussions that have been going on about the relative values of the so-called methods of Halley & Delisle is that it is important to employ both methods. No doubt either method is capable of giving a good result, but by the employment of both, the weight of the resulting determination of the parallax will be materially increased" (emphasis in original). J. C. Adams to Airy, May 5, 1873, RGO 6/271, file 4, leaves 122–126.

16. "Mr. Proctor is a vain man who can carry but one idea at a time, and is a wonderful scribbler." Airy to Richards, July 30, 1873, RGO 6/268, file 3, leaf 163. Johns has characterized the professional "scribbler" as a mercenary who prostituted himself by "selling his honor to booksellers by the line." Johns, *The Nature of the Book,* 183.

17. Proctor, *Transits of Venus,* 193–194.

18. When December 1874 came, of the several nations that had dispatched transit observers, the English were the only ones who made direct provision for the use of Delisle's method; and (Proctor wrote) the only Delilean stations "properly so termed" were those occupied by the British observing team in the Sandwich Islands. Proctor, *Transits of Venus,* 206.

9. Cambridge Connections

1. Regarding the "unknown hands at Cambridge University" that put together a set of instructions for observing the transit of Venus of 1761, see Woolf, *The Transits of Venus,* 78–79.

2. William Gooch, a graduate of Caius College, Cambridge, was the astronomer

appointed by the Board of Longitude aboard the supply ship *Daedalus* attached to a four-year (1791–1795) surveying expedition under the command of George Vancouver. On May 13, 1792, Gooch was—along with the commander of the *Daedalus*, Lt. Richard Hergest—murdered by a group of Hawaiian natives at Waimea Bay, on the island of O'ahu, while getting water for the ship. He was twenty-two. The circumstances surrounding Gooch's death have been investigated by Dening, *The Death of William Gooch*.

3. Edward Wright (1561–1615), a graduate of Caius College, Cambridge, was a mathematician and cartographer whose most important work was his *Certaine Errors in Navigation*. John Dee (1527–1608), a graduate of St. John's College, Cambridge, was a mathematician who wrote treatises on navigation and navigational instruments and for more than twenty-five years served as an adviser to various English voyages of discovery. Thomas Digges (1546?–1595), a mathematician and student of John Dee, was the leader of the English Copernicans. William Gilbert (1540–1603), a graduate of St. John's College, Cambridge, was physician to Elizabeth I and James I and author of *De Magnete* (1600), a book postulating that the Earth is a giant lodestone with magnetic properties. John Bainbridge (1582–1643), of Emmanuel College, Cambridge (B.A., 1603; M.A., 1607; M.D., 1614), became, in 1619, the first Savilian Professor of Astronomy at Oxford.

4. Gresham College was named for Sir Thomas Gresham, financial advisor to Queen Elizabeth and founder of the Royal Exchange, who died in 1579. In his will, Gresham bequeathed all the revenues from the land and buildings comprising the Royal Exchange, along with his mansion in Bishopsgate Street, jointly to the City of London and the Company of Mercers. In return, they were charged with supporting, from the revenues of the Royal Exchange, seven professors who were to be lodged in his Bishopsgate mansion. These seven scholars—one each in Law, Rhetoric, Divinity, Music, Physic, Geometry, and Astronomy—were to give weekly public lectures in their respective subjects. After the death in 1596 of the widow Lady Gresham, the seven professors were at last installed and their lectures commenced. This took place in 1598 as Gresham's mansion became Gresham College. Several decades later—in 1657, and only five years before the formal incorporation in 1662 of the Royal Society, of which Gresham College was a precursor—Christopher Wren (1632–1723) was appointed professor of astronomy at Gresham College. Although Wren would go on to serve from 1661 until 1673 as Savilian Professor of Astronomy at Oxford, he is best remembered not as an astronomer but as an architect: the designer of, inter alia, St. Paul's Cathedral in London, several buildings at Oxford and Cambridge, and the Royal Observatory at Greenwich. Andrade, *A Brief History of the Royal Society*, 3–4; Francis R. Johnson, "Gresham College."

5. It is widely accepted that it was William Caxton who, in or about the year 1471, established the first printing press in England. In 1481 he published his first scientific book, *The Mirror of the World*, his own translation of a thirteenth-century French poem describing the physical universe. Johns, *The Nature of the Book*, 329; Ronan, *Their Majesties' Astronomers*, 26. Writing of the early history of Cambridge University, Leedham-Green has noted that:

> Newly written texts in the medieval period were both scarce and costly, and there can be no doubt that in early years texts were handed down, often in the form of extracts or abstracts, from one generation to

another, as indeed they continued to be even after the introduction of printing in the late fifteenth century had increased the availability of relatively cheap books. Nor would the average medieval undergraduate, or indeed the average BA, have owned copies of the actual texts he studied, but rather slim volumes of *tabulae* and of *quaestiones*: synopses of, and standard discussions of problems arising from, the text. (Leedham-Green, *History of the University of Cambridge,* 16)

A modern scholar can still find physical evidence at Cambridge of the high value once imparted to the printed word: In the old library at Trinity Hall, some texts are still chained—or show evidence of former chaining—to the shelves.

6. Russell, "English Astronomy Before 1675." Francis Johnson, in his essay on Gresham College noted above, writes (p. 429): "From the early years of the seventeenth century there is evidence of a close association, in scientific investigations, of the Gresham College professors and the sea captains, the shipbuilders, and the administrative officials of the English Navy." This focus on utilitarian astronomy—and the more general notion that science should be useful—is firmly within the British tradition championed by Francis Bacon and the Royal Society and embodied in the history of the Royal Observatory at Greenwich. The contrary notion—that astronomy is or ought to be pursued first and foremost to banish a man's ignorance and not for some other narrowly conceived utilitarian end—is represented by Aristotle (*Metaphysics,* bk. 1, chap. 2).

7. Murdin, *Under Newton's Shadow,* 39; Gunther, *Early Science in Oxford,* vol. 2, 68; Gunther, *Early Science in Cambridge,* 161.

8. Whatton tells us that when Horrocks attended Cambridge, no branch of mathematical or physical science was taught there. Whatton, *Memoir of Jeremiah Horrox,* 9. More than two centuries later, George Airy wrote: "Most of my contemporaries [at Cambridge], being intended for the church, attended also divinity lectures: but I never did." W. Airy, *Autobiography,* 25. For a discussion of European universities as "ecclesiastical corporations" instituted for the education of churchmen and having a curriculum that was subservient to theology, see Adam Smith, "Of the Expense of the Institutions for the Education of Youth," in *The Wealth of Nations,* bk. 5, chap. 1, pt. 3, art. 2. The licensing and printing of books—and of more divinity books than of any other single subject (including law and medicine)—seems to have been, in seventeenth-century England at least, consistent with such a theologically laden curriculum. See Johns, *The Nature of the Book,* 239. Colleges and universities in post-revolutionary America may be said to have followed the English model by educating "many of their Youth in . . . those Sciences that qualify men for the Professions of Divinity, Law, or Physick [Medicine]." Franklin, *Autobiography,* 239. It is to be remembered that John Harvard, the founder of Harvard University, was a graduate of Emmanuel College, Cambridge.

9. Murdin, *Under Newton's Shadow,* chap. 3.

10. The seven liberal arts consisted of the trivium (grammar, rhetoric, and logic) and the quadrivium (arithmetic, geometry, astronomy, and music). Together with the three philosophies—natural philosophy, moral philosophy, and metaphysics—they once formed the core of a liberal arts curriculum, a scheme that can be traced back to antiquity and was supposed to culminate ideally in theology. Leedham-Green, *History of the University of Cambridge,* 2, 17–18.

11. Proctor, *Transits of Venus,* 19.

12. To some Englishmen for whom astronomy was not a distinct profession—to medieval churchmen and physicians, for example—it was nevertheless more than a mere ornament. For to calculate the variable feast days of the Church year—the principal aim of astronomy in Christendom since late antiquity—gave astronomy (in the first case) an ecclesiastical use. And (in the second case) because the study and practice of medicine in late medieval England was grounded upon both astronomical and astrological teachings, university-trained physicians could apply to the care of the human body suppositions of celestial influences. Leader, *A History of the University of Cambridge,* vol. 1, 140, 146–154, 204–208.

13. Murdin, *Under Newton's Shadow,* 10.

14. When Robert Main of Queens' College came aboard as Airy's chosen assistant, a Cambridge hegemony was put into place at Greenwich that was to continue into the twentieth century. Edward Stone (1831–1897), who was like Main a graduate (in 1859) of Queens', was appointed chief assistant in 1860. When in 1870 Stone became the Royal Astronomer at the Cape of Good Hope, William Christie became Airy's chief assistant at Greenwich—and not long thereafter, his successor as Astronomer Royal (1881–1910), the post having been declined by the Cambridge-educated John Adams (St. John's, 1843). Christie was, like Airy, a graduate of Trinity.

15. Krisciunas, *Astronomical Centers of the World,* 194; Fernie, *The Whisper and the Vision,* 63.

16. Dreyer and Turner, *History of the Royal Astronomical Society 1820–1920.*

17. This statement by Airy is dated February 26, 1828. "Observatory," *Cambridge University Reporter* 29. See also Leedham-Green, *History of the University of Cambridge,* 114.

18. The Natural Sciences Tripos was assimilated into the Cambridge curriculum in 1851. Brooke, *A History of the University of Cambridge,* vol. 4: 1870–1990, 153.

19. Airy once wrote:

> I consider it as most important that the First Assistant [at Greenwich] should be a man of respectable rank in society. This alone can give a hope of security against the danger of being corrupted with money . . . and of losing authority over the subordinate assistants. . . . It was partly for this reason and partly for the general object of raising the tone of science in the Royal Observatory by introducing a person of high mathematical attainments that I have strongly recommended a Cambridge man. With respect to habits of patient industry, they may sometimes be found among Cambridge men in a very eminent degree. (Meadows, *Greenwich Observatory,* 2)

20. W. Airy, *Autobiography,* 9–10. Airy claimed that his predecessor at Greenwich, John Pond, "understood nothing of physical astronomy; but neither did anybody else, in England." W. Airy, *Autobiography,* 128.

21. W. Airy, *Autobiography,* 26.

22. Krisciunas, *Astronomical Centers of the World,* 195.

23. George Forbes, *David Gill,* 233.

24. Maskelyne—who, like Airy, was an alumnus of Trinity College and thus a part of the Cambridge network—had attempted a similar strategy for the 1769 transit, asking both Shepherd and Ludlam at Cambridge (as well as Hornsby at Oxford) to recommend likely candidates for voyages to foreign parts. Woolf, *The Transits of Venus,* 165.

25. A brief biography of Leonard Darwin can be found in *Nature* 151, April 17, 1943, 442. A more extended though still brief account of his life, *Leonard Darwin 1850–1943,* was written by his niece Margaret Keynes.

26. The five sons were: William (1839–1914), George (1845–1912), Francis (1848–1925), Leonard (1850–1943), and Horace (1851–1928). William was a classmate at Cambridge of the missionary to Hawai'i and transit of Venus observer Robert Dunn. George became Plumian Professor and director of the Cambridge Observatory. Francis edited his father's autobiography. Horace was cofounder of the Cambridge Scientific Instruments Company. George, Francis, and Horace all became fellows of the Royal Society. An affectionate portrait of each of the five sons of Charles Darwin can be found in Gwen Raverat's *Period Piece,* chap. 10. Raverat was George Darwin's daughter and the sister of Margaret Keynes (see the preceding note).

27. While away on the expeditions of 1874, 1882, and 1886, Leonard Darwin frequently wrote to his mother. These letters are preserved at the Cambridge University Library in DAR 239 (LD/1/2; LD/1/6; and LD/1/7). Although Leonard Darwin's name is not mentioned, some discussion of Lockyer's work as "head" of the British expedition to Grenada can be found in Lockyer and Lockyer, *Life and Work of Sir Norman Lockyer,* 126–128. Leonard Darwin's own account of the expedition to Grenada and of Lockyer's part in it is found in LD/1/7.

28. The degree of doctor of science, *honoris causa,* was conferred upon Leonard Darwin in May of 1912. *Cambridge University Reporter,* May 28, 1912, 1,107.

29. Leonard Darwin, *The Need for Eugenic Reform.* Leonard's motivation to write this book was, by his own admission, derived from the work of his father, who wrote: "Man scans with scrupulous care the character and pedigree of his horses, cattle, and dogs before he matches them; but when he comes to his own marriage he rarely, or never, takes any such care. He is impelled by nearly the same motives as the lower animals. . . . Yet he might by selection do something not only for the bodily constitution and frame of his offspring, but for their intellectual and moral qualities. . . . Everyone does good service, who aids toward this end." Charles Darwin, *The Descent of Man,* chap. 21. The dedication page of *The Need for Eugenic Reform* reads: "Dedicated to the memory of MY FATHER for if I had not believed that he would have wished me to give such help as I could towards making his life's work of service to mankind, I should never have been led to write this book."

30. The riddle of the universe for Leonard Darwin seems to have been both the *origin* of life and its *aim.* For him, "evolution" meant something cosmic, not merely organic: It meant not only "the gradual building up, in accordance with the laws of nature, of the world as we now find it from some unknown beginning" but also taught that "the universe is normally not stable but in a state of flux." The philosophy of "emergent evolution"—which holds that when sentience, intellect, conscience, and possibly other human attributes first made their appearance, "some-

thing new came into this universe of ours . . . which had not been there before"—underscored Leonard's riddle but did not solve it. For although man's "mind" and its associated faculties might be explained prima facie on evolutionary principles, the inductively established laws of science could never by themselves guide a man's conduct, give him aims and ideals, solve his ethical problems—tell him, in short, how he *ought* to behave. "Paradoxical as it may sound," Leonard wrote, "we get no clue to [the] underlying foundations of our moral sense from a knowledge of the natural origin of the brain." Here, he concluded, we are "knocking our heads against the stone wall" of an "impenetrable mystery." His father Charles wrestled with similar problems (Chauvin, "Darwin's Delay: Minds and Materialism"). Leonard Darwin's discussion of his riddle can be found in a separate essay, "Eugenics and the Riddle of the Universe" (DAR 239, LD/37, undated typescript, 17 pp., at the Cambridge University Library), as well as in his book chapter of the same title. Citations given here are from his *Need for Eugenic Reform,* pp. 2, 8, 507, 515.

31. Because the voyage of the *Beagle* (1831–1836) was primarily a surveying expedition, Charles Darwin was very likely instructed in the practice of the relevant astronomy by the ship's captain, Robert FitzRoy, with whom he shared accommodations. Moreover, when the *Beagle* was in the Southern Hemisphere, Darwin sought out astronomer John Herschel, whom he esteemed highly, and dined with him at the Cape of Good Hope. Later, his reference in the opening paragraph of his introduction to the *Origin* to "one of our greatest philosophers" was a reference to this same astronomer, and when the book was published in 1859 he had a copy sent to Herschel, saying: "I have taken the liberty of directing Murray [the publisher] to send you a copy of my book on the Origin of species, with the hope that you may still retain some interest on this question. . . . I cannot resist the temptation of showing in this feeble manner my respect, & the deep obligation, which I owe to your Introduction to Natural Philosophy. Scarcely anything in my life made so deep an impression on me." Herschel's *Introduction to Natural Philosophy* appeared in 1831. Darwin read the book soon after it was published and in his autobiography refers to the great influence it had on him. Darwin and Herschel are entombed next to each other at Westminster Abbey. Burkhardt, *The Correspondence of Charles Darwin,* vol. 7, 370–371; Francis Darwin, *The Autobiography of Charles Darwin and Selected Letters,* 24, 36; Chauvin, "Darwin's Delay: Minds and Materialism."

32. If the surviving correspondence between Charles Darwin and his five sons is indicative of Charles' interest in each son's chosen profession, it is telling that George, the astronomer, seems to have been his father's most prolific correspondent. Burkhardt, et al., (see note 35) have indexed the number of pieces of correspondence between Charles Darwin and his sons as follows: Francis, 175; George, 232; Horace, 17; Leonard, 27; William Erasmus, 231.

33. Letter to Airy from Leonard Darwin, Brompton Barracks, Chatham, August 21, 1872, RGO 6/273, leaf 347.

34. Darwin's letter to Hubert Airy (August 24, 1872, RGO 6/273, leaves 348–349) reads:

> My dear sir,
>
> I have thought that you would excuse my begging a favour of you; that is if you think it a proper one to grant, of which I am not at all sure.

One of my sons Leonard Darwin of the Royal Engineers has sent in an application to Sir G. Airy to be one of the observers in the Transit of Venus expedition. I find that he has not mentioned any of his qualifications; and perhaps you could find an opportunity of mentioning the few following particulars to your father.

In the preliminary examination for Woolwich he entered as 2nd man, and he likewise passed out as Second. These examinations are well known to be very severe; and Success in them implies some knowledge & aptitude for Mathematics. On this head I believe that Prof. Sylvester would speak in his favour. At Woolwich & since he has been at Chatham he has worked hard at Surveying, drawing fortifications &.c; and he is very neat handed in making maps plans &.c. I mention this as I suppose a steady hand and a good eye are important requisites for observation. I can speak from my own knowledge that he is energetic, industrious and accurate in details; & that he has a very clear intellect; so that I should think he would make a good observer; but I must add that he has had no experience in Astronomical observations. I hope that you will excuse me for thus troubling you, & do what you can to aid me.

35. Burkhardt et al., *A Calendar of the Correspondence of Charles Darwin, 1821–1882*, 325. See also Prodger, "Photography and *The Expression of the Emotions*." Prodger's remark—that *The Expression of the Emotions* was one of the first scientific books ever published with photographic illustrations and that the photographs reproduced therein constitute "one of the first public attempts to use photography to freeze motion for analysis and study"—is not without interest when considered in the context of the 1874 transit of Venus photographic efforts.

36. Leonard Darwin's population figures for Hawai'i are found among the voluminous Darwiniana at the Cambridge University Library, in DAR 90. The statement that he sent them to his father from the Naval College at Greenwich in "1873[?]" is found in Burkhardt, et al., *Correspondence of Charles Darwin*, p. 377, although the assigned date of 1873 appears speculative. On the other hand, the date of Titus Munson Coan's transmission to Charles Darwin of population figures for the Hawaiian Islands (in DAR 90, 40–43) is clear: February 14, 1874. Here's the rub: In a letter that seems to have been written to Thomas N. Staley, Anglican Bishop of Honolulu, in January 1874 (i.e., *after* Leonard's communiqué to his father, but *before* Coan's), Charles Darwin still appears altogether ignorant of Hawaiian census figures, though he does acknowledge the general admission "that the natives have largely decreased since the time of Cook." This letter is now preserved in Honolulu in the archives of the Hawaiian Historical Society; and although its addressee, as well as its date, cannot be unambiguously determined, Plews assigns to it a January 1874 date, an assignation that even subsequent scholarship (by Garber) does not dispute. See Plews, "Charles Darwin and Hawaiian Sex Ratios," and Garber, "Darwin's Correspondents in the Pacific."

Just as interesting are the following facts. Leonard Darwin's Hawaiian population figures are seven in number, the first for the year 1832 and the last for the year 1872; Titus Munson Coan gives nine figures, beginning with the year 1779 (400,000) and ending with the year 1872; but the six numbers given in a table in *Descent*—for the years 1832 (130,313), 1836 (108,579), 1853 (71,019), 1860 (67,084), 1866 (58,765), and 1872 (51,531)—match precisely those of both men.

Charles Darwin's own statement regarding the decline of the Native Hawaiian population (from 300,000—the number he adopts for 1779), including his reference to Coan, can be found in *The Descent of Man*, chap. 7.

For a recent discussion of population growth and arrest in prehistoric Hawai'i—including the notions that the 1778–1779 Native Hawaiian population may have been as low as 110,000 or as high as 1 million, that the population may have already suffered decline before Captain Cook's arrival, and that such decline as may be attributed to foreign diseases (syphilis in particular) may have had a pre-Cook source in voyages of Spanish or Japanese origin—see Dye, "Population Trends in Hawaii Before 1778."

10. The Sandwich Island Seven

1. Short biographical sketches of George Forbes can be found in: *Obituary Notices of Fellows of the Royal Society,* 1936–1938, vol. 2, 283–286; MNRAS 97 (1937), 269–270; *Nature* 138 (3498): 830–831 (November 14, 1936).

2. J. A. Fleming and D'Arcy W. Thompson, "George Forbes 1849–1936," *Obituary Notices of Fellows of The Royal Society,* 1936–1938, vol. 2, 284–285.

3. Having been appointed to a chair in Natural Philosophy at Glasgow in 1846, William Thomson (Lord Kelvin) was in 1849 (the year of George Forbes' birth) assisting George's father James David Forbes in measuring underground temperatures and the thermal properties of rocks. Burchfield, *Lord Kelvin,* 34.

4. Airy's letter, dated August 30, 1872, reads:

Gentlemen

Understanding that M^r. George Forbes is candidate for the Professorship of Natural Philosophy in the Andersonian University, I ask leave to lay before you my Testimonial in support of his application.

I have long known M^r. George Forbes (as the son of my old friend Professor James Forbes), and have remarked his desire to enter into subjects possessing the character of Natural Philosophy and to treat them mathematically where it was necessary. M^r. Forbes went through the usual course of Cambridge education; and since its termination he has employed himself on physical studies and practice, and in making the acquaintance of continental philosophers. He called attention, in this country, to some of the labours of Palmieri and Respighi; he discussed the observations of meteor-shower at the Cape of Good Hope, and he has since proposed a theory on a point of refraction which had escaped general attention.

Lately M^r. Forbes has spent some time at this observatory in practicing the use of instruments applicable to the observations of the Transit of Venus 1874, for employment in which he desires to offer himself as candidate.

I believe that M^r. Forbes' talents, and inclinations, and education, would suit him well for the Professorship in the Andersonian University.

The testimonial letter of Airy, together with those of J. C. Adams, William Thomson, Warren De la Rue, et al., are among the George Forbes Papers (Incoming Correspondence, 1872), located at the University Library, St. Andrews, Scotland.

5. Forbes to Airy, January 17, 1872, RGO 6/273, leaves 491–492.

6. Airy's quick response politely suggested that in an expedition that would likely engross much of Forbes' attention, "it may not be easy to find time for geology." Airy to Forbes, February 9, 1872, RGO 6/273, leaf 494.

7. Airy to Forbes, October 17, 1873, RGO 6/277, leaf 661.

8. Biographical information on Barnacle can be found in *Alumni Cantabrigienses* and in Tanner, *The Historical Register.*

9. Barnacle to Airy, December 10, 1873, RGO 6/273, leaves 151–152.

10. Airy to Barnacle, December 11, 1873, RGO 6/273, leaf 153.

11. Barnacle to Airy, December 12, 1873, RGO 6/273, leaves 154–155.

12. Barnacle to Airy, December 22, 1873, RGO 6/273, leaves 157–159.

13. W^{m}. H. H. Hudson to Sir George Airy, December 24, 1873, RGO 6/273, leaves 162–163.

14. Airy to Barnacle, January 23, 1874, RGO 6/273, leaf 166.

15. Barnacle to Airy, March 31, 1874, RGO 6/273, leaf 168.

16. "John Walter Nichol," MNRAS 39 (February 1879), 237.

17. Gunther, *Early Science in Cambridge,* 175, 179.

18. Challis to Airy, July 18, 1873, RGO 6/273, leaf 755.

19. Airy to Challis, July 19, 1873, RGO 6/273, leaf 756.

20. Nichol to Challis, July 29, 1873, RGO 6/273, leaf 757.

21. Airy to Nichol, October 14, 1873, RGO 6/273, leaf 759; Nichol to Airy, October 15, 1873, RGO 6/273, leaf 760.

22. Airy, "Instructions to Observers," 3–4.

23. F. E. Ramsden, "Photographer's Journal at Honolulu," September 24, 1874, to February 6, 1875, RGO 59/68. The Airy-Ramsden correspondence regarding the transit of Venus encompasses but seven leaves: RGO 6/273, leaves 985–991.

24. Airy, "Instructions to Observers," 3.

25. The largely unilluminating Airy-Noble correspondence is found in RGO 6/273, leaves 776–786.

26. In addition to what is found in the introduction to Airy's *Account,* biographical information on Tupman is given in MNRAS 83 (1923), 247–248.

27. Airy to Tupman, April 25, 1872, RGO 6/270, file 1, leaf 4; George Tupman, "Journal of Captain G. L. Tupman R. M. A. in connection with the Transit of Venus 1874" (hereafter referred to as Tupman's "Home Journal"), vol. 1, RGO 59/56, entry for May 15, 1872. Tupman's "Home Journal" is an essentially diarylike record, in four volumes, of Tupman's 1874 transit-related work and encompasses a period of more than eight years, from May 1872 to October 1880, excepting that period of time when the author was away from home (i.e., from the RGO) on the expedition to

Hawai'i. Among its early entries, one reads that Tupman commenced his work at the RGO on May 15, 1872; that F[orbes] observed there on May 21; and that Tupman was—for some unexplained reason—away at Cambridge from August 24 to 26.

28. Only scanty biographical information is available on Richard Johnson, and none at all was found during a personal visit by the author to the library of Trinity College, Dublin, in September of 1996. The sources used here include: MNRAS 55:4 (February 1895), 194–195; Jane Maxwell (Trinity College Library, Dublin) to Michael Chauvin, June 29, 1995, personal correspondence; P. A. Wayman (Dunsink Observatory, Dublin) to Michael Chauvin, March 25, 1996, personal correspondence.

29. Johnson to Airy, January 31, 1874, RGO 6/273, leaves 455–456.

30. Airy to Johnson, February 3, 1874, RGO 6/273, leaf 457.

31. Johnson to Airy, February 4, 1874, RGO 6/273, leaves 458–459.

32. Airy to Johnson, February 6, 1874, RGO 6/273, leaf 461.

33. Johnson to Airy, February 7, 1874, RGO 6/273, leaf 462.

11. Practice at Greenwich

1. George Forbes, "The Coming Transit of Venus," *Nature,* May 28, 1874, 67.

2. As Chapman has pointed out, one reason why astronomical instruments of precision were rare and expensive in Horrocks' day was because demand was not yet sufficient to stimulate and sustain regular commercial manufacture. Chapman, "Jeremiah Horrocks," 340.

3. King, *History of the Telescope,* 251–252; McConnell, *Instrument Makers to the World.* McConnell records (p. 47) that Troughton & Simms also worked to improve George Forbes' patented design for a rifle range finder; but after more than a decade of experimentation, it was the Zeiss company that finally brought it into production for him. For a detailed account of the Chance Brothers' business, see Chance, *A History of the Firm of Chance Brothers & Co.* Chapter 8 discusses the production and use of optical glass. Something of the Chance family's connection with Cambridge University can be found on page 119. The statement that Airy, in about 1828 when he was still at Cambridge, "had to wait for years for a 4-inch object glass," is found on page 172. Information about the 25-inch discs supplied by the Chance Brothers to T. Cooke & Sons, worked by them into an object glass for R. S. Newall, and eventually bequeathed to Cambridge University, is given on page 178. Something of the production, by Alvan Clark & Sons, of the U.S. Naval Observatory's 26-inch telescope, using a disc supplied by the Chance Brothers, is given on pages 178–179. RGO 6/279, leaves 555–574, contain correspondence with the Chance Brothers, who, for the British transit of Venus expeditions, supplied the Astronomer Royal (in March 1874) with the 6 x 6–inch-square patent glass plates and (in April 1874) with the 8.3-inch diameter circular patent glass plates for the Janssen—thirty dozen of the latter, and more than twice that number of the former.

4. Airy's 1874 transit of Venus correspondence with the Admiralty can be found in

RGO 6/267. The first letter in this file—a file that covers a period of eleven years (1869 to 1880)—is dated February 15, 1869, and is addressed to Childers.

5. The Admiralty to Airy, June 22, 1869, RGO 6/267, file 1, leaf 14; W. Airy, *Autobiography*, 286–287.

6. W. Airy, *Autobiography*, 289.

7. Hind, "Particulars of the Transit of Venus," 17–22. Airy was in communication with Hind as early as February 1870 with respect to what particulars the 1874 *Nautical Almanac* ought to contain regarding the transit of Venus. RGO 6/269, file 14, leaves 321ff.

8. Airy, "Report of the Astronomer Royal to the Board of Visitors of the Royal Observatory, Greenwich," (1871): 21, (1872): 21–22.

9. Forbes responded with a private letter to Airy expressing his annoyance with his (Airy's) rash judgment and hoping that he (Airy) would alter his opinion. Forbes to Airy, July 11, 1872, RGO 6/273, leaves 501–502.

10. Airy had twice expressed his opinion to Captain G. H. Richards, R.N.—once in 1869 ("You know that Regular Service Men and Civilians rarely work well together") and again in 1871 ("I well know the belief, and I join in it, that regular-service-men and civilians do not work well together."). Airy to Richards, May 5, 1869 and October 10, 1871, RGO 6/268, file 1, leaves 26–27, 60.

11. Airy to the secretary of the Admiralty, March 21, 1873, RGO 6/267, file 3, leaves 95–104.

12. "I am glad of the opportunity you have afforded me of testifying to the complete knowledge possessed by Prof. G. Forbes of all our Instruments, Methods of Observation, Adjustments and Reductions. He also thoroughly understands Photography generally, as well as its application to Heliography, and appears to be conversant with Electrical Apparatus. . . . I think it very unlikely that we shall be so fortunate as to secure the services of . . . [other] gentlemen with the qualifications of Prof. Forbes." Tupman to Airy, June 23, 1873, RGO 6/270, file 2, leaf 59.

13. Airy to Forbes, July 29, 1873, RGO 6/273, leaf 513.

14. Airy to Tupman, September 22, 1873, RGO 6/270, file 3, leaf 103.

15. Airy to Barnacle, December 11, 1873, RGO 6/273, leaf 153; Airy to Johnson, February 6, 1874, RGO 6/273, leaf 461.

16. THJ, vol. 1, entries for August 7 and September 5, 10, 18, 19, and 27 (1873).

17. Nearly matching his flattering assessment of Forbes' abilities was Tupman's judgment of Ramsden: A "remarkably steady and accurate observer, and [a] certain computer," he wrote of a man who was always "much interested in his work without being at all excited." THJ, vol. 2, entry for November 17, 1873.

18. Airy, "Report of the Astronomer Royal to the Board of Visitors of the Royal Observatory, Greenwich," (1873), 22. When Airy eventually recognized the desirability of supplementing the five head stations with three auxiliary stations (two at Hawai'i, one at Kerguelen), the additional required instruments were borrowed from various sources. Tupman, Barnacle, and the Cambridge Observatory Syndicate all lent telescopes. Airy, "Report of the Astronomer Royal to the Board of Visitors of the Royal Observatory, Greenwich," (1874), 19; W. Airy, *Autobiography*, 305.

19. A mechanical model of this or similar kind was previously suggested by Bevis in anticipation of the 1769 transit. Woolf, *The Transits of Venus,* 164.

20. RGO 6/277, leaf 632.

21. RGO 6/277, file 14, leaves 631, 633, 658.

22. George Forbes, "The appearances presented by the Model Transit of Venus, mounted at the Royal Observatory, with a cloudy sky," RGO 6/277, leaves 664–675.

23. On October 30, 1873, Forbes suggested to Airy that he provide a transit model for practice at each station. Airy replied that (before this) he "had no idea of making a Model for each station." RGO 6/277, file 14, leaves 676–677, 678.

24. Tupman to Airy, April 4, 1874, RGO 6/272, file 2, leaf 110. Some weeks earlier, Tupman had written that he had "inspected Mr Barnacle's transit work" and found it "very unsatisfactory." THJ, vol. 2, entry for February 28, 1874.

25. "The Journal of H. G. Barnacle regarding the 1874 Transit of Venus, observations made from Hawaii," RGO 59/67.

26. Meadows, *Greenwich Observatory,* 4. Another story of Airy's sometimes incredible behavior relates of the occasion when he sent some of his assistants to Harton Colliery to measure the behavior of a pendulum deep underground in an attempt to determine the change of gravity with depth. Not only did he tell them, as if they were children going on their first journey alone, precisely which trains to take and where to change, but he also packed soap and towels with the instruments in order to be sure they had everything they needed. Ronan, *Their Majesties' Astronomers,* 145; Ronan, *Astronomers Royal,* 130.

12. Astrophotography

1. Hentschel, "Drawing;" Winkler and Van Helden, "Representing the Heavens;" Johns, *The Nature of the Book,* 436–440.

2. Carpenter, "British Preparations."

3. Lankford writes that the reluctance exhibited by some astronomers to employ photography in their research was due to social as well as technical factors. Lankford, "Photography and the 19th-Century Transits of Venus."

4. Even though his life and work had antedated the advent of photography, Johannes Hevelius (1611–1687) expressed a similar concern over the uneven shrinkage of the paper ("ten parts in width to six parts in length") on which were printed the lunar representations of his *Selenographia* (1647). Winkler and Van Helden, "Johannes Hevelius," 110.

5. The coining of the word "photography" is ascribed to the astronomer John Herschel.

6. Rehbock, "The History of Photographic Invention;" Norman, "The Development of Astronomical Photography." Norman writes (p. 562) that in or about 1849, Faye had enough confidence in daguerreotypes that he recommended a photographic method

that "shortly thereafter yielded a very satisfactory value for the solar parallax."

7. Rehbock, "The History of Photographic Invention," 7.

8. From the Astronomer Royal to the secretary of the Admiralty, July 27, 1871, RGO 6/267, file 2.

9. Rothermel, "Images of the Sun."

10. Rothermel, "Images of the Sun," 160.

11. W. De W. Abney, "Dry Plate Process for Solar Photography," March 7, 1874. A copy of Abney's four-page essay can be found in RGO 6/273, leaves 49–50. Abney was a member of the team eventually dispatched to Egypt for the 1874 transit observations.

12. Airy, "Report of the Astronomer Royal to the Board of Visitors of the Royal Observatory, Greenwich," (1872), 21–22.

13. Having come to England in 1851 from his native Westphalia, Dallmeyer (1830–1883) had his name first brought before the public by Sir John Herschel in the article on "Telescopes" in the eighth edition of the *Encyclopedia Britannica,* and several of his telescopes were eventually used by government expeditions sent out to observe eclipses of the sun. But from about 1862, the greater part of his fame and fortune was derived from his reputation as a manufacturer of photographic lenses and from the instruments he supplied to photographers in all parts of the world, of which more than thirty thousand had been sold up to the time of his death. In 1863, in the service of celestial photography, he successfully constructed a photoheliograph for Russia's Wilna Observatory for taking 4-inch pictures of the sun, and he supplied a similar instrument to the observatory at Harvard the following year. At various exhibitions in the 1860s and 1870s at Dublin, Berlin, Paris, and Philadelphia, Dallmeyer's lenses received the highest awards. "John Henry Dallmeyer," DNB.

14. A description of a Dallmeyer photoheliograph can be found in the *Catalogue of the Special Loan Collection of Scientific Apparatus at the South Kensington Museum,* 3rd ed., 1876 (London, 1877), 421–422. See also Carpenter, "British Preparations."

15. About Janssen's apparatus, Airy wrote:

> When the preparations for the Transit Expedition were far advanced, a proposal was published by M. Janssen for taking a photograph of Venus and a portion of the Sun's limb near to it at every second of time, or other short interval, near to the times of ingress or egress. It appeared desirable to make trial of this proposal; and, under my general superintendence, an apparatus was prepared by Mr. Dallmeyer, with great skill, which appeared likely to carry out M. Janssen's proposals perfectly well. A circular photographic glass plate, $10\frac{3}{4}$ inches in diameter, mounted in a large ring whose circumference was cut in teeth, was so arranged that, when its frame was fixed upon the photographic end of the photoheliograph, with the photographic plane transversal to the optical axis of the instrument, it could be made to rotate by a small toothed-wheel spindle. . . . During a portion of the rotation of the spindle the large ring and photographic plate stood still; and the plate was exposed to the Sun, and an image was formed. . . . During the remaining portion of the rotation the sun-light was

stopped, and the motion of the spindle gave motion to the ring and plate so as to expose a new part for a new photographic image. (Airy, *Account,* appendix 5, 19)

16. Airy elsewhere gives the number as ten fewer: "A Janssen slide, capable of taking 50 photographs of Venus and the neighbouring part of the Sun's limb at intervals of one second, has been made by Mr Dallmeyer for each of the five photoheliographs." W. Airy, *Autobiography,* 305.

17. Proctor, *Transits of Venus,* 2nd ed. (1875), 210; George Forbes, "The Coming Transit of Venus," *Nature,* May 7, 1874, 14.

18. From the Admiralty to Airy, April 26, 1873, RGO 6/267.

19. Airy, "Report of the Astronomer Royal to the Board of Visitors of the Royal Observatory, Greenwich," (1874), 20; W. Airy, *Autobiography,* 302, 305.

20. Carpenter, "British Preparations."

21. Airy, "Instructions to Observers," 13.

22. Davis, *Na Pa'i Ki'i.* Davis has laid out some of the historical, political, and social issues surrounding the use of photography in Hawai'i in *History of Photography* 25:3 (autumn) 2001.

13. Supplies

1. Late in 1873, with but a year remaining before transit day, the question of providing proper emoluments to the expedition's members had still not been resolved to the satisfaction of the one man who seemed most intimately acquainted with that question: Captain Tupman. What was at issue, as Tupman saw it, was more than a matter of economics, it was a matter of morale. For too long the conduct of the government in its relations with the transit of Venus volunteers had been, he felt, calculated to drive them away rather than to encourage them. The resignation of several officers from among the volunteers earlier in the year was already a sign that something was amiss, and in December Tupman wrote to Airy detailing the ill treatment (financial and otherwise) accorded to them. He then said this of the civilian volunteers:

> The Civilians, most of whom are gentlemen of some reputation as Astronomers, have been treated with still less consideration. A learned Professor comes all the way from Scotland several times, resides away from home for many months, and devotes his whole time and energy to the furtherance of a <u>Government</u> Enterprize—and (I believe I am right in saying) actually pays a substitute to do his duty in his absence. Astronomers come from Stoneyhurst and Edinburgh—remain here for months, devoting themselves to <u>Government</u> Work with an energy truly surprising—and—receive nothing—not even a lodging allowance [emphasis in original]. (Tupman to Airy, December 10, 1873, RGO 6/270, file 3, leaves 142–145)

The astronomers alluded to are probably Forbes (the "learned Professor" from Scotland), Perry (the director of the Stoneyhurst Observatory), and Nichol (from Edinburgh). Tupman's concluding admonition to Airy—"If we are to have good men they must be paid, and paid well"—probably contributed to the resolution of the issue by the Admiralty in January 1874. Civilian observers—including Nichol, Johnson, Barnacle, and Forbes—would be paid a salary of £300 per annum for their transit-related work; military personnel—Captain Tupman and Lieutenants Ramsden and Noble—would receive the full pay of their rank, with Tupman, the head of the enterprise, receiving a special allowance of £1 per diem from the date of embarkation. The observers would, in addition, receive proper compensation sufficient to cover the actual expenses of travel and subsistence. The Admiralty to Airy, January 2, 1874, RGO 6/267, file 4, leaves 157–160; Airy to Forbes, January 6, 1874, RGO 6/273, leaf 524; Airy to Nichol, October 14, 1873, RGO 6/273, leaf 759; Airy to Barnacle, December 11, 1873, RGO 6/273, leaf 153; RGO 6/267, file 5, leaf 202. When, in April of 1873, Airy was still putting transit matters in order with the government and could not state the terms on which volunteers would be paid, he asked Forbes if he would be satisfied in simply being relieved of all expense from his time of leaving England until the time of his return, but without other stipend. Forbes' response was even more generous than requested: Not only would he be satisfied with such an arrangement, but he was prepared to devote two full years—from the beginning of 1874 to the end of 1875—to the transit work. Airy to Forbes, April 2, 1873, RGO 6/273, leaf 507; Forbes to Airy, April 8, 1873, RGO 6/273, leaf 509.

2. The material used in this chapter has largely been culled from Tupman's "Transit of Venus: List of Government Stores for All Stations," Royal Observatory, May 30, 1874, RGO 59/58.

3. G. L. Tupman, "Transit of Venus, 1874, British Observations," pt. 6, an item dated November 22, 1873, RGO 59/57.

4. Abney's prescription for the processing of the photographic plates (see chapter 12, note 11), which called for the use of distilled water, also noted the utility of bottled beer. Though the distilled water clearly had a large number of photographic uses, from cleaning collodion bottles to preparing baths, precisely how much of the Guinness Stout supplied to the expedition was used by anyone for any photographic work is not a matter of public record.

14. Gifts

1. Bird, *The Hawaiian Archipelago.*

2. George Forbes Papers, Incoming Correspondence, 1874, no. 14, University Library, St. Andrews, Scotland.

15. Instructions

1. Airy, "British Expeditions for the Observation of the Transit of Venus, 1874, December 8: Instructions to Observers," May 4, 1874. This thirteen-part set of instructions can be found in its entirety among the Report[s] of the Astronomer Royal, 1871–1881, RGO 17/3.

2. Airy's interest in making chronometric (longitudinal) connections extended far beyond Honolulu and San Francisco: His greater ambition was to "interconnect all the [transit of Venus] stations, British and foreign, as completely as possible." Airy, "Preparations."

16. Military and Political Maneuvers

1. Buck, *Explorers of the Pacific,* 44.

2. Daws, *Shoal of Time,* 73–74.

3. *PCA,* September 8, 1866; "British Consular Service Completes More Than 100 Years Existence in Honolulu," *Honolulu Advertiser,* September 4, 1930, 4.

4. "Kamaaina Back for Isle Visit," *Honolulu Star-Bulletin,* April 5, 1939, 7.

5. Daws, *Shoal of Time,* 197–199.

6. Daws, *Shoal of Time,* 200–201.

7. "The Transit of Venus," *HG,* January 28, 1874; *Aliiolani Hale,* 49.

8. Daws, *Shoal of Time,* 199–202.

9. James H. Wodehouse to the earl of Derby, April 30, 1874, ADM 1/6302, PRO. Edward Henry Stanley (1826–1893), the fifteenth earl of Derby, was secretary of Foreign Affairs in 1874.

17. A Royal Reception

1. Venus reached superior conjunction on February 22, 1874, at 23:00 UT (Universal Time) and greatest eastern elongation on September 30, 1874, at 01:00 UT. Data kindly provided by Kevin Polk, manager, NASA Pacific Regional Planetary Data Center, University of Hawai'i.

2. Airy, *Account,* 5; Airy to Forbes, May 5, 1874, RGO 6/273, leaves 532, 533; Forbes to Airy, June 3, 1874, RGO 6/273, leaf 540; Airy to Barnacle, May 5, 1874, RGO 6/273, leaf 177; Forbes to Airy, July 22, 1874, RGO 6/273, leaves 542–545; FJ (RGO 59/69): June 1 and 3 and July 18 and 28, 1874; Tupman to Airy, July 31, 1874, RGO

6/270, file 5, leaf 209. Tupman states elsewhere (THJ, vol. 2) that the *Illimani* sailed from Liverpool with 68 tons of baggage and the *Britannia* with 25 tons.

3. The three sappers were George Currie, Mark Meins, and Edward Meyers—all of them Royal Engineers.

4. Bird, *The Hawaiian Archipelago,* 14.

5. This included 30 officers, 49 petty officers, 115 seamen, 45 marines, and 36 boys. Ship's Log, HMS *Scout,* (Captain) Ralph P. Cator, February 7 to November 17, 1874, ADM 53/10399, PRO.

6. Tupman to Airy, September 17, 1874, RGO 6/270, file 5, leaves 212–217.

7. That Kalākaua was among those who studied Olmsted's *Rudiments* is reported in Menton, 162. Hoffleit writes that Olmsted's *Rudiments* (1842) went through more than fifty editions, including one in raised type for the blind. Hoffleit, *Astronomy at Yale,* 25.

8. Lyman, "Hawaiian Journals." The HMCS papers on Lyman include a brief biographical sketch, reportedly culled from an 1887 issue of *Popular Science Monthly.*

9. James H. Wodehouse to the earl of Derby, September 28, 1874, RGO 6/269, leaf 85.

10. "Audiences at the Palace," *PCA,* September 19, 1874. Captain Cator, who was among those presented to Kalākaua on September 15, was not soon to forget the king's kindness nor the proper obeisance deserving of a king: Two months later, on November 16, he would have his ship dressed in honor of King Kalākaua's birthday and would fire a twenty-one-gun salute to the Hawaiian flag at 12 noon—a ritual he would repeat on November 28 in honor of Hawaiian independence. Ship's Log, HMS *Scout,* February 7 to November 17, 1874 (ADM 53/10399) and November 18, 1874, to June 2, 1875 (ADM 53/10400), PRO.

11. *PCA,* September 19, 1874.

18. The Observatory at 'Āpua

1. Tupman to Airy, September 17, 1874, RGO 6/270, file 5, leaves 212–217.

2. Airy, *Account,* 7.

3. Tupman to Airy, September 17, 1874.

4. Tupman wrote: "Although high-water mark was half a mile distant, the tide percolated through the coral and rose many inches above its surface, but in no way interfered with the stability of the piers, which were set with cement." Tupman to Airy, September 17, 1874.

5. Airy, *Account,* 8; Tupman to Airy, September 17, 1874. Tupman later reported: "The arrangements in case of fire are believed to be satisfactory, but Captain Cator intends to send us one of the 'Scouts' Fire engines as an additional Security." Tupman to Airy, October 13, 1874, RGO 6/270, file 5, leaf 226. In addition to its many other purposes, Tupman thought that water might be used to wet the floor of

the photographer's darkroom to allay the dust. Tupman, "Transit of Venus, 1874, British Observations," pt. 2, "Photoheliograph," RGO 59/57.

6. It is to Tupman's journal (RGO 59/70) that one must turn for an authoritative description of the regimen: After a 9:00 A.M. breakfast, Tupman would issue the orders for the day and post them in the computing room, examine the observing books for the preceding night, write up his journal, copy some of the astronomical observations onto the printed forms, calculate the mean time (if necessary), inspect the carpenter's work, check the instruments and the photographic proceedings, and attend to household matters. This continued until about 5:00 P.M. Noble, meanwhile, was busy reducing the previous night's work with the transit instrument, including the meridional transits of Greenwich clock stars. These reductions included those for azimuth error, collimation error, and level error. He copied his work, in duplicate, on printed forms. These tasks kept him employed for six to eight hours. Ramsden attended to photographic matters all day and kept his own journal, separate from Tupman's. Nichol was made "generally useful" in astronomical and other matters. Practice on the model was carried out daily, weather permitting, and for this exercise, during which the model was observed through several telescopes, the men assigned to the auxiliary stations (Barnacle, Forbes, and Johnson) joined in. After a 5:30 supper, work continued into the night: Two or three polar stars, ten or twelve clock stars, and six zenith distances of the moon and two of a star near the moon were observed nightly. The meridian mark, after its erection, was observed when possible at sunrise (having been observed at sunset as well). TJ, 34–37.

7. "The ground between the telescopes and the model is light sandy earth covered more or less with grass which native horses find in sufficient quantity to live upon." Tupman to Airy, November 1, 1874, RGO 6/270, file 5, leaves 228–232.

8. Airy, *Account,* 32, 54–56.

9. RJ, entries for November 11, 13, and 14. Experiments using the Janssen vis-à-vis the model were already underway in November, and by mid-month five days had already been devoted to such labors, four Janssen plates being exposed each day. "Progress of the Transit of Venus Expedition Honolulu, 1874 November 16," RGO 59/60. Tupman, in his own journal (TJ), records that practice with the photoheliograph on the model began November 11.

10. Although the sappers Meins and Meyers, who lived directly on the observatory grounds (together with Corporal Currie), can be credited with assisting Ramsden in the photographic department (the former preparing solutions for the dry plates, the latter distilling water), it is probably largely due to Ramsden that this photographic part of the historical record—scanty as the surviving fragments may be—provides a still-extant supplement to a bare textual account. RJ, entries for October 1, 5, and 14.

19. The Adversities of Nature and Society

1. Tupman to Airy, September 17, 1874.

2. Tupman to Airy, October 13, 1874, RGO 6/270, file 5, leaves 222–227.

3. Captain Ralph Cator to the secretary of the Admiralty, September 27, 1874, RGO 6/267, file 6; report of (Captain) R. P. Cator, HMS *Scout*, Honolulu, October 14, 1874, RGO 6/267, file 7, leaves 292–296.

4. Tupman's second letter to Airy—that of October 13—contained the simple statement, "A good deal of wet weather," but he would frequently repeat that lament, in refrainlike fashion, in his journal (TJ)—as, for example, in the entries for October 27 and 31; November 2, 8, 9, 18, and 19; and December 3 and 4.

5. HAA for 1875, 29.

6. G. L. Tupman, "Meteorological Register," June 1874 to February 1875, National Meteorological Library and Archive, Bracknell. The rainfall data recorded in the register are as follows: November 19, 1874: 3.040 (4 P.M.), 3.710 (8 P.M.); November 20, 1874: 3.500 (4 A.M.), 2.000 (8 A.M.), 1.000 (noon)—totaling 13.25 (inches) within this period of time. Tupman, however, has added for November 19 the illuminating remark that the "Rain Guage [*sic*] overflowed for hours," and elsewhere in the register he says: "When rain was falling heavily the guage was emptied every four hours, but occasionally the whole fall was not measured. On the night of 1874 Nov 19, the guage was filled to overflowing several times, [and] the amount recorded is probably not more than one third of what fell."

7. Tupman to the Astronomer Royal, December 3, 1874, RGO 6/270, file 5, leaves 238–248.

8. Tupman to Airy, November 1, 1874, RGO 6/270, file 5. In his own private journal (TJ), Tupman further records (on November 7): "Repaired the Model Sun-shade which had been blown away & smashed. Natives engaged repairing the rush-roofing which has been much damaged by the gales of wind & rain."

9. Mosquitoes were introduced at Lahaina (Maui) in 1826. Mitchell, *Resource Units in Hawaiian Culture*, 208.

10. Tupman to Airy, October 13, 1874, RGO 6/270, file 5, leaves 222–227.

11. Tupman to Airy, October 13, 1874, RGO 6/270, file 5, leaves 222–227.

12. TJ, September 21.

13. TJ, p. 37.

14. TJ, October 3.

15. Tupman to Airy, November 1, 1874, RGO 6/270, file 5.

20. Measuring Heaven and Earth

1. Bennett, "Practical Mathematics in the Age of Discoveries."

2. That land surveying could be not only a geographically but a socially divisive practice had already been bemoaned in England by John Dee (b. 1527), who wrote: "Of these feates (of mathematics) is sprong the feate of Geodesie, or Land Measuring: more cunning to measure and survey Land, Woods, and Waters, afarre

off. More cunning, I say: But God knoweth, hitherto, in these Realmes of England and Ireland, whether through ignorance or fraude, I can not tell, in every particular, how great wrong and injurie hath in my time bene committed by untrue measuring and surveying." Mason, *A History of the Sciences,* 250.

3. Airy, *Account,* 20.

4. The Government Survey began in 1870 when the Hawai'i Legislature appropriated $5,000 to procure the requisite instruments and to make a beginning. An order for the instruments was sent to Troughton & Simms of London—the same makers of some of the equipment used by the British transit of Venus team. When the instruments arrived in Hawai'i in 1871, they "proved to be first class in every respect." The theodolite excited special admiration: It could read horizontal angles to an accuracy of one arc second and vertical angles to five seconds, and its telescopic sight could distinguish a bare signal pole at a distance of over 20 miles. Alexander, "A Brief Account of the Hawaiian Government Survey," 12–14.

5. Airy, *Account,* 21.

6. Alexander, "A Brief Account of the Hawaiian Government Survey;" Chinen, *The Great Mahele;* Daws, *Shoal of Time,* 124–128.

7. Alexander, "A Brief Account of the Hawaiian Government Survey," 11.

8. Gay, "Surveys in Honolulu." This small book apparently served as Gay's field book. Along with a sketch of the "Traverse from Captain Tupman's Transit Instrument to Flitner's or Lyman's Observatory—also to about where Fleurier's [sic] Observatory stood," it contains a pencil sketch of the Honolulu "Transit Station" together with related sketches of the ground plan of the observatory at the 'Āpua site.

9. Fleuriais, "Sur la longitude d'Honolulu."

10. Gay, "Surveys in Honolulu." Gay's (undated) letter to Tupman reads:

> My dear sir
>
> I have made further search for Fleurier's [sic] transit st[ation], and by sinking in a spot named by the Man who lived in the old house at the time of Fleurier's stay here, I find old pieces of Coral rock, Brick and wood, but no solid kind of Masonry. [I]f Convenient for you—or one of your party to come up & see what they think of it—you would much oblige yours
>
> Respectfully
>
> J W Gay

11. Tupman's journal records the fuller story of the disinterment:

> In the years 1867-8 M. Fleuriais, a Lieutenant in the French Navy, determined the Longitude of Honolulu by Moon Culminations, his observations extending over several months. His results are published (I believe) in the 'Connaissance des Temps.' Considering it desirable that the Station of the Transit of Venus Instruments should be geodetically connected with Mr. Flitner's observatory and the site of Fleuriais' transit, I instituted a search for the latter. In a few days, chiefly through the friendly and energetic cooperation of Mr. James W. Gay, Surveyor,

of Honolulu, the foundations of his (Fleuriais') pier were found upon the Coral, 5 feet below the surface, on the North side of Emma Street, immediately opposite the end of Adam's Lane. His observatory stood in the road just clear of the carriage track. The Mason who built the pier & who afterwards removed the material identified the spot, and pointed out to me some portion of the fencing which had been removed to clear his North Meridian line. Using our own Meridian line as a basis of Azimuth, Mr. Gay, with theodolite and chain ran a traverse along the streets to Flitner's & Fleuriais' piers, and back again by a different route. Mr. Gay also connected our station with surrounding permanent objects & localities and also with the nearer Government Trig. Stations, on Diamond Head & Punch Bowl Hills. According to the traverse, Flitner's pier (which was Lyman's) is 2370¼ feet <u>North</u> and 12½ feet <u>East</u> of the centre of the 'Transit of Venus' transit pier. Fleuriais' pier was 2474 feet <u>North</u> and 456 <u>East</u> of our pier [Emphasis in original]. (TJ, 92–94)

Although "Emma" (Street) has been deleted in Tupman's journal (and replaced by "Union"), it remains intact in Airy's *Account* (pp. 8, 30) as marking the relevant place of intersection with Adam's Lane.

12. TJ, 94. D. G. Rushford's unsuccessful search in 1964 to recover the 1874 transit of Venus station in Honolulu was thwarted by the same cause that is believed to have destroyed Tupman's bottle: the urbanization of downtown Honolulu.

13. Airy, *Account,* 30.

14. Gay, "Surveys in Honolulu."

15. *PCA*, July 21, 1877, 2.

16. Airy, *Account,* 6, 31.

17. Barnacle to Airy, April 14, 1875, RGO 6/273, leaves 188–193.

18. Other *ali'i* who visited Lyman at different times at his New Haven home were Queen Emma (Rooke) and Bernice Pauahi (Bishop). Lyman, *Around the Horn,* xii.

19. Lyman's "Hawaiian Journals" detail, in diarylike fashion, his travels through the Islands. And although they reveal only a glimmer of his astronomical interests, there is enough therein to corroborate and to amend the groping account of the traveling astronomer given by Tupman, who mistakenly writes:

> In or about the year 1845 Professor Lyman, now of Yale College, Connecticut, then residing in Honolulu for the benefit of his health, made a number of meridional observations of the Moon in order to determine the longitude. It is supposed that these observations have never been published, but their utility was such that in 1874 the Hawaiian Surveyor-General was still using the longitude communicated to him by Professor Lyman. The observatory and transit instrument of Professor Lyman passed into the hands of David Flitner, Esq., chronometer maker, of Honolulu, and in 1874 they were in perfect order. (Airy, *Account,* 7)

Lyman's own account is somewhat different. Between May 15 and June 17 of 1846, we find Lyman, by his own rendering, paying several calls on "Mr.

Boardman, watchmaker." On May 25, 1846, Lyman saw Boardman's "fine new Transit," and by June 1 he was "assisting Mr. Boardman part of the day in adjusting his Transit Instrument." On the evenings of June 4 and 5, he was making transit observations of stars (not of the moon, as is stated in Tupman's account), which he then reduced the following mornings (June 5 and 6), obtaining thereby longitude figures of 157° 45′ 25″ and 157° 47′ 50″. Lyman, "Hawaiian Journals."

See also: "Flitner's Transit Instrument," *The Friend,* January 1, 1875, 4; and HAA for 1882, 5. Biographical information on Lyman can be found in DSB and in BDAS. In both places, Lyman is credited as being the first to obtain convincing evidence of an atmosphere around Venus. In fact, however, evidence was already available a century earlier. See Dunn, "Some Observations of the Planet Venus." That it is Mikhail Vasilievitch Lomonosov (1711–1765) who should be credited with the discovery of Venus' atmosphere during the 1761 transit is advanced by Maor, *June 8, 2004: Venus in Transit,* 88–91. Lyman's 1874 observations of Venus are recorded in his essay "On Venus as a Luminous Ring." He states there that his observations on December 8 were made less than five hours before the beginning of the transit (an event that, at Yale, would not have commenced until after sunset) when Venus was in close proximity to the sun; that he made his observations using a 5-foot Clark telescope of 4⅔ inches aperture; and that a larger 9-inch equatorial (presumably the Sheffield telescope acquired in 1866, also by Alvan Clark) could not be used on this occasion because there were "no means of excluding the direct sunlight." Something of the history of the Sheffield Observatory, where Lyman served as director, can be found in Hoffleit, *Astronomy at Yale,* 42–46.

21. Kailua-Kona

1. Tupman to Airy, September 17, 1874.

2. Bird, *The Hawaiian Archipelago,* 23–24.

3. Forbes to Clerk-Maxwell, October 1, 1874, Box 11, part 11, leaves 71–72, St. Andrews University Library, Scotland.

4. Tupman to Airy, September 17, 1874; TJ, 17. Tupman records in his journal (October 6) that he interviewed with a Mr. Clark of Maui, who strongly recommended Haleakalā.

5. This instrument, by Messrs. T. Cooke and Sons, had been lent to the Astronomer Royal by William Garnett. It had a 2.57-inch objective and a focal length of approximately 3 feet and was eventually used at the Kailua-Kona station together with a clock by Earnshaw made some years previously for the Royal Observatory at Greenwich. To shelter the Garnett transit instrument and the Earnshaw clock, a Honolulu carpenter, Mr. Lucas, built a commodious wooden observatory, 13 feet by 10 feet, complete with a shutter that, according to Forbes' description, left "an open view of the sky on the meridian for a considerable angle, including all good clock stars." It also had a panel "to the north of the instrument [that] can be removed from the side of the hut, thus giving a clear view of polar stars." It is recorded elsewhere that: "Regular observations were commenced with the Transit Instrument for local

time on September 26th . . . . Trial observations were commenced with the Hawaii Transit mounted in the grounds of the [Hawaiian] Hotel, by Professor Forbes Octr 3^d, and with the Atooi Transit at the Head station by Mr Johnson Octr 8th." From a copy of a report of (Captain) R. P. Cator, HMS *Scout*, Honolulu, October 14, 1874, enclosed in a letter to Airy from the Admiralty, November 19, 1874, RGO 6/267, file 7, leaves 292–296. Tupman, in his own letter to Airy of October 13, 1874 (RGO 6/270, file 5, leaf 224), gives these dates as October 2 and 5.

6. In his September 17, 1874, letter to Airy, Tupman had articulated his own reasons for ordering this arrangement: He had decided to keep the observers intended for the auxiliary stations at work with their own instruments until their departure for those stations in November.

7. FJ, September 9 and October 1–4 and 5–7, 1874; Airy, *Account,* 213.

8. TJ, 39.

9. BJ, October 27–30, November 2; FJ, November 2.

10. Ship's Log, HMS *Scout,* ADM 53/10399, PRO; FJ, November 2, 3, 4, and 5; BJ, November 2, 3, 4, and 5.

11. Airy, "Preparations."

12. Forbes to Tupman, November 11, 1874, RGO 6/270, file 5, leaf 237.

13. FJ, November 11.

14. FJ, November 5.

15. Here is the full quote:

> Having taken the opinion of every one acquainted with the locality who could be communicated with, either personally or by letter, I decided upon stationing Prof. Forbes in the district of Kona on the West Coast of Hawaii. The only habitation available is a coral-built house on the shore of Kailua Bay, some 12 miles to the North of Kalakakua [sic] Bay, the property of the Princess Ruth, Governess of Hawaii, who has given permission for the Transit party to occupy it. It is <u>furnished</u> in the native sense of the word, but wholly unfit for Europeans [emphasis in original]. (Tupman to Airy, November 1, 1874, RGO 6/270, file 5)

16. TJ, 94.

17. Forbes to Tupman, November 11, 1874; extract from Wodehouse's Despatch No. 26, November 26, 1874, RGO 6/269, leaves 90–91.

18. "Cook's Monument at Kealakekua," HAA for 1912, 60–71.

19. Ship's Log, HMS *Scout,* ADM 53/10399, PRO, "Remarks" for Friday, October 30, 1874.

20. Extract from Wodehouse's Despatch No. 26.

21. Ship's Log, HMS *Scout,* ADM 53/10399, PRO; FJ, November 14; "Monument to Cook," *PCA,* October 31, 1874, 3. The cost of the project was partly borne by subscribers in England, one of whom was both an inveterate correspondent with George Airy on transit of Venus matters and the erstwhile captain of the HMS *Hecate,* which had once plied Hawaiian waters—viz., Admiral Richards. "Cook's Monument at Kealakekua," HAA for 1912, 67.

22. Cook, King, and Bayly, *The Original Astronomical Observations,* 57–61.

23. FJ, November 14–19; BJ, November 14–19. Barnacle's journal, which contains several references to "my telescope"—an instrument that Barnacle brought from Cheshire to Greenwich and, evidently, from there to Hawai'i—specifies neither the maker nor the size of the instrument. Tupman, however, describes it as a Cooke 4-inch. See BJ entries for March 7, 9, 11, and 16, November 24, and December 8, 1874; and Tupman's "Transit of Venus: List of Government Stores for All Stations," RGO 59/58.

24. On November 16, King Kalākaua's birthday, "Simon Kaai's natives" arrived at the transit station with presents of fruit, vegetables, and fowls.

25. Forbes to Tupman, November 11, 1874, RGO 6/270, file 5, leaf 237.

26. Forbes to Tupman, November 11, 1874.

27. FJ, November 20.

28. FJ, November 20, 21; BJ, November 20, 21.

29. FJ, November 22, marginalia.

30. FJ, November 24. Regarding the mention of cigars in this passage, there is, in RGO 59/61, a bill to Forbes from Henry Cooper (a "Storekeeper" and "Cleghorn's Agent") headed "Kailua February 1st 1875" and showing a purchase on December 12 of "75 Manilla Cigars" (cost: $2.25) after a "Bundle" of the same had been purchased on December 10 (cost: $0.60). It seems a fair presumption that Forbes enjoyed these himself. Barnacle, in a post-transit letter to Airy dated April 14, 1875 (RGO 6/273, leaves 188–193), accuses Forbes of "smoking" on transit day.

31. FJ, November 25.

32. FJ, November 24.

33. This condition caused such anxiety that, after Barnacle returned from Honolulu, Forbes arranged watches of three hours' duration to be taken by himself, Barnacle, and Lieutenant Bigge of HMS *Tenedos,* who had been assigned to assist in the operations on transit day. FJ, November 25 to December 7; BJ, November 25 and 30 and December 2.

34. Airy, *Account,* 218–219, 223. The given longitude figure for Forbes' site is equivalent—in degrees, minutes, and seconds of arc—to 156° 0' 25".5.

22. Waimea

1. Captain R. Cator to the secretary of the Admiralty, November 16, 1874, RGO 6/267, file 8; JJ, November 6. Note: On the title page of JJ (Johnson's journal) is found the note: "Mr Wellings Kept a weather Journal, in which are many interesting notes." This note appears to have been added by Airy. The fate of the Wellings journal is unknown.

2. JJ, November 7. See also: Johnson to Tupman, November 9, 1874, RGO 6/270, file 5.

3. JJ, November 7.

4. JJ, November 7; Johnson to Tupman, November 9, 1874, RGO 6/270, file 5.

5. Johnson's transit instrument, made by Troughton & Simms, had been lent to the Astronomer Royal by Reginald Bushell. It had an aperture of 2⅛ inches and a focal length of 31 inches and stood upon a stone slab that rested atop the pier that was sunk 6 feet into the red clay. The three chronometers, which were wound and compared regularly each day, also rested on the pier inside the small transit hut. The hut was almost entirely removed when astronomical observations were being made. Airy, *Account,* 237–238; JJ, November 21 and 22.

6. Airy, *Account,* 237; TJ, 94.

7. Airy, *Account,* 240–241. The given longitude figure for Johnson's site is equivalent—in degrees, minutes, and seconds of arc—to 159° 39′ 57″ (±30″).

8. Airy, *Account,* 237.

9. "Lehau Island" suggests Lehua, but it probably refers to Ni'ihau.

10. JJ, November 10, 13, 14, 16, and 17.

11. JJ, November 7, 8, 14, 15, 17, and 19.

12. JJ, November 7 to December 7.

13. In early 1874, Dunn wrote to Airy, saying: "I am going out as a Missionary to Honolulu Hawaiian Islands by the mail of [the] 13th instant:—As I understand that Honolulu is to be a post of observation for the transit of Venus—I venture to offer my services, subject to my duties there & the Mrs. sanction, if I can be useful in any way[.] I have some Knowledge of Astr[L]. Instruments—and Photography & am used to the use of my fingers &—Jun[r]. Opt. Can. 1862 so I might help if any is needed[.]" Airy replied: "I thank you for your proffer, and will not fail when the time approaches to make you acquainted with the Officer in charge of that expedition." Dunn to Airy, January 6, 1874, RGO 6/274, file 2, section 4, leaf 178; Airy to Dunn, January 17, 1874, RGO 6/274, file 2, section 4, leaf 179. Dunn had been a classmate of William Erasmus Darwin (1839–1914), the eldest son of Charles, and a graduate of Christ's College. Both Robert Dunn and William Darwin had been junior optimes of the class of 1862, and both had undertaken the Mathematical Tripos. Dunn had arrived in Honolulu in March of 1874 to assume ecclesiastical duties. Restarick, *Hawaii 1778–1920,* 143; "Hawaiian Church Monthly Messenger," Honolulu, March 1, 1874, 24.

14. Airy, *Account,* 243. Johnson describes Dunn's telescope as a 2.5-inch, while Tupman gives it an aperture of 2¾ inches. JJ, December 8; Tupman, "Transit of Venus: List of Government Stores for All Stations," RGO 59/58, 23.

15. JJ, November 25 and 27, December 2, 3, 4, 7, and 8; Airy, *Account,* 243–244.

23. An Absentee King

1. TJ, 33, 53.

2. Among the notes found in "Transit of Venus, 1874, Honolulu, Original Observations on scraps of paper" (RGO 59/59), Tupman has twice written "blasted fireworks" between/among the numerical data of November 16, 1874, Kalākaua's birthday. It is unclear whether Tupman intended these words to record observations or imprecations.

3. For the 1761 transit, astronomer James Short had made his observations from London in the presence of "His Royal Highness the Duke of York, accompanied by Their Royal Highnesses Prince William, Prince Henry, and Prince Frederick." To this account, Richard Proctor added in 1874, and with biting sarcasm, this comment: "We are not told whether the Duke of York actually honoured Venus by directing His Royal gaze upon her during her transit, or whether Their Other Royal Highnesses made any observations; but as Venus was under observation for about 3½ hours, we may suppose that these exalted persons did not lose the opportunity of witnessing a phenomenon so seldom seen. Venus, all unconscious of the honour, moved onwards." Proctor, *Transits of Venus,* 52. For the 1769 event, King George III responded with even greater enthusiasm, as reported thusly by Sellers:

> He commanded that an observatory be built at Richmond (now Kew), so that he too could observe the transit. The observatory was designed by Sir William Chambers, with no expense spared: a magnificent build- ing of Portland stone, surmounted by a moveable dome. It was ready by the time of the transit and was placed under the superintendence of Stephen Demainbray, a one-time itinerant lecturer on popular science. It had been Demainbray's lectures many years earlier which had kin- dled a keen interest in science in the youthful king. On the day of the transit, the King was accompanied at the telescope by Queen Charlotte and a number of other notables. Demainbray was charged with taking a note of the time, as the King observed. Strangely, although the obser- vatory, as can be imagined, was equipped with the best instruments for the purpose, the results were never published. Whether the King had considered, like the young Tycho [Brahe], that publishing was beneath the dignity of his station, or whether his reticence to go into print was for fear of submitting his efforts to scrutiny by others, we can only speculate. (Sellers, *The Transit of Venus,* 151–152)

4. When the Reciprocity Treaty was renewed in 1887, a provision was added per- mitting the United States to use Pearl Harbor as a naval base. Lili'uokalani, King Kalākaua's sister, responded to the 1887 episode by writing into her diary, first on September 25: "King told me that efforts were being made to cede pearl river to U.S.—He would resist it—"; then on September 26: "Today—a day of importance in H. History. King signed a lease of Pearl river to U. States for eight years to get R. Treaty. It should not have been done." Lili'uokalani, "Diaries" (1887), M 93, folder 117, Hawai'i State Archives. The diary entry for September 26 is cited in a discus- sion of "Reciprocity and Annexation" in Menton and Tamura, *A History of Hawaii,*

63–67.

5. Lili'uokalani, *Hawaii's Story*, 178–179.

6. Judd, *Hawaii*, 93–96; Daws, *Shoal of Time*, 201–206.

7. Lyman, *Around the Horn*, xii, 168.

8. Wright, *James Lick's Monument*, 98.

9. Letter from Lili'uokalani to Kalākaua, November 26, 1874, Hawai'i State Archives.

24. Military Fortification

1. Ship's Log, HMS *Scout*, ADM 53/10400, PRO; FJ, December 7–8; JJ, December 7–8.

2. Airy, "Instructions to Observers," part 10.

3. FJ, December 8; Memorandum (of George Forbes) of operations at Kailua, December 8, 1874, in connection with the Transit of Venus, RGO 6/267, file 8.

4. JJ, December 8.

5. James H. Wodehouse to minister of Foreign Affairs W. L. Green, December 8, 1874, Hawai'i State Archives; W. L. Green to James H. Wodehouse, December 8, 1874, FO 331/40, folios 227–229, PRO.

6. TJ, 65.

25. All Honolulu Was Awake

1. *PCA*, December 5, 1874, "Notes of the Week."

2. TJ, December 3, 4.

3. "Transit of Venus," *PCA*, December 12, 1874.

4. *Ka Nūpepa Kū'oko'a*, Honolulu, September 19 and December 5 and 12, 1874. *Ka Nūpepa Kū'oko'a* (The Independent Newspaper) was reportedly the longest-lived, most widely circulated, and most distinguished Hawaiian language newspaper ever published. It ran for sixty-six years, from 1861 to 1927, and was the only Hawaiian language newspaper actually in print in the latter part of 1874 when the transit of Venus occurred. Mookini, "The Hawaiian Newspapers."

5. "Transit of Venus," *PCA*, December 12, 1874.

6. "Transit of Venus," *PCA*, December 12, 1874.

7. Cleghorn, "Diaries," December 8, 1874.

8. Dwight Baldwin (1798–1886) had arrived in Honolulu in 1831 as a member of the

Fourth Company of American missionaries. Between late November and mid-December of 1874, this would be his only journal entry. Baldwin, "Missionary journals;" Day, *History Makers of Hawaii*, 7.

26. *Hōkūloa i Mua o ka Lā*

1. FJ, December 8.

2. FJ, December 8; Airy, *Account*, 219–220.

3. FJ, December 8; BJ, December 8; Airy, *Account*, 220–222; Forbes to Airy, December 9, 1874, RGO 6/273, leaves 546–548.

4. JJ, December 8; TJ, December 9; Airy, *Account*, 241–244.

5. This instrument was probably the 3-inch Cooke owned by Tupman. See Stories Behind the Figures (this volume), note 27.

6. NAAE for the year 1874, Appendix, 22.

7. Tupman to Cator, December 9, 1874, RGO 6/267, file 8.

8. Forbes wrote:

> It is probable that the observations of contact will be very materially supported by additional observations made with the double-image micrometer. This instrument was devised many years ago by Sir George Airy. It is the most convenient eye-piece micrometer which can be used for measuring the distance between a pair of stars, or, as in the present case, between the limbs of the sun and Venus. . . . It is easy to see that after the internal contact at ingress, and before the internal contact at egress, measurements may thus be made of the distance of Venus from the sun's limb, from which the true time of contact may be deduced, just as in the Janssen photographic method. But, besides, this double-image micrometer gives a means of estimating the true time of contact in a manner which may possibly be one of very great accuracy indeed. Consider the case of ingress two minutes before the time of true contact. From this time up to the actual contact the distance between the cusps, where the limbs of Venus and the sun meet, will diminish with very great rapidity. By turning the micrometer so that the line of junction of the half-lenses is in a line with the points of these two cusps, the distance between them may be very accurately measured. The observation may be repeated a number of times. The great rapidity with which these cusps approach, with a very slight motion of the planet, makes it probable that each of these observations will give the means of determining very closely the true time of contact. (George Forbes, "The Coming Transit of Venus," *Nature*, May 21, 1874, 49)

9. TJ, 69–70. Concerning the application of the double-image micrometer to the transit of Venus, Tupman thought that just before internal contact about six minutes of time might be devoted to measuring cusps with it, though internal contact itself should be observed without it. "Each measure with the micrometer either of cusps

or limbs," he wrote, "will, by applying the proper correction, give a determination of the time of internal contact. It must not, however, be supposed that a micrometer measure, or even the mean of several, is as good as the telescopic observation of contact. The latter admits of great precision, observers side by side generally agreeing within one or two seconds of time." Tupman, "Transit of Venus, 1874, British Observations," RGO 59/57.

Tupman's prescription failed to produce the desired result on transit day as he, like Nichol, appears to have spent too much time measuring cusps with the double-image micrometer and, consequently, after withdrawing it and inserting the eyepiece intended for the observation of contact, actually missed that observation while focusing. The time given by Tupman for his and Noble's observation of contact (3h 35m 54s) is therefore probably not precise. (Relevant criticisms by Stone can be found in chapter 32.)

Adhering to the inveterate practice still in use in 1874, the Honolulu transit of Venus party began its day at astronomical noon, local mean solar time, 10 hours and 31 minutes later than noon at Greenwich. This was a convenient habit for astronomers—and one not abandoned until the twentieth century—because it did not require that the calendar date be changed in the middle of a night's observing, as would have been the case had civil time (in which the day begins at midnight) been used. Tupman's recording of the moment of internal contact on December 8— as well as the recorded times in his journal—reflect his practice of using astronomical time rather than civil time. Airy, *Account,* 16; TJ, "Abbreviations;" Howse, *Greenwich Time,* 149.

10. RJ, December 8.

11. RJ, November 11, 13, 14.

12. The material in this section, unless otherwise noted, is taken from the TJ entry of December 8 and from Tupman's letter to Airy dated December 3, 1874 (but continuing through transit day), RGO 6/270, file 5, leaves 241–247.

13. "Some had climbed up into the trees commanding a view of our enclosure." Tupman to Airy, December 3, 1874, RGO 6/270, file 5, leaf 243.

14. Captain Cator gave the time of external contact as 3h 11m 52s and of internal contact as 3h 34m 53s. Ship's Log, HMS *Scout,* ADM 53/10400, PRO, "Remarks" of Tuesday, December 8, 1874. Cator's observations were made with a 2.8-inch telescope made by Ross, at a magnification of 70x. Airy, "Report on the Telescopic Observations of the Transit of Venus."

15. "Transit of Venus," *The Friend,* Honolulu, January 1, 1875, 2; *Aliiolani Hale,* 50; "Transit of Venus," *PCA,* December 12, 1874.

16. Tupman to Cator, December 9, 1874.

17. Tupman to Cator, December 9, 1874.

27. A Memorial in Westminster Abbey

1. "A Monument to Jeremiah Horrocks," *Nature,* July 9, 1874, 190.

2. *Westminster Abbey: Official Guide,* revised edition, 1988.

3. Newton's tribute to Horrocks is found in Book 3 of the *Principia* in the context of his discussion of the motion of the moon's nodes. He writes: "Our countryman, Horrox, was the first who advanced the theory of the moon's moving in an ellipse about the earth placed in its lower focus." Newton, *Mathematical Principles of Natural Philosophy,* 322. Flamsteed evidently held Horrocks in higher esteem than he did Newton and at one point even characterized the work that Newton had done as a mere tinkering with Horrocks' existing lunar theory. Johns, *The Nature of the Book,* 573; Chapman, "Jeremiah Horrocks," 350 n. 2.

4. Although the monument is dated December 9, 1874, it was reportedly not actually set in its place in Westminster Abbey until sometime the following year. "Jeremiah Horrocks," DNB. The description of Horrocks as "the pride and boast of British astronomy" is attributed to John Herschel. Chapman, "Jeremiah Horrocks," 333.

28. To the Top of the Mountain

1. Tupman to Cator, December 9, 1874. Although it was understood that an essential part of the expedition's efforts in Hawai'i would include the determination of the relative longitudes of some of the outer islands and that this would have been done (though perhaps not so thoroughly) had the transit observations themselves failed on December 8, Tupman had decided by early December that the local inter-island service, by steamer or schooner, was "altogether unsuited for running chronometers for [the] longitude," and he had postponed the costly chronometer runs until after the transit in case of possible failures at either Kaua'i or Hawai'i on transit day. Having realized that this task would be better undertaken by the conveniently positioned British men-of-war, by December 11 he was making arrangements for shipping the chronometers in the HMS *Tenedos.* Airy, *Account,* 30; Tupman to Airy, December 3, 1874, RGO 6/270, file 5, leaves 238–248.

2. TJ, December 9, 10.

3. The transit of Venus expedition in Hawai'i used a total of thirty-one chronometers. Of these, sixteen had been supplied by the Royal Greenwich Observatory and three each belonged to the *Tenedos* and the *Reindeer*. David Flitner, Honolulu's own chronometer expert, lent six to the expedition; and Captain Daniel Smith, Honolulu's harbormaster, lent one. Of the two remaining, one belonged to Tupman, the other to Warren De la Rue. Of these thirty-one chronometers, eighteen (the sixteen RGO, the Tupman, and the De la Rue) had been lodged on October 2 under the stage inside the 'Āpua observatory whence the transit of Venus model was observed. Early in November, two RGO chronometers went with Forbes to Kailua-

Kona and two RGO and the De la Rue were sent with Johnson to Waimea. Airy, *Account*, 31, 32.

4. Airy, *Account*, 33.

5. FJ, December 15. Barnacle's journal entry for the same date reads simply: "Tenedos arrived with 29 chronometers"—a number at variance with information given elsewhere.

6. Early on the morning of December 16, George Forbes joined Captain Van der Meulen and some officers of the ship who went to hunt wild game. This was apparently much appreciated by Forbes, who had experienced difficulty obtaining supplies of fresh meat and who thought of game birds—ducks, plovers, snipe, and geese—as "great delicacies." FJ, December 16.

7. Beaglehole, *The Journals of Captain James Cook*, vol. 3, cxlv, 507, 1,160, and 1,161.

8. FJ, December 16. Barnacle's journal entry for December 16 records merely: "Went in Tenedos to Kealakakoa [*sic*]."

9. On December 15, 1874, Kalākaua was introduced to President Grant, and three days later he was received by the houses of Congress in joint session. Daws, *Shoal of Time*, 202.

10. Daws, *Shoal of Time*, 200.

11. To Charles Darwin, Hawai'i's sagging native population was alarming—and worse. It also augured racial extinction, or so he conjectured in the 1870s in *The Descent of Man* where he wrote: "The decrease of the native population of the Sandwich Islands is . . . notorious." Between the time of Cook's arrival in 1778–1779 and the year 1872, the native population of Hawai'i had dwindled from an estimated 300,000 to fewer than 60,000—a loss in less than one century of almost 83 percent. The loss could only be explained, as Darwin had learned from Malthus, by two causes: an increase in the death rate or a decrease in the birth rate. Darwin's own explanation of Hawai'i's alarming demographics included both factors: Bloody wars, severe labor imposed on conquered tribes, and newly introduced diseases (including measles) were the probable causes, he thought, of the accelerated death rate; but a low birth rate, excited by the lessened fertility of the natives—male and female—was cited as "the most potent of all the causes" of the population decrease. Moreover, "Lessened fertility," he wrote, ". . . as in the case of the . . . Sandwich Islanders . . . is still more interesting than their liability to ill-health and death; for even a slight degree of infertility, combined with those other causes which tend to check the increase of every population, would sooner or later lead to extinction." Charles Darwin, *The Descent of Man*, 352–354.

12. Forbes to Tupman, December 9, 1874, RGO 6/273, leaves 549–551.

13. The *Tenedos* returned to Kailua-Kona on Sunday, January 3, 1875, for her third and final chronometer run to that station. Astronomers Nichol and Noble and British commissioner Wodehouse were all aboard. The ship's stay at Kailua-Kona was brief; but before it left for Honolulu the next day, January 4, Nichol—who now was Tupman's replacement in charge of the chronometers—rode to the place of Captain Cook's death and memorialization, Kealakekua Bay. Noble, who remained behind with Forbes until January 20, was to pay similar respects on Sunday, January 17, with Forbes. FJ, December 29 and January 3, 4, 17, 20; Airy, *Account*, 34.

14. Tupman to Barnacle, December 17, 1874, RGO 6/273, leaf 194.

15. Tupman to Airy, December 28, 1874, RGO 6/270, file 6, leaf 253; Tupman to Airy, January 10, 1875, RGO 6/270, file 6, leaves 256–258. Tupman's more private musings on the "mad" astronomer were equally scathing: "Mr Barnacle . . . is no manner of use here and brings daily fresh discredit on the expedition." TJ, January 11, 1875. On page 1 of Tupman's journal, where a list of the personnel at Station B (Hawai'i) is given, a note has been penciled in next to Barnacle's name that reads, "went mad."

16. On the morning of December 9, Forbes commenced building a brick pier for his meridian mark, which was finally set up on December 12 and used for the first time on December 17. Situated on a ridge to the north of his transit instrument at a distance of just under 1,230 feet (see Fig. 47), the meridian mark—which Forbes thought "likely to be tolerably permanent"—consisted of a copper plate perforated with a horizontal line of circular holes 1.875 inches apart from center to center. The mark was used to check the collimation and azimuth errors of the transit instrument, from which the distance between its holes, center to center, subtended an angle of a mere 26.23 arc seconds—less than the apparent semidiameter of Venus during the transit. The center of the meridian mark was itself but "a few inches from the true meridian"—76.6 arc seconds west of true north. In addition, Forbes observed meridional transits of the moon and of Polaris, as well as numerous stars in Cetus, Pisces, Andromeda, Aries, Sextans, Leo, Hydra, Crater, Taurus, Ursa Minor, Eridanus, Orion, Gemini, and Lepus. The determinations for longitude having been completed with the last visit of the *Tenedos* in early January, Forbes could reflect, on January 5, that his only remaining task was the determination of his latitude. To this end, he attempted to use, on January 13, a reflecting circle of his own and a mercury horizon, taking altitudes of Polaris and observing both Capella and Alpha Columbae (Phact) near the meridian. The following day, using the same reflecting circle, he took nine altitudes of the sun near noon; but, unsatisfied with the results, he pronounced the instrument "troublesome" and soon began to resort to the Sheepshanks Repeating Circle of the Royal Astronomical Society, which he found "very pleasant to work with." On January 18, 19, and 20—following a few days of cloudy, rainy weather and a Sunday outing to Kealakekua Bay with Noble on January 17—the Forbes-Noble team successfully observed numerous "circum-meridian altitudes" of the sun with the repeating circle. Airy, *Account*, 215–216; FJ, various entries from December 9, 1874 to January 20, 1875.

17. On Kaua'i, a meridian mark (consisting of two parallel vertical wooden posts) was erected on December 14 with the help of Lieutenant Wellings and Mr. Gay. About ¾ of a mile distant, the angular separation between the two posts, as seen from Johnson's transit instrument, was only a little greater than the angular breadth of the instrument's micrometer wire and permitted him to cleverly position that wire on the meridian "by seeing a thin slice of the light of the sky on either side of it." Later in the month, the moon lit up the sky, and Johnson dutifully and regularly observed it transiting his meridian. But the dark tropical skies of Waimea also yielded their token pleasures: the appearance of the zodiacal light—which Johnson described as "very brilliant"—as well as the flashing of "several meteors" (possibly the Geminids) on the night of December 11. After the *Tenedos* arrived, on December 20 and with Tupman aboard for the first of three chronometer runs connecting Waimea's longitude with Honolulu's, the ship returned—with Nichol and the chronometers—on December 23 and again, after a long absence and much bad

weather, on January 10. Still, after Johnson's sunny success on December 8, the rest was anticlimactic; and with the anxiety diminished, he found time to have Christmas dinner with Judge McBride, take some photographs, and even visit "a remarkable waterfall." Then, after dismounting and packing the transit instrument and piers and the telescope and disposing of the superfluous stores, Johnson left Kaua'i aboard the *Reindeer* on January 25 bound for Honolulu. JJ, December 9, 11, 14–21, 23, 25 and January 5, 10, 15–17; Airy, *Account*, 33–34.

18. Measured from its base on the ocean floor, Mauna Loa rises approximately 8,700 meters to sea level, continuing 4,170 meters (13,677 feet) farther to its summit.

19. FJ, January 24. Information regarding Mauna Loa is taken from Macdonald, Abbott, and Peterson, *Volcanoes in the Sea*, 60–74. Isabella Bird's discussion of her visit to Mauna Loa is given in her *Hawaiian Archipelago*, letters 28–29. Although Forbes did not name in his journal the crater he intended to visit, that it was Moku'āweoweo rather than the more distant Kīlauea is corroborated by two facts: (1) A glowing Mauna Loa summit is visible from Kona; and (2) Isabella Bird's statement (*The Hawaiian Archipelago*, letter 29, 265n) that Forbes himself informed her that he reached Moku'āweoweo when ascending Mauna Loa in 1875. Forbes returned to Honolulu aboard the *Reindeer* on February 4. TJ, February 4.

29. More Attention from the King

1. Tupman to Captain Van der Meulen, January 14, 1875, RGO 6/267, file 9. A month later, Airy, having been at least partially apprised of the assistance rendered to the transit expedition by British naval vessels, wrote to the secretary of the Admiralty:

> I have the honor to acknowledge receipt of your letter . . . of February 15, including a copy of Captain Van der Meulen's Report dated January 8; on the services which had been rendered by the 'Tenedos' to the operations of the Observers of the Transit of Venus, especially in the carriage of chronometers among the group of the Sandwich Islands. . . .
>
> The determinations of difference of longitude thus obtained between the three principal islands of the group will be of the greatest value for the scientific enterprise: for which indeed they are indispensable. And, when combined with [the] longitude of the fundamental station [at] Honolulu, which I hope to extract from the numerous lunar observations made under Captain Tupman's directions, I anticipate that they will furnish materials of very high importance for Nautical Astronomy and Hydrography. (Airy to the secretary of the Admiralty, February 17, 1875, RGO 6/267, file 8, leaves 376–377)

2. February was the month during which Tupman inspected Flitner's transit instrument and took some observations with it for the determination of its constants. "Mr Flitner," Tupman wrote with gratitude, "having rendered important & gratuitous services to the Expedition when the Chronometers were being transported to Kauai and Hawaii, I am anxious to leave him as much information as possible regarding his instrument." TJ, February 11, 14.

3. At a height of 1,540 feet and a distance of 21,218 feet from the transit instrument, the meridian mark consisted principally of two vertical posts of timber, 4 x 3 inches and 16 feet in length. A clear space of 9.94 inches between the inner surfaces of the posts subtended an angle of 8.05 arc seconds as seen from the transit instrument. Yet even at the altitude and distance selected for its placement, the center of the meridian mark was only about 10 inches east of true north. Airy, *Account,* 13–15; TJ, November 4, February 4, 6.

4. In a letter to Airy, Tupman wrote: "An earthquake occurred here yesterday morning while I was levelling the Transit Instrument. At the Hawaiian Hotel, people were much frightened, although the shocks must have been very slight. The transit piers rocked about one-eighth of an inch in an east and west direction. . . . There were 3 shocks, perhaps more." Tupman to Airy, December 28, 1874, RGO 6/270, file 6, leaf 253. In a fuller description of the incident, Tupman wrote that the first shock disturbed the bubble in the level for more than a minute; the second for a minute; and the third for many minutes. He gave December 28 as the date of the earthquake, and about 12^h to 13^h as the (sidereal) time. "Transit of Venus, 1874, Honolulu, Original Observations on scraps of paper," RGO 59/59.

5. Tupman records: "H. M. Queen Emma, accompanied by the British Commissioner, Mrs Wodehouse & party of ladies spent the evening in the observatories, looking at the Moon Etc."; and "Visitors all day—most annoying." TJ, January 14, 27. See also entry for February 2.

6. TJ, February 5, 9, 10.

7. Forbes and Johnson left Hawai'i aboard the *Tenedos* on February 6. TJ, February 6.

8. TJ, February 12, 15, 19, 22, 24, 26 and March 1.

9. Tupman estimated the sum generated by the sale to be "about £500." Tupman to Airy, April 15, 1875, RGO 6/270, file 6, leaves 266–267. Several items were purchased at the sale by Archibald Cleghorn. Cleghorn, "Diaries," March 13, 1875.

10. TJ, March 13.

11. Airy, *Account,* 36. Another ship—*Ka Moi*—would be responsible, through Messrs. Hackfield & Co., for transporting instruments and stores directly to England via Cape Horn. Tupman to Capt. Anson, HMS *Reindeer,* March 2, 1875, RGO 59/60; Tupman to Airy, April 15, 1875, RGO 6/270, file 6, leaves 266–267. *Ka Moi* left Honolulu on May 15 with seventy-three packages of astronomical instruments and other materials and arrived at Falmouth in September. RGO 6/274, file 3, leaves 229, 232.

12. TJ, March 16.

13. *PCA,* March 20, 1875, 3.

14. *PCA,* March 20, 1875, 3. The Edinburgh-born Cleghorn, who had taken a personal interest in the expedition since its arrival in September of the previous year and who was much a part of Honolulu's social scene, had dined with his fellow Scotsmen Nichol and Forbes, as well as with Captain Tupman, on earlier occasions. Cleghorn, "Diaries" entries for September 10, October 11, and October 29, 1874, and February 4 and March 18, 1875.

15. Wodehouse correspondence (to the earl of Derby?), March 9, 1875, F. O. 331/8, folio 110, PRO.

16. TJ, 120. Tupman's courtesy to the French appears consistent with the British desire, as expressed by Airy, that the 1874 pursuit of the astronomical unit be one of international scope and cooperation.

17. Airy, *Account*, 6.

18. Tupman to Airy, April 15, 1875, RGO 6/270, file 6, leaves 266–267.

30. Homeward Bound

1. TJ, February 6, 1875.

2. The party conveyed to San Francisco by the *Reindeer* consisted of Ramsden, Nichol, Noble, and Tupman, together with three sappers. They arrived at Mare Island on April 9. Tupman immediately notified Airy by telegram of the party's arrival. Both Ramsden and Nichol were immediately discharged on April 9 for passage to England. The three sappers were discharged on April 12. On April 16, Tupman and Noble left Mare Island with the chronometers, negatives, and personal baggage, and went to a hotel in San Francisco where they waited until the railway line was reported clear, excessive floods having washed away the track in the vicinity of the Green River in Wyoming. On April 29, they at last began their transcontinental journey via Salt Lake City and Chicago. Telegram, Tupman to Airy, San Francisco, April 9, 1875, RGO 6/270, file 6, leaf 265; letters, Tupman to Airy, April 15 and May 15, 1875, RGO 6/270, file 6, leaves 266–267, 268. Regarding Honolulu's longitudinal connection with San Francisco, W. D. Alexander later wrote: "During the latter half of 1884, by the courtesy of Prof. Davidson, and of the commanders of the steamers of the Oceanic Co., their chronometers were compared at every trip with the standard time at the Lafayette Park Observatory, in San Francisco, and similar comparisons were made here [in Honolulu] in order to determine the difference of longitude between the two stations. The result agrees within a second with the former determination by Major Tupman in 1874." Alexander, *Minister of the Interior—Biennial Report—1886*, Appendix F, xlvii.

3. Such a journey was made possible only six years earlier when the driving of the Golden Spike at Promontory Point, Utah, marked the completion in 1869 of the first transcontinental train route. Passing through Salt Lake City and Omaha, the train arrived in Chicago on May 6, whence Noble went on alone to New York. Tupman, being taken ill, stayed behind convalescing in Chicago but followed to New York soon thereafter and on June 16 sailed for England, arriving at Liverpool on June 27. Information on Tupman's return to England via the United States can be found in a folder labeled "Accountant-General of the Navy" in RGO 59/60.

4. Leonard Darwin was sustained on his journey across America by his sense of humor, as well as by several cards and letters of introduction. On April 21, 1875, he had addressed to someone named Jim a letter from Yosemite Valley that read, in part: "I arrived in America on [Sunday] April 11th. . . . I am fatter and balder than ever and I have a scrubby beard 3.1415962 inches long or thereabouts. Old William S. told a whopper when he said that a rose by another name would smell as sweet. This one would not if his name were not Darwin. I have been given lots of cards

and letters of introduction in San Francisco." Leonard Darwin's reported beard length is actually an (intentionally?) *incorrect* estimation of π, which should be 3.1415926(53589793 . . .). The letter quoted here is found among the papers of Leonard Darwin, LD/1/2, "Letters to my Mother, 1874–75, Transit of Venus," at the Cambridge University Library. These will hereafter be cited as DAR 239, LD/1/2. Leonard Darwin had commenced his transit-related work at Greenwich on September 15, 1873. THJ, vol. 1.

5. DAR 239: LD/1/2/5.

6. DAR 239: LD/1/2/6.

7. DAR 239: LD/1/2. The letter cited here consists of six leaves, beginning February 23, 1875 and continuing into April. The picturesque cliff described by Leonard is probably the Nu'uanu Pali, where Hawai'i's *first* king (Kamehameha the Great) legendarily performed the deed mentioned. In Newcomb's *Observations* (1881, pt. 2, sec. 5, p. 275), there is a statement by William Harkness that reads: "In company with me they sailed from Sydney for the United States upon the steamer *Mikado*, March 13, 1875." This suggests that Harkness was already aboard the *Mikado* with Darwin when it reached Honolulu—a statement seemingly at odds with Darwin's report that Harkness "came on board" there.

8. Darwin's letter reads as follows:

> I waited longer at San Francisco than I had intended—more than a week altogether—in order that two Transit of Venus men from the Sandwich Islands might have time to join me in my trip to the Yosemite, but they threw me over at the last minute, and I started off alone. I was rather glad they did on the whole as they would probably not have cared to go about as much as I did, or to walk up any of the hills. Hardly anyone thinks of walking here and the wretched horses have to pack heavier people than me up these hills, some of them over 4000 ft from the starting point. I was the first person to go up one of the mountains—the Clouds Rest—this year simply because it envolved about two hours walk up hill the regular path being blocked up with snow. I had four days in the valley which I enjoyed as much as possible, though I think the American estimate of the beauty of the views are a little exaggerated.
>
> There have been great floods on the railway, and for some time all traffic was stopped[;] in fact it had only been opened for two days before I crossed[.] In coming here our train was delayed in every possible way[:] first a train in front of us had an accident in which three men were killed—4 hours[;] then our engine broke down 2 hours; the way was bad and we had to go slowly where the floods had been—4 hours—and lastly some men took to fighting and we had to wait till the police came and locked them up. This railway travelling might be pleasant in summer when sitting outside on the platform, but now it is too cold to be enjoyable. I came across the two Transit men in the same train which made it much pleasanter. . . . My plans are to go from here [Chicago] to Washington—Philadelphia—New York—Boston and then a round trip to the [Niagara] Falls, down the St Laurence and back to N. York and then home. I was walking with one of my transit friends last night and we both confessed that if our inclinations were merely con-

sulted, we should go straight to New York and take the first steamer home and that it was only a strong sense of duty that kept us to our work. (Leonard Darwin to his mother, Chicago, May 6, 1875, DAR 239, LD/1/2)

Although Darwin does not mention by name the "two Transit of Venus men from the Sandwich Islands," that they were Tupman and Noble is substantiated by other documents: Barnacle, who left Hawai'i in January 1875, was already back in England by February; Johnson departed from Honolulu on February 6 and journeyed home via Canada; and Forbes took a trans-Asia route. Tupman and Noble, however, were in San Francisco in April 1875, from whence they journeyed eastward by train, arriving in Chicago on May 6 (the place and date of Darwin's letter to his mother) via Salt Lake (where Darwin—as he mentions in the same letter—also stopped for a day).

9. Leonard Darwin to his mother, Boston, May 15, 1875, DAR 239, LD/1/2. The "great telescope" mentioned by Darwin was the 26-inch refractor by Alvan Clark & Sons, newly received by the U.S. Naval Observatory in 1873 and partly English in origin (see chapter 11, note 3). In the observer's notebook for that instrument ("VII. 26 inch Equatorial. 1875. April 9 to July 24.") I found, during a personal visit to the USNO in June 2001, a remark for May 26 that adds a measure of plausibility to Leonard Darwin's witticism about Uranus, a remark written in the hand of Asaph Hall: "too much haze for Uranus." By 1875, four moons of Uranus had been discovered: Titania and Oberon (by William Herschel in 1787) and Ariel and Umbriel (by William Lassell in 1851). In 1877, two years after Leonard Darwin's visit, Hall, using the Clark 26-inch, discovered the two moons of Mars—Phobos and Deimos.

10. In New England, Leonard Darwin would call on the Nortons at the American Cambridge, and visit the Grays and the Sedgwicks. Leonard's brother, William Erasmus Darwin (Charles' eldest child), married in 1877 the American Sara Sedgwick, whose sister Theodora was the wife of Charles Elliot Norton, professor of Italian at Harvard (Freeman, *Darwin Pedigrees,* 53). Asa Gray (1810–1888) was the leading botanical taxonomist in America in the nineteenth century. After a brief tenure at the University of Michigan, he accepted in 1842 a professorship of natural history at Harvard. While on a visit to Europe in 1851, he had lunch with Leonard's father Charles at Kew, and by 1857 he had been let in on the secret of the trend of Charles' theory of the origin of species by natural selection. When Charles Darwin published *The Different Forms of Flowers on Plants of the Same Species* in 1877, he dedicated it to Gray "as a small tribute of respect and affection."

11. Before July passed, Tupman would be spending his entire Sundays reducing the Honolulu transit of Venus observations. THJ, vol. 3, entries for June 29, July 11, and July 25, 1875. A note on the back of page 98 of this volume states that L. Darwin returned to England on June 19, 1875. See also: RGO 6/269, file 10, leaf 239.

31. Some Challenging Correspondence

1. THJ, vol. 3, entry for October 13, 1875.

2. THJ, vol. 3, entry for October 14, 1875. Johnson replied to Tupman from Trinity College, Dublin, saying that it would take him longer than he thought to finish his reductions, disclosing that he had found some errors in the calculations and elsewhere, and suggesting that a second copy of his observations could be made if he only had the proper forms. He excused himself by noting that he did not expect any pay for such work because (as he put it), "I might have done it before this." Johnson to Tupman, October 20, 1875, RGO 6/273, leaves 470–471.

3. Airy to Johnson, November 20, 1875, RGO 6/273, leaf 474. The full text of Chapter 2, Article 1 of Airy's "Instructions to Observers" reads: "All books, papers, journals (so far as they relate to the Official Expedition), notes of observations in all stages, notes of calculations in all stages, are the property of the British Government; and are to be delivered to the Local Chief, and through him to the Head of the Enterprise if present, for deposit in the Royal Observatory, Greenwich, whenever either of these Officers shall require them, and not later than the day of landing in England."

4. Johnson to Airy, November 22, 1875, RGO 6/273, leaves 475–476; Johnson to Airy, November 27, 1875, RGO 6/273, leaf 477.

5. On March 7, 1877, Airy wrote to Johnson saying: "We are greatly in want of your Transits Vol 1 . . . and of your Zenith Distances, of which we have not a single figure. Could you send both these speedily? You will remember that it was understood in all the regulations of the Transit of Venus that observations were to be delivered up as quickly as possible after your return. Pray allow me to urge very strongly on you the necessity of attending to this matter as soon as possible." Airy to Johnson, March 7, 1877, RGO 6/273, leaf 484. On March 16, 1877, Airy again wrote to Johnson:

> The evening before last, I received two quarto copy books, marked respectively "Transit of Venus 1874 Station B3 Sandwich Islands, Latitudes and Time by Equal Altitudes of . . . [the sun's upper limb]. Observations by R. Johnson and Lieut. Welling[s]: Waimea, Atooi (Kauai)" [and] "Meteorological Journal by R. H. Wellings." And yesterday I received a small memorandum book, marked "Sextant and Circle, Waimea, Kauai {Atooi}, Sandwich Islands. R. Johnson"[.] I am obliged by your sending these, the first and third appear to contain every thing relating to latitude. But still there is wanting "The first volume of transit-reductions" (mentioned in my note of March 7) and I should further be glad to receive "The official journal." You will I am sure excuse my urgency in this matter when you consider the position in which I stand. You are responsible <u>through me</u> to the Government for the delivery of all official books (which strictly ought to have been delivered as early as possible after your return), and I am therefore responsible for seeing that every effort is made for delivering those books, and I shall be subject to severe censure if it is not done properly [emphasis in original].(Airy to Johnson, March 16, 1877, RGO 6/273, leaves 485–486)

See also: Airy to Johnson, April 10, 1877, RGO 6/273, leaf 488; and Airy to Johnson, April 14, 1877, RGO 6/273, leaf 489. Still later, questions were raised regarding Johnson's transit-related expenditures and his seeming disregard of his indebtedness to the Government. Tupman, who thought that Johnson had professed "a shabby claim . . . for two months salary while living as the guest of his brother in Canada" while returning to Britain, told the accountant general of the navy: "The accounts of Mr Richard Johnson . . . were never submitted to the Astronomer Royal or to me for examination as were those of other observers. . . . It would be a satisfaction to myself to be permitted to examine his Cash Account, but I am unable to suggest any gentle means of recovering the Balance [7 pounds and 6 pence], Mr Johnson having taken no notice of the last two or three letters I had occasion to write to him." Accountant general of the navy to Tupman, November 14, 1877, RGO 59/60; and Tupman's reply, November 16, 1877.

6. Barnacle to Airy, February 26, 1875, RGO 6/273, leaf 181.

7. Tupman to Barnacle, December 17, 1874, RGO 6/273, leaf 194; Airy to Barnacle, February 27, 1875, RGO 6/273, leaf 185.

8. Barnacle to Airy, March 6, 1875, RGO 6/273, leaves 186–187.

9. Barnacle to Airy, April 14, 1875, RGO 6/273, leaves 188–193.

10. Barnacle to Airy, May 10, 1875, RGO 6/273, leaves 196–197.

11. Airy to Barnacle, May 11, 1875, RGO 6/273, leaf 198.

12. Barnacle to Airy, November 17, 1875, RGO 6/273, leaves 204–206.

13. Airy to Barnacle, November 20, 1875, RGO 6/273, leaf 207.

14. Barnacle to Airy, November 23, 1875, RGO 6/273, leaves 208–209.

15. Barnacle to Airy, February 3, 1876, RGO 6/273, leaves 210–211.

16. Airy to Barnacle, February 7, 1876, RGO 6/273, leaves 212–213.

17. Tupman to Airy, November 6, 1875, RGO 6/270, file 7, leaf 303.

18. Tupman to Airy, February 5, 1876, RGO 6/270, file 7, leaf 325.

19. "Henry Glanville Barnacle," AC.

32. Reducing the Data

1. Airy, "Report of the Astronomer Royal to the Board of Visitors of the Royal Observatory, Greenwich," 1876, 24.

2. W. Airy, *Autobiography,* 317. See also: Airy, "Report of the Astronomer Royal to the Board of Visitors of the Royal Observatory, Greenwich," 1876, 24.

3. Tupman appears to have suffered from ill health on several post-transit occasions and was once incapacitated for three months. Airy(?), "Reduction of the Observations," 184.

4. "The longitudes of Honolulu and Rodrigues by the observations of the Moon in zenith distance, are completely reduced. These two calculations required the use of three millions of figures." Airy(?), "Reduction of the Observations," 181.

5. Airy, "On the Method."

6. A table of the more than fifty stations where the transit was "more or less" successfully observed can be found in MNRAS 36 (4): 180–181 (February 11, 1876). If one includes as "British"—as this table does—Australia, India, and the Cape of Good Hope, then the British successfully observed the transit from some twenty stations, far more than any other nation. Other successful participants included the Russians (11), Americans (8), Germans (7), French (5), Italians (1), Dutch (1), and Mexicans (1). The principal locations of the stations were Australia, India, Japan, China, Russia, Persia, Egypt, and several islands including Hawai'i, New Zealand, and Tasmania. There were, notably, no stations in Western Europe or anywhere in North or South America.

7. The agitation in the House of Commons with regard to making public the results of the 1874 transit of Venus observations actually began, apparently, as early as the summer of 1876. RGO 6/267, file 11, leaves 486–497. It was later asked if a report could be made to the House without having to wait for the calculations. F. I. Evans (Hydrographic Department, Admiralty) to Airy, April 23, 1877, RGO 6/268, file 5, leaf 346. See also Airy, *Account,* v–vi.

8. Airy, "Report on the Telescopic Observations of the Transit of Venus, 1874, made in the Expedition of the British Government, and on the Conclusion derived from those Observations," ordered by the House of Commons to be printed July 16, 1877 and hereafter referred to as the *1877 House Report.* Although the *1877 House Report* appeared under Airy's name, Tupman elsewhere claims to have done all the calculations himself. Airy essentially acknowledged as much when saying: "Under a demand from the House of Commons, a strong effort was made to finish all introductory calculations; and to effect computations of Solar Parallax, by comparing all eye-observations of ingress of Venus among themselves, and all eye-observations of egress of Venus among themselves. The operation was in fact entirely conducted by Captain Tupman, though always under my cognizance." Airy, "Report of the Astronomer Royal to the Board of Visitors of the Royal Observatory, Greenwich," 1878, 19.

9. By July 16, 1877, the *1877 House Report* had been amended to include the New Zealand observations, Airy saying:

> The strong language in which Major Palmer, R. E., [the head of the New Zealand observing team] had expressed his sense of the failure of the observations in New Zealand, induced me to state, in . . . the Report . . . that 'the observations failed totally.' On examining strictly the details of Major Palmer's report, I find that this expression is not supported. The supposed visible contacts of the limbs (to which probably Major Palmer alluded), of which there is no trustworthy observation at any station, were lost; but the phenomena preliminary to internal contact at ingress of Venus . . . were very well observed.

The *Report* then proceeded to exhibit the results of the comparison of the observations at New Zealand with those of three other stations: Hawai'i, Rodriguez, and Kerguelen. Although the combination of *ingress retarded* at Burnham, New

Zealand, with *ingress accelerated* in the Hawaiian Islands yielded a mean solar parallax of 8″.677, the mean of all three means—8″.764—showed close agreement with the previous general result, 8″.760. Airy, *1877 House Report,* Supplement.

10. The *1877 House Report* contains the following description of the various phases used in the reductions:

> At *Ingress* the observers generally perceived the sun-light refracted by the planet's atmosphere some time before internal contact, and they recorded "circular contact". . . . The next appearance is that when the planet appears just within the Sun's disc, but the light between the two limbs is very obscure; this is the first phase employed in the reductions, viz., α. After a certain interval, about 20 seconds, this light begins to clear, and observers generally think the contact is passed, this is called β. Still, however, the light between the limbs is not equal to that of the adjacent Sun's limb, and after another interval of about 20 seconds, no more shadow is seen, this is γ.
>
> Of these phases, β is the most precise. In the absence of clouds, and even through clouds not varying in density, observers agree within 3^S or 4^S. For the other phases, discordances many times greater exist.
>
> At *Egress* the first appearance of "faint shadow," or "a single fine line," is called δ; this becoming definite, or "brown haze" appearing, is called ε. When the gathering reaches its maximum intensity, and most observers record "contact," it is ζ, and probably corresponds with α of *Ingress.* There is an agreement among observers as to the phase ζ many times closer than the other phases. . . .
>
> . . . Treble weight has been given to the phases β and ζ

11. One voice that would not be silenced was that of Richard Proctor. In the third edition of his *Transits of Venus,* published in London in 1878, Proctor added a section on the "Results of the British Expedition" of 1874 and openly impugned both Airy and his recently promulgated value(s) for the AU:

> Now the net result of the British expeditions, so far as of themselves they can determine the sun's distance, is to give a solar parallax of between 8″.75 [and] 8″.76, corresponding to a mean distance of 93,375,000 miles. This is far outside the limits between which all other results show that the true distance lies. Of course Sir G. Airy considers that this result should displace all previous ones. . . . I venture to predict [however] that . . . continental and American astronomers will not be very ready to adopt the new estimate of the sun's distance; nor will British astronomers, outside official ranks. . . . It is [furthermore] worth mentioning that the results obtained from ingress observations do not agree so closely with those from egress observations as we should expect if the results of the entire series were worthy of the exaggerated confidence placed in them. It appears from Sir G. Airy's own statement that, if the ingress observations alone were taken, the sun's distance would be estimated at 93,550,000 miles, but if the egress observations alone were taken the estimated distance would be 92,395,000 miles—a rather wide discrepancy. (Proctor, *Transits of Venus,* 3rd ed., 240–241)

12. Using the parallax values and corresponding weights given in Table 5, the mean value for ingress (8″.739) checks, but the mean for egress (8″.847) does not. The

combination of those two given values, however, together with their assigned weights (10.46 for ingress, 2.53 for egress), does yield the more general value of 8".760. This discrepancy may simply be the result, therefore, of a misprint in the tabulated data contained in the *1877 House Report* rather than of any devious intent.

13. *1877 House Report*.

14. Airy, *Account*, vi.

15. Stone, "On the Telescopic Observations."

16. Stone defined "real" contact as "the phase at which the observer first perceives the formation or disappearance of any permanent connection between the limbs of *Venus* and the Sun." He went on to say: "When we come to examine the observations made in 1874 we find that the apparent contacts have not been observed at the Sandwich Islands, one of the principal stations. It would almost appear from Mr. Nichol's remarks, and those of Capt. Tupman, that the measures of the cusps were run too close to the time of contact to allow of any successful attempt to observe the apparent contacts."

17. Tupman, "Note." A value of 8".813 is only one of the many solutions realized more privately by Tupman and recorded in his "Transit of Venus 1874, Determination of the Mean Solar Parallax," RGO 59/76.

18. Tupman, "On the Mean Solar Parallax."

19. Airy, "Report of the Astronomer Royal to the Board of Visitors of the Royal Observatory, Greenwich," 1879, 19–20.

20. Airy, "Report of the Astronomer Royal to the Board of Visitors of the Royal Observatory, Greenwich," 1880, 19.

21. RGO 59/56.

22. Airy, *Account*, vi.

33. Publishing and Retiring

1. Airy to Noble, August 5, 1875, RGO 6/273, leaf 786.

2. RJ, February 6.

3. "John Walter Nichol," MNRAS 39, February 1879, 237. Information regarding Nichol's post-transit work at Greenwich can be found in THJ, vol. 3.

4. The museum was also the site of a post-transit lecture given on June 12, 1876, by S. J. Perry, the chief of the British team observing the 1874 transit of Venus from Kerguelen. Perry, "The Methods."

5. RGO 6/278, file 16, leaf 670. Here, the following particulars are disclosed regarding the stations from which came the assortment of instruments and huts lent to the South Kensington Museum: The photoheliograph instrument was from B, but its hut and/or roof was from A; the transit instrument was from E, its hut from A; the altazimuth instrument was from E, its hut from C; the equatorial and its hut (com-

plete) were both from C; and, in addition to a transit of Venus model, the clocks lent to the museum were four in number. Although nothing from station D appears to have been included, the close uniformity of the instrumentation for all stations is evident. Further information regarding the loan of the instruments to the museum can be found in RGO 6/278, leaves 652–687.

6. W. Airy, *Autobiography*, 317–318.

7. "Mr. C. E. Burton continued the measurement of the photographs until the end of April 1876, when, unable any longer to support the great strain upon his eyesight, he was compelled to abandon the work. During the seven months he was engaged upon it he made upwards of 38,000 bisections with the microscopes." Burton recovered from the strain at the Dunsink Observatory, where he acted as first assistant. Among the photographs of the actual transit measured by him were fifty square plates from Honolulu. Airy(?), "Reduction of the Observations," 182.

8. Rothermel, "Images of the Sun," 166.

9. Tupman, "On the Photographs."

10. Airy, *Account,* appendix 5, 18.

11. W. Airy, *Autobiography,* 323; Meadows, *Greenwich Observatory,* vol. 2, 46.

12. Airy, "Report of the Astronomer Royal to the Board of Visitors of the Royal Observatory, Greenwich," 1878, 19–20.

13. Rothermel, "Images of the Sun," 169. P. M. Janiczek of the U.S. Naval Observatory opines that the international effort to use the 1874 transit of Venus for the determination of the solar parallax resulted in such widespread disappointment—and not merely from the failure of photography—that by 1882 transit expeditions were sent out "principally for the reason that it was the thing to do." And even then (as has been noted by Lankford, 656), photography was not entirely abandoned. More importantly, the published American value(s) for the solar parallax derived from the 1874 transit of Venus were either "premature" or "preliminary," and the work (including the reductions) was apparently never finished. Of a four-part work entitled *Observations of the Transit of Venus, December 8–9, 1874, Made and Reduced under the Direction of the Commission Created by Congress,* part 1, "General Discussion of Results," by Simon Newcomb, was printed in 1880; of part 2, "Observations" (also edited by Newcomb), only a single copy exists as two bound volumes of page and type proofs; neither part 3, containing a discussion of the longitudes of the stations, nor part 4, containing photographic plate measures, have been found in any form. Moreover, Todd's value for solar parallax (8".883 ± 0".034) derived from the American photographs and published in 1881 contains the illuminating statement: "Hitherto no value of the solar parallax has been derived from the observations of the transit of Venus made at the American stations in 1874." Janiczek, "Remarks," 52–53, 68, 70; Todd, "The Solar Parallax."

14. Airy, "Report of the Astronomer Royal to the Board of Visitors of the Royal Observatory, Greenwich," 1880, 20; W. Airy, *Autobiography,* 331.

15. Airy, *Account,* vii.

16. W. Airy, *Autobiography,* 324.

17. George Forbes, *David Gill,* 137. Airy's letter to Gill is dated June 2, 1883.

18. Tupman's last entry in his Home Journal, dated September 27 to October 2, 1880,

reads: "Wrote the Astronomer Royal on subject of reducing the bulk of the matter originally intended, and already prepared, for publication."

19. Airy, "On the Method." Simon Newcomb expressed a like opinion when he wrote:

> If the observations on the transit of 1874 had been made in the same way as those of the transit of 1769, they could be very speedily worked up, and we should soon expect to see the solar parallax deduced from the combination of them all. But the investigation and measurement of the photographs is so laborious an operation that the American results can hardly be published before 1878. The definitive value of the parallax must then be deduced, not from the observations of any one nation, but so far as possible from the combination of those of all nations. We must, therefore, wait for the final publication and discussion of all the observations before the definitive value of the parallax can be announced. (Newcomb, *Popular Astronomy*, 193)

20. Airy, "On the Inferences." To what extent the final numbers given by Airy in this work are truly the results of his own labor may be subject to some skepticism. Among a "List of Publications written wholly or in part by G. L. Tupman" (in RGO 59/62), Tupman has written: "The Astronomer Royal's paper in the *Monthly Notices* on the Inferences for the value of the Solar Parallax from the British Observations of the Transit of Venus, all the Calculations were made by me."

21. The value for solar parallax given by Airy in 1877 was further refined before the close of the nineteenth century. In 1895, Simon Newcomb's discussion of the observations of the transits of Venus of 1761, 1769, 1874, and 1882 yielded a value of 8".794; but Richard Proctor's earlier statement of its value (see the note immediately following this) had already been in close agreement with this, and the value adopted by international agreement (Paris, 1896) turned out to be exactly that given by him—8".80.

During the first half (and more) of the twentieth century, a value of 8".80 was adopted, but the number continued to be fine-tuned. By 1961 one author (de Vaucouleurs), having examined a variety of methods—trigonometric, dynamical, optical, and radio—used in the determination of the solar parallax, concluded by assigning it a value of 8".7979 ± 0".0002. De Vaucouleurs further found that the average probable error of individual determinations of the solar parallax was historically about 1" in 1700, 0".1 in 1800, and 0".01 in 1900, and he opined that because the consistency and accuracy of solar parallax determinations increases tenfold per century, it would drop to 0".001 by the year 2000.

But by the middle of the twentieth century, advances in technology had already made it possible to determine astronomical values to a much higher precision than before. The introduction of electronic computers, the development of radar astronomy, and the launching of artificial satellites and space probes had made it quite clear that the astronomy of the second half of the twentieth century could not be based on the achievements of the nineteenth. Already among the efforts used to pinpoint the solar parallax were: the close-to-Earth approach (in the 1930s) of the minor planet Eros; radio echoes from the planet Venus after its close-to-Earth approach in 1958 and 1959; and observations of the Pioneer 5 space probe in 1960. So by the time the International Astronomical Union (set up in 1919) held a symposium in Paris in 1963 on "The System of Astronomical Constants," it was already understood that such a system of constants was wanted that would satisfy the requirements of geophysics and space research, as well as of classical astronomy, and serve as a common link among these disciplines. Among the quantities recommended by the symposium to be treated as fundamental constants was the ratio of the astronomical unit to the meter. Yet even as the 1960s drew to a close, American doctoral candidates in astronomy were still trying to determine the value of the AU and the solar parallax by modern means: Yale awarded two Ph.D.'s in 1968 for studies devoted to this very subject.

A recently given value for the AU in meters is $1.49597870 \times 10^{11}$ m (= 92,955,807 miles); and for the solar parallax, 8".794148 (= the Earth's equatorial radius ÷ 1AU). Though the astronomical unit continues to be roughly defined as the mean distance separating the sun from the Earth, it is more precisely defined as the semimajor axis of the orbit around the sun of the Earth-moon barycenter, neglecting planetary perturbations. De Vaucouleurs, *The Astronomical Unit of Distance;* Wilkins, "The System of Astronomical Constants;" Bishop, *Observer's Handbook 1995,* 16; Hoffleit, *Astronomy at Yale,* 198–199.

22. Richard Proctor's adversarial posture seems to have softened as the years passed. His earlier criticisms of Airy, as they appeared in the third edition of his *Transits of Venus,* were expunged from the fourth edition of the same book, printed in 1882, though his brief preface remained challenging: "The estimates now regarded as probably nearest the truth assign to the sun a distance of about 92,885,000 miles, corresponding to a mean equatorial long horizontal solar parallax of 8".80. It remains to be seen whether observations made on the approaching transit [of December 6, 1882] will modify this value." Proctor, *Transits of Venus,* 4th ed., 1882. See also: Clerke, *History of Astronomy,* 236–237.

23. Proctor, *Transits of Venus,* 231–232.

24. Airy to the hydrographer of the Admiralty, October 10, 1868, RGO 6/267, file 1.

34. Reaffirmations

1. Sousa's "Transit of Venus March" premiered in Washington in 1883 on the occasion of the unveiling of a statue of Joseph Henry (1797–1878), the American physicist and first secretary of the Smithsonian Institution and, as president of the National Academy of Sciences, the man responsible for the proper observations by American participants of the 1874 transit. It is not known whether the Washington-born Sousa (1854–1932), whose life encompassed both nineteenth-century transits, witnessed either of them: The first, in 1874, was not visible from Washington; the second, in 1882, was. Somewhat of a celebrity in his own right—and, by at least one account, a Mason with possible interests in astrology—Sousa seems to have befriended several other historical figures of his day, Thomas Edison and Charlie Chaplin among them. But musical, not literary, composition remained his talent: His third and last novel, *The Transit of Venus* (1919), never enjoyed great popularity, whereas his "Stars and Stripes Forever" is now identified as the national march of the United States. Bierley, *The Works of John Philip Sousa,* 90, 189–190; Ovason, *The Secret Architecture of Our Nation's Capital,* 15–22, 193.

2. "Leis; Their Variety and Change," HAA for 1922, 90.

3. "Cook's Monument at Kealakekua," HAA for 1912, 69. Regarding the later trans-fer from Ernest Wodehouse to the British government of the title to the site of Cook's Monument, see the *Honolulu Star-Bulletin,* January 4, 1939, 4.

4. A photograph bearing the caption "Kalakaua and Liliuokalani Visit the Cook Monument" appeared in the *Honolulu Advertiser* on August 12, 1928, together with a statement that King Kalākaua had visited the monument sometime in the 1870s on Kamehameha Day (June 11).

5. Crowe, *The Extraterrestrial Life Debate,* 372; Armstrong, *Around the World with a King,* 13; "King Kalakaua's Tour Round the World," Honolulu: P. C. Advertiser Co., October 1881, 13–14. England was one of many countries visited during this trip by King Kalākaua, the first reigning monarch of any nation to travel around the world.

6. Warner, *Alvan Clark & Sons,* 57–58, 76, 93; Fraser, "Diary;" Wright, *James Lick's Monument,* 87, 95, 98; Osterbrock, Gustafson, and Unruh, *Eye on the Sky,* 42. In a letter dated November 22, 1880, and addressed to the president of the Lick Trust (Capt. Richard S. Floyd), King Kalākaua wrote of the Lick Observatory: "Something of the kind is needed here very much but we have so few people who take interest in scientific matters. Everybody is bent upon making money on sugar and the all mighty <u>dollar</u>" (emphasis in original). Kalākaua's original letter is in the Bancroft Library at the University of California at Berkeley.

7. "Interest in Venus transits for determining the solar parallax waned after 1874 . . . [as] the years between 1874 and 1882 saw preference being shifted to other methods for determining the parallax. By the time of the 1882 event, the level of urgency had declined to the point where expeditions were sent principally for the reason that it was the thing to do." Janiczek, "Remarks," 68.

8. George Forbes, *David Gill.* Forbes gives (p. 193) a mean solar distance of 92,876,000 miles and a corresponding horizontal equatorial parallax of 8".802 as Gill's definitive values. The lasting significance of these values has been acknowl-edged in Krisciunas' *Astronomical Centers of the World* (p. 195), where Gill is called "the most significant Astronomer Royal at the Cape." An engaging story of Gill's astronomical adventures at Mauritius, Ascension, and the Cape of Good Hope can be found in Fernie, *The Whisper and the Vision,* chapter 3. An alternative to Forbes' book-length biography of Gill is in the DSB.

9. DAR 239, LD/1/6/10, letter from Leonard Darwin to his mother, December 10, 1882. The year 1882 was marked by three major events in Leonard's life: his father's death, his marriage to Elizabeth Fraser, and his transit of Venus expedition to Australia.

10. In May 1878, the death of Oxford's Robert Main left the position of Radcliffe Observer vacant. Candidates to fill the position were Gill, Stone, Christie, Pogson, and Tupman. The trustees gave the appointment to Stone—leaving a vacancy at the Cape of Good Hope, to which Gill then succeeded. In 1881, Christie replaced Airy as Astronomer Royal. George Forbes, *David Gill,* 100–102.

11. Among his notes regarding the 1882 expedition, Tupman has written: "It will be remembered that the Expedition in 1874 under Major Palmer R. E. [with Leonard Darwin in the observing party] was located near Christchurch. Finding the piers and wooden observatories left by him in perfect condition, I decided to reoccupy his

site at Burnham, some 18 miles from Christchurch, on the Southern Railway." Tupman, "Transit of Venus 1882: Account of the Expedition to New Zealand," RGO 59/79, pt. 1.

12. HAA for 1882, 4; *HG,* December 13, 1882; *Aliiolani Hale,* 50; Daws, *Shoal of Time,* 218.

13. Howse, *Greenwich Time,* 120–121.

14. "Standard Time and Local Time," HAA for 1897, 7.

15. In 1874, having eagerly anticipated the arrival of the British transit of Venus expedition, Alexander had made his own calculations of the times of external and internal contact and had set up equipment at Punahou School (where he had been an erstwhile teacher of astronomy) so that teachers and students there might observe the phenomenon. He also visited the 'Āpua observatory and even corresponded with Tupman over longitudinal matters several years subsequent to the captain's departure from Honolulu. *Aliiolani Hale,* 50; TJ, January 23. In a letter dated April 19, 1878, Alexander wrote to Tupman from Makawao, Maui, saying:

> I cannot thank you sufficiently for the valuable information which you have furnished us, and which will be of immediate service to our Survey. After carefully connecting your transit station and meridian mark with our system of triangulation, we found that our previous azimuths had been in error 2". . . . We will consider it a great favor if you will furnish us the differences of longitude between your observatory at Honolulu and your stations at Waimea, Kauai, and Kailua, Hawaii, respectively, as determined by your chronometric expeditions. By so doing you can render an important service to our Survey.

Tupman soon supplied the requested information, giving the difference of longitude between the Honolulu and Kailua stations as 7 minutes 24.53 seconds and that between the Honolulu and Waimea stations as 7 minutes 13.48 seconds. Tupman's response included in addition a corroboration of the pretransit insight of George Forbes with regard to the need for refinement of the lunar data given in the *Nautical Almanac,* for when Alexander wrote "The difference between your final result for longitude and the preliminary determination, I imagine is due to the difference between the predicted places of the Moon as given in the Nautical Almanac and the true places as actually observed at Greenwich and other European observatories," Tupman replied, "You are quite right in supposing that the difference between the preliminary Longitude of our Transit Station in Honolulu and the final adopted Longitude was due to the errors of the Lunar Tables. Those errors in 1874-5 were on the average about 0^S.5 of R. A. which would be equivalent to about 13^S of Longitude." "Honolulu—Chronometers—Longitude," RGO 59/60, letters of April 19, 1878 (Alexander to Tupman), and June 11, 1878 (Tupman to Alexander).

16. Alexander, "The Meridian Conference," v.

17. Biographical information on Adams can be found in Harrison, *Voyager in Time and Space,* and in AC. Letters to Adams from both George Airy and Richard Proctor regarding transit of Venus matters are preserved at the St. John's College Library, Cambridge.

18. "I am perfectly satisfied with the results of our Congress at Washington in which I took a more prominent part than I expected to do" (emphasis in original). J. C.

Adams to Francis Bashforth, from the observatory, Cambridge, November 21, 1884, ref. 4/26/4, St. John's College Library, Cambridge.

19. *International Conference.* The seven resolutions of the conference and how the participating nations voted on each of them are summarized in Howse, *Greenwich Time,* 138–151.

20. Alexander, "The Meridian Conference," x, xi.

21. In 1896, standard time was established in Hawai'i. It was 10 hours 30 minutes behind Greenwich Time and was based on the meridian central to the island group at 157° 30'. Lyons, *History of the Hawaiian Government Survey,* 17–18.

35. A Meeting in Siberia

1. George Forbes' "Dynamo-Electric Machinery" appeared in the December 1884 issue of the *Journal of the Franklin Institute.* The same *Journal* (vol. 132, no. 4, October 1891, p. 320; and vol. 132, no. 6, December 1891, p. 480) records Forbes' election in 1891 as an honorary member of the Franklin Institute. Of the National Conference of Electricians that also met in Philadelphia in September 1884, and of Forbes' attendance thereat, see the *Report of the Electrical Conference at Philadelphia in September, 1884,* 3–10.

2. TJ, February 6.

3. Forbes to Airy, May 29, 1874, RGO 6/273, leaves 536–537.

4. Among the Russian 1874 transit of Venus observers were those stationed in Yokohama, Habarowka, Jalta (Yalta), Kiachta (Kyakhta), Nertschinsk (Nerchinsk), Orianda, Port Possuet, Tschita (Chita), and Wladiwostok (Vladivostok). MNRAS 36 (4): 179–181, (February 11, 1876).

5. Airy to Forbes, May 30, 1874, RGO 6/273, leaf 538.

6. The account of George Forbes' journey home via Siberia is taken from his own 47-page, handwritten, first-person narrative, composed from memory twenty-two years after the events had taken place—that is, in 1897—when he was forty-eight years of age. Forbes' manuscript is now held among the George Forbes Papers, Box 11, no. 12, University of St. Andrews Library, Scotland.

7. Alatau Tamchiboulac Atkinson (1848–1906) was born on the Kirghiz steppes of Siberia when his English parents were making an exploration trip. Educated at Rugby School in England, he came to Hawai'i in 1868 and subsequently became editor of the *Hawaiian Gazette* (in 1881) and inspector general of public schools (in 1887). He served in the House of Representatives in 1898, the year that Hawai'i was annexed by the United States. Atkinson Drive, in Honolulu, is named in his honor. Day, *History Makers of Hawaii,* 6; Pukui, Elbert, and Mookini, *Place Names of Hawaii,* 14. Forbes writes in his narrative that he again saw Atkinson in Honolulu "two years ago"—that is, in or about 1895—meaning that he returned to Hawai'i at least once after the 1874 transit of Venus. Although he was in New Zealand in 1896 for his work at Huka Falls and may therefore have passed through Hawai'i just

prior to that time, further documentation of his return visit(s) to Hawai'i has not been discovered.

8. Forbes writes: "No European traders were then allowed in Pekin, but I found a Dane named Kieralph [?] who helped me to gain access to places where no European had ever been, even inside the Temple of Heaven, now burnt, and I photographed these places. For although there were no Kodaks in those days and we generally used the wet collodion process I luckily had with me some Liverpool dry plates as they were called by which you could get a picture by exposing in a good light for 3 minutes."

9. A verst is a Russian unit of linear measure equal to about 3,500 feet, or 2/3 mile.

10. Forbes to Airy, September 2, 1875, RGO 6/273, leaves 558–559.

11. Josef Szlenker to George Forbes, February 1876, George Forbes Papers, Incoming Correspondence, 1876, no. 2, St. Andrews University Library.

Appendix A. Measuring the Earth

1. Heath, *Greek Astronomy*, 121–123.

2. Assuming that one stade is equivalent to approximately one-tenth of a mile, Posidonius' figure for the Earth's circumference would be 24,000 miles—very close to the true value.

3. Heath, *Greek Astronomy*, 110.

4. Heath believes Eratosthenes' estimate to be remarkably accurate—more accurate than Posidonius'. Berry, however, gives a more cautious interpretation depending on the value assigned to the stade. Berry, *History of Astronomy*, 40.

5. Bryan, *Stars over Hawaii*, 41–42.

6. Like the moon, the sun was represented in Hawaiian myth either as the habitation of a god who descends from the sky to live on Earth in human form or as the divine body of a god who is worshipped by his descendants. Thus we are told: "At noon when the body casts no shadow the full strength of the sun passes into its worshiper. Ka la i ka lolo (the hour of triumph, or, literally, the sun on the brain) it is called." Beckwith, *Hawaiian Mythology*, 85.

Appendix C. The Circumstances of a Transit of Venus

1. Meeus, "The Transits of Venus;" Maor, *June 8, 2004: Venus in Transit*, 51–66.

Appendix D. Geometry and the Astronomical Unit

1. For Proctor's explanation of what he calls the *direct method,* see his *Transits of Venus,* 93–96.

2. Proctor, *Transits of Venus,* 101.

Stories Behind the Figures

1. For a characterization of European universities as "ecclesiastical corporations" where both moral philosophy and natural philosophy (natural science) were subservient to theology, and where apprentices (students) "neither are taught, nor always can find any proper means of being taught, the sciences," see Adam Smith, *The Wealth of Nations,* bk. 5, chap. 1, pt. 3, art. 2.

2. For a discussion of Bacon's "Great Instauration," see Tiles and Tiles, *Historical Epistemology,* 24–36.

3. The *Philosophical Transactions* in due course was publishing scientific papers on a bewildering assortment of subjects. More than two dozen papers would appear in the *Transactions* on the 1761 transit of Venus alone, and by the middle of the following century, it would publish more than five thousand papers on subjects ranging from mathematics to acoustics, chemistry to mineralogy, and anatomy to zoology—including 206 papers on optics and 621 on astronomy. Weld, *History of the Royal Society,* 19n, 565.

4. Halley, "De Visibili."

5. Halley, "Methodus Singularis."

6. "It has long been recognized that central to the Society's success (such as it was) was its publishing record—a record encompassing not just the first 'scientific' journal, the *Philosophical Transactions,* but the invention of the experimental paper, and above all the successful production of Newton's *Principia.*" Johns, *The Nature of the Book,* 466.

7. Among the many instruments mentioned by Sprat were these:

> An Instrument for finding a second of Time by the Sun . . . several Quadrants. . . . A new Instrument for taking Angles by reflection . . . which is of great use for making exact Observations at Sea. A new kind of Back-staff for taking the Suns altitude. . . . A Hoop of all the fix'd Stars in the Zodiac. . . . A Copernican Sphere, representing the whirling Motion of the Sun, and the Motion of the several Planets. . . . Many new wayes of making Instruments, for keeping time very exactly, both with Pendulums, and without them: whereby the intervals of time may be measur'd on the Land, and Sea. . . . An Instrument for grinding Optick-glasses: a double Telescope: several excellent Telescopes of divers lengths . . . with a convenient Apparatus for the managing of them: and

several contrivances in them for measuring the Diameters, and parts of the Planets, and for finding the true position, and distance of the small fix'd Stars, and Satellites. (Sprat, *History of the Royal Society*, 246–250)

At least some of this work was likely encouraged, if not recompensed, by Charles II, who, Sprat tells us (p. 150), "has been most ready to reward those, that shall discover the Meridian [i.e., the longitude]."

8. Weld, *History*, vol. 2, 566–572. In honor of the Royal Society, Cook had named the islands that neighbored his 1769 transit of Venus observing site at Tahiti the Society Islands. Buck, *Explorers of the Pacific*, 26.

9. Howse, *Greenwich Time*, 27–28.

10. Howse, *Greenwich Time*, 41, 42.

11. NAAE for the year 1874, 538.

12. Wilson and Fiske, *Appletons' Cyclopedia*, 388. The letters to Airy from Sands are dated April 17, 1872, and March 19, 1873, and are found in RGO 6/271, file 15, leaves 710–712 and 722–724.

13. Forbes, *David Gill.* Forbes' description of his "shed" as "a hermit's library in a pleasant grove" together with a mention of his two visits to South Africa are found on page viii. Comments regarding Gill's working in the "shed" are given on pages viii and 352–353.

14. Clerke, *History of Astronomy*, 235; George Forbes, "The Coming Transit of Venus," *Nature*, May 14, 1874, 28.

15. George Forbes, "The Coming Transit of Venus," *Nature*, May 14, 1874, 28–29.

16. "Janssen, Pierre Jules Cesar," DSB.

17. Bird, *The Hawaiian Archipelago*, 23.

18. Airy, *Account*, 20–30.

19. Airy, *Account*, 7.

20. The huts that sheltered other instruments, including the altazimuth and the photoheliograph, were similarly stenciled. Tupman, "Transit of Venus. List of Government Stores for all Stations," RGO 59/58, pp. 9, 13, 37.

21. The rotation of the Earth from west to east, and the consequent passage of successive stars across the observer's meridian from east to west, provides a natural clock by which a mechanical clock can be accurately set. At the instant a particular star, called a *clock star*, crosses (transits) the meridian, the clock can be set to 0 and other clocks (or watches, or chronometers) can be similarly set, checked, and regulated. Because the difference between local time thus established (at the observer's meridian) and Greenwich Time (at the prime meridian) can be translated directly into a difference in longitude (4 minutes of time = 1° of longitude), and because longitudinal determinations were critical to the success of the transit of Venus method for finding the AU, much attention was given to accurate determinations of time at the various observing stations.

About clock stars, Tupman wrote: "Certain stars known as Greenwich clock stars have had their places determined with consummate accuracy, and they continue to be observed more frequently than any other stars (excepting a few close polars) for the express purpose of rating clocks. They are chosen in the Equatorial zone of the heavens, most of them with less than 30° declination, for the sake of rapidity of motion across the field of the transit instrument." Tupman, "Transit of Venus, 1874, British Observations," RGO 59/57, pt. 5 ("Transit"), 32.

22. Tupman, "Transit of Venus, 1874, British Observations," RGO 59/57, pt. 5 ("Transit"), 4; Airy, *Account,* 9–15. One author has described the three corrections that must be applied to a transit instrument as follows:

> If the pivots are not due east and west, but slightly north of east and south of west, stars north of the zenith will be seen after the time of transit, while those south will be observed to transit early. By observing stars both north and south of the zenith, and plotting the results on a graph, these errors, known as azimuth errors, can be detected and the appropriate corrections applied. If the east pivot is lower than the west pivot, the telescope is tilted towards the east and all stars, north or south, will be observed to transit early. This level error is measured by means of a spirit level which is placed astride the pivots or by nadir observations in a bowl of mercury. The collimation error is caused when the optical axis of the telescope is not at right angles to the axis of the pivots; this is eliminated by reversing the telescope on its bearings. (Howse, *Greenwich Observatory,* 32)

23. This clock had undergone protracted tests at the Royal Observatory under very demanding variations of temperature, for which the zinc-and-steel pendulum was built to compensate, and its performance was excellent. At Honolulu, it was mounted on a tripod of mahogany and iron that rested upon three stakes driven into the ground. Though the pendulum's suspension spring was changed in early November 1874, only a month before transit day, the clock remained remarkably accurate, to within less than 1 second of time, from November 1874 to February 1875. Airy, *Account,* 9, 108–112.

24. Dent No. 2013 was used in tandem with Noble's observations at the Dolland altazimuth. TJ, 72. But there was another transit of Venus clock in Hawai'i that had by 1874 already acquired its own distinctive history. This clock (by Earnshaw), which was with Richard Johnson on Kaua'i for the transit, was visiting the Islands for the second time. Having been purchased by the Board of Longitude in 1791, it had sailed to Hawai'i with astronomer William Gooch aboard the *Daedalus.* After Gooch's murder on O'ahu, it was transferred to the *Discovery* (Capt. George Vancouver) and returned to Greenwich in 1795—only to be back in Hawai'i in 1874. It has since passed into private hands. Something of the history of the various transit of Venus instruments, including the Dent clocks, can be learned from Howse, *Greenwich Observatory.*

25. Airy, *Account,* 18–20.

26. Such an observing seat had reportedly been made for each telescope. Tupman to Airy, December 3, 1874, RGO 6/270, file 5, leaf 241.

27. A third telescope, of 3-inch aperture—also made by Cooke and owned by Tupman—was brought to Honolulu, but being the most inferior of the available instruments, it probably saw but limited use. A fourth telescope—this one made by Dolland—was used by Noble; though mounted on a simple tripod and having an aperture of only about 3.5 inches, its focal length approached 6 feet and it was capable of motion in both vertical and horizontal planes. All four telescopes were fitted

with a special apparatus for observing the sun: a double-image micrometer, by Messrs. Troughton and Simms. Airy, *Account,* 38–39, 41, 59, 62. The Dolland telescope used by Noble is variously described as having had an aperture of 3½, 3⅝, and 3¾ inches. See: TJ, 67, 70.

28. Yale Misc. MSS, Group No. 1258, Box 12, Folder 478. The seventeen letters include six from Bernice Pauahi, three from Lot Kamehameha, three from Alexander Liholiho, three from William Lunalilo, one from Emma Rooke, and one from Mary Kepaʻaʻāina. Subjects discussed in the letters include: surveying, a wedding, a school examination, the plotting of a field, a celebration of Hawaiian independence, music, politics and religion, the improved Pali Road, measles, deaths in Honolulu, California gold, and the ruinous effect of heavy rain on adobe.

29. Lyman, "Hawaiian Journals." On Thursday, August 27, 1846, Lyman reports: "Making Sundial for Bro. Paris." His journal records the following day: "Finished the Sundial and made a meridian line by which to adjust it."

30. Information about the transit of Venus monument at Huliheʻe Palace (including a copy of a letter to Mrs. Timothy Montgomery, curator of the palace, from James M. Dunn, surveyor, State of Hawaiʻi, dated 11 October 1961) was kindly provided by Marjorie Erway of Kailua-Kona.

31. HAA for 1912, 68.

32. Richard Hodgson to Airy, May 22, 1873, RGO 6/277, file 15, leaves 719–720; Airy, *Account,* 213–223 (esp. 222).

33. JJ, December 15.

34. In 1888, fourteen years after the transit of Venus, E. D. Preston of the U.S. Coast and Geodetic Survey erected a pier at Waimea for the determination of latitude and gravity. His pier was located only 11.8 feet due East of Johnson's transit pier. In 1903–1904, W. D. Alexander occupied and reestablished Preston's station, known as the Waimea Latitude Station. In 1910, O. B. French recovered what presumably were the remains of Johnson's transit pier and reestablished the Waimea Latitude Station therefrom. The station was again reestablished in 1917 by Messrs. Thrum and Evans in their survey of Waimea Village, and was again marked in 1928 by R. M. Towill. By this time, a tradition had arisen that Captain Cook himself—who had landed at Waimea in 1778—had made observations near this place, and a mark 169.72 feet from the station, in azimuth 197° 18′ 30″, was now being called "Cook's Arrow." Towill, in reestablishing the Waimea Latitude Station in 1928, tied it to "Cook's Arrow"—possibly the arrow made by Johnson and marked "c" on Gay's map. But in 1966, "Cook's Arrow" was recovered again, a proper 169.8 feet from the station, but this time in azimuth 277° 19′ 38″.2 (measured from south)—suggesting arrow "b" on the Johnson-Gay chart. Tax maps for the Territory of Hawaiʻi, which in the 1930s continued to show the "Transit of Venus" site, led Rebecca Nadler and the author in September of 1993 to the Waimea hillside, where a small concrete pier bearing the inscription "Transit of Venus" and dated "March 23, [19]32," was found. But thick and forbidding vegetation had by then concealed the last vestiges of whatever arrow(s) remain on the hillside above Waimea, and none were seen. (Information regarding "Cook's Arrow" and the Waimea Latitude Station was graciously provided by Donald Oyama, Survey Division, Department of Accounting and General Services, State of Hawaiʻi.)

35. In his journal (TJ, p. 71) Tupman has written: "Between the two contacts [external and internal] 12 square plates were exposed A 1 to 6 and B 1 to 6. After second contact 48 plates were exposed all more or less good, but damaged by the 'boiling'." The photograph shown here—labeled C.1—must therefore be the first one taken after internal contact had passed.

36. BDAS, 117. For a detailed account of William Harkness' involvement in transit of Venus matters, see Dick, *Sky and Ocean Joined*, 238–273.

37. Medcalf, *Hawaiian Royal Orders.*

38. Meadows, "Airy and After;" Satterthwaite, "Airy's Transit Circle."

Bibliography

· · · · ·

Airy, George Biddell. *Popular Astronomy: A Series of Lectures Delivered at Ipswich*. 6th ed. rev. London: Macmillan, 1868.

————. "Report of the Astronomer Royal to the Board of Visitors of the Royal Observatory, Greenwich." Annual reports for the years 1871, 1872, 1873, 1874, 1875, 1876, 1878, 1879, and 1880.

————. "British Expeditions for the Observation of the Transit of Venus, 1874, December 8: Instructions to Observers." May 4, 1874. This thirteen-part set of instructions can be found in its entirety among the Report[s] of the Astronomer Royal, 1871–1881, RGO 17/3.

————. "On the Means Which Will Be Available for Correcting the Measure of the Sun's Distance, in the Next Twenty-Five Years." MNRAS 17:7 (May 8, 1857): 208–221.

————. "On the Preparatory Arrangements Which Will Be Necessary for Efficient Observation of the Transits of Venus in the Years 1874 and 1882." MNRAS 29:2 (December 11, 1868): 33–43.

————. "Copy of a Letter from the Astronomer Royal to the Secretary of the Admiralty Expressing His Views on Certain Articles Which Had Appeared in the Public Newspapers in Regard to the Approaching Transit of Venus." MNRAS 33:5 (March 14, 1873): 269–273.

————. "Preparations for the Observation of the Transit of Venus, 1874, December 8–9." MNRAS 35:1 (November 13, 1874): 1–10.

————. "On the Method to be used in Reducing the Observations of the Transit of Venus, 1874, December 8." MNRAS 35:5 (March 12, 1875): 277–288.

————(?). "Reduction of the Observations of the Transit of Venus, December 8, 1874." MNRAS 37:4 (February 1877): 181–184.

————. "Report on the Telescopic Observations of the Transit of Venus, 1874, Made in the Expedition of the British Government, and on the Conclusion Derived from Those Observations." Ordered by the House of Commons to be printed July 16, 1877.

————. "On the Inferences for the Value of Mean Solar Parallax and Other Elements Deducible from the Telescopic Observations of the Transit of Venus, 1874, December 8, Which Were Made in the British Expedition for the Observation of that Transit." MNRAS 38:1 (November 1877): 11–16.

————, ed. *Account of Observations of the Transit of Venus, 1874, December 8, Made under the Authority of the British Government: And of the Reduction of the Observations.* Printed for Her Majesty's Stationery Office, 1881.

Airy, Wilfrid, ed. *Autobiography of Sir George Biddell Airy.* Cambridge: Cambridge University Press, 1896.

Alexander, W. D. "The Meridian Conference." Appendix to the *Report of the Minister of Foreign Affairs*. April 1886.

————. *Minister of the Interior—Biennial Report—1886*. Appendix F.

————. "A Brief Account of the Hawaiian Government Survey, Its Objects, Methods and Results." Honolulu: Bulletin Steam Print, 1889.

Aliiolani Hale: A Century of Growth and Change. N.p.: Frost and Frost, 1977.

Allen, Richard Hinckley. *Star Names: Their Lore and Meaning*. New York: Dover, 1963.

Andrade, Edward Neville de Costa. *A Brief History of the Royal Society*. London: Royal Society, 1960.

Armstrong, William N. *Around the World with a King*. Rutland, VT: Charles E. Tuttle, 1977.

Ashbrook, Joseph. "The Reputation of Father Hell." *Sky & Telescope* (April 1961): 213–214.

————. "Father Perry's Expedition to Kerguelen Island." *Sky & Telescope* (June 1966): 340–341.

Baldwin, Dwight. "Missionary Journals." Mission Houses Museum Library, Honolulu.

Beaglehole, J. C., ed. *The Journals of Captain James Cook on His Voyages of Discovery*. Vol. 3. *The Voyage of the* Resolution *and* Discovery, *1776–1780*. Cambridge: Published for the Hakluyt Society at the University Press, 1967.

————. *The Life of Captain James Cook*. Stanford, CA: Stanford University Press, 1974.

Beckwith, Martha. *Hawaiian Mythology*. Honolulu: University of Hawai'i Press, 1970.

Bennett, J. A. "Practical Mathematics in the Age of Discoveries." Four wall charts published by the Whipple Museum of the History of Science, University of Cambridge (1992?).

Berry, Arthur. *A Short History of Astronomy from Earliest Times through the Nineteenth Century*. New York: Dover, 1961. Originally published by John Murray in 1898.

Bierley, Paul E. *The Works of John Philip Sousa*. Columbus, OH: Integrity Press, 1984.

Bird, Isabella L. *The Hawaiian Archipelago: Six Months among the Palm Groves, Coral Reefs and Volcanoes of the Sandwich Islands*. 7th ed., 10th printing. Rutland, VT: Charles E. Tuttle, 1992.

Bishop, Roy L., ed. *Observer's Handbook, 1993*. Toronto: University of Toronto Press, 1992.

————. *Observer's Handbook, 1995*. Toronto: University of Toronto Press, 1994.

Brooke, Christopher N. L. *A History of the University of Cambridge*. Vol. 4: 1870–1990. Cambridge: Cambridge University Press, 1993.

Bryan, E. H., Jr. *Stars over Hawaii*. Hilo, HI: Petroglyph Press, 1955, 1977.

Buck, Peter H. *Explorers of the Pacific: European and American Discoveries in Polynesia*. Honolulu: Bernice P. Bishop Museum, 1953.

Burchfield, Joe D. *Lord Kelvin and the Age of the Earth*. Chicago: University of Chicago Press, 1975, 1990.

Burkhardt, Frederick, and Sydney Smith, eds. *The Correspondence of Charles Darwin. Vol. 7, 1858–1859*. Cambridge: Cambridge University Press, 1991.

Burkhardt, Frederick, Sydney Smith, David Kohn, and William Montgomery, eds. *A Calendar of the Correspondence of Charles Darwin, 1821–1882*. Garland Reference Library of the Humanities, 369. 1985. New York: Garland Publishing, 1993.

Carlyle, Thomas. *On Heroes, Hero-Worship, and the Heroic in History*. With notes and introduction by Michael K. Goldberg. Berkeley and Los Angeles: University of California Press, 1993.

Carpenter, J. "British Preparations for the Approaching Transit of Venus." *Nature* (January 4, 1872): 177–179.

Catalogue of the Special Loan Collection of Scientific Apparatus at the South Kensington Museum. 3rd ed. London: 1877.

Chance, James Frederick. *A History of the Firm of Chance Brothers and Co., Glass and Alkali Manufacturers*. London: Spottiswoode, Ballantyne, 1919.

Chapman, Allan. "Jeremiah Horrocks, the Transit of Venus, and the 'New Astronomy' in Early Seventeenth-Century England." *Quarterly Journal of the Royal Astronomical Society* 31:3 (September 1990): 333–357.

Chauvin, Michael E. "Lunars and Automatons: Navigational Practices during the Voyages of Captain Cook." Unpublished manuscript. Cambridge, England: 1987.

———. "Darwin's Delay: Minds and Materialism." Unpublished manuscript. Cambridge, England: 1987.

———. "Useful and Conceptual Astronomy in Ancient Hawaii." In *Astronomy Across Cultures: The History of Non-Western Astronomy*, Helaine Selin, ed., 91–125. Dordrecht: Kluwer Academic Publishers, 2000.

Chinen, Jon J. *The Great Mahele: Hawaii's Land Division of 1848*. Honolulu: University of Hawai'i Press, 1958.

Cleghorn, Archibald. "Diaries" (1874–1877). MFL 46, Reel 2, Hawai'i State Archives.

Clerke, Agnes M. *A Popular History of Astronomy during the Nineteenth Century*. 4th ed. London: Adam and Charles Black, 1902.

Cook, James, and Charles Green. "Observations Made, by Appointment of the Royal Society, at King George's Island in the South Sea; by Mr. Charles Green, Formerly Assistant at the Royal Observatory at Greenwich, and Lieut. James Cook, of His Majesty's Ship the Endeavour." *Philosophical Transactions* 61 (1771): 397–421.

Cooke [*sic*], James, James King, and William Bayly. *The Original Astronomical Observations Made in the Course of a Voyage to the Northern Pacific Ocean, for the Discovery of a North East or North West Passage: Wherein the North West Coast of America and North East Coast of Asia were Explored. In His Majesty's Ships the Resolution and Discovery, in the years 1776, 1777, 1778, 1779, and 1780.* London, 1782.

Crowe, Michael J. *The Extraterrestrial Life Debate, 1750–1900.* Cambridge: Cambridge University Press, 1986.

Darwin, Charles. *The Descent of Man.* Great Books of the Western World, vol. 49. Chicago: Encyclopedia Britannica, 1952.

Darwin, Francis, ed. *The Autobiography of Charles Darwin and Selected Letters.* New York: Dover, 1958.

Darwin, Leonard. *The Need for Eugenic Reform.* London: John Murray, 1926.

Davis, Lynn. *Na Pa'i Ki'i: The Photographers in the Hawaiian Islands, 1845–1900.* Honolulu: Bishop Museum Press, 1980.

Daws, Gavan. *Shoal of Time: A History of the Hawaiian Islands.* Honolulu: University Press of Hawai'i, 1968.

Day, A. Grove. *History Makers of Hawaii.* Honolulu: Mutual Publishing, 1984.

Dening, Greg. *The Death of William Gooch.* Honolulu: University of Hawai'i Press, 1995.

Dick, Steven J. *Sky and Ocean Joined: The U.S. Naval Observatory, 1830–2000.* Cambridge: Cambridge University Press, 2003.

Drake, Stillman. *Discoveries and Opinions of Galileo.* Garden City, NY: Doubleday Anchor Books, 1957.

Dreyer, J. L. E., and H. H. Turner, eds. *History of the Royal Astronomical Society, 1820–1920.* London: Royal Astronomical Society, 1923.

Dunn, Samuel. "Some Observations of the Planet Venus, on the Disk of the Sun, June 6th, 1761; with a Preceding Account of the Method Taken for Verifying the Time of That Phaenomenon; and Certain Reasons for an Atmosphere about Venus." *Philosophical Transactions* 52:1 (1761): 184–195.

Dye, Tom. "Population Trends in Hawaii Before 1778." *The Hawaiian Journal of History* 28 (1994): 1–20.

Elliot, Clark A. *Biographical Dictionary of American Science: The Seventeenth through the Nineteenth Centuries.* Westport, CT: Greenwood Press, 1979.

Fernie, Donald. *The Whisper and the Vision: The Voyages of the Astronomers.* Toronto: Clarke, Irwin, 1976.

Fleuriais, M. G. "Sur la longitude d'Honolulu (île Oahu, archipel des Sandwich) déduite des observations méridiennes de la Lune faites par M. G. Fleuriais, Lieutenant de vaisseau." In *Connaissance des Temps ou des Mouvements Célestes, a L'usage des Astronomes et des Navigateurs, pour l'an 1872,* 46–65. Paris: Bureau des Longitudes, 1871.

Forbes, Eric G. "The Greenwich Observatory: Origins and Early Development, 1675–1835." *Nature* 255 (June 19, 1975): 587–592.

———. *Greenwich Observatory.* Vol. 1. London: Taylor and Francis, 1975.

Forbes, George. *History of Astronomy.* London: Watts, 1909.

———. *David Gill: Man and Astronomer.* London: John Murray, 1916.

———. "The Transit of Venus in 1874." PPSG (1872–1873): 373–394.

———. "The Coming Transit of Venus." Parts 1–7. *Nature* (April 9 to June 4, 1874).

———. "Dynamo-Electric Machinery." *Journal of the Franklin Institute* 118:6 (December 1884): 401–426.

Franklin, Benjamin. *The Autobiography and Other Writings.* Kenneth Silverman, ed. New York: Penguin Books, 1986.

Fraser, Thomas E. "Diary." In the Mary Lea Shane Archives of the Lick Observatory, University Library, University of California at Santa Cruz.

Freeman, R. B. *Darwin Pedigrees.* London: Printed for the Author, 1984.

Garber, Janet. "Darwin's Correspondents in the Pacific." In *Darwin's Laboratory,* Roy MacLeod and Philip F. Rehbock, eds., 169–211. Honolulu: University of Hawai'i Press, 1994.

Gay, Jas. W. "Surveys in Honolulu." At the Honolulu offices of the Survey Division of the Department of Accounting and General Services, State of Hawai'i. Undated manuscript.

Gillispie, Charles Coulston, ed. *Dictionary of Scientific Biography.* New York: Charles Scribner's Sons, 1972, 1973.

Gould, R. T. *Captain Cook.* London: Gerald Duckworth, 1978.

Gunther, R. T. *Early Science in Oxford.* Vol. 2. London: Dawsons, 1967. First published in 1923.

———. *Early Science in Cambridge.* London: Dawsons, 1969. First printed in Oxford, 1937.

Halley, Edmond. "De Visibili Conjunctione Inferiorum Planetarum cum Sole Dissertatio Astronomica." *Philosophical Transactions* 17:193 (1691): 511–522.

———. "Methodus Singularis qua Solis Parallaxis sive Distantia a Terra, ope Veneris intra Solem conspicienda, tuto determinari poterit." *Philosophical Transactions* 29:348 (1716): 454–464.

Hansen, Peter Andreas. "On the Construction of New Lunar Tables, and on Some Points in the Lunar Theory Depending on the Conformation of the Moon with Respect to Its Centre of Gravity." MNRAS 15:1 (November 10, 1854).

Harrison, H. M. *Voyager in Time and Space: The Life of John Couch Adams, Cambridge Astronomer.* Sussex: Book Guild, 1994.

Heath, Thomas L. *Greek Astronomy.* New York: Dover, 1991. Originally published in 1932 by Dent, London.

————. *Aristarchus of Samos: The Ancient Copernicus.* New York: Dover, 1981. Originally published in 1913 by the Clarendon Press, Oxford.

Hentschel, Klaus. "Drawing, Engraving, Photographing, Plotting, Printing: Historical Studies of Visual Representations, Esp. in Astronomy." In *The Role of Visual Representations in Astronomy: History and Research Practice,* Klaus Hentschel and Axel D. Wittman, eds., 11–43. Thun und Frankfurt am Main: Verlag Harri Deutsch, 2000.

Hind, J. R. "Particulars of the Transit of Venus over the Sun's Disc at the Stations Selected for Observation by Great Britain, France, the North German Confederation, and Russia." Appendix to the *Nautical Almanac and Astronomical Ephemeris for the Year 1874.* London: 1870.

Hoffleit, Dorrit. *Astronomy at Yale, 1701–1968.* New Haven: Connecticut Academy of Arts and Sciences, 1992.

Hornsby, Thomas. "A Discourse on the Parallax of the Sun." *Philosophical Transactions* 53 (1763): 467–495.

Howse, Derek. *Greenwich Time and the Discovery of the Longitude.* Oxford: Oxford University Press, 1980.

————. *Nevil Maskelyne: The Seaman's Astronomer.* Cambridge: Cambridge University Press, 1989.

————. *Greenwich Observatory.* Vol. 3. London: Taylor and Francis, 1975.

Hoyle, Fred. *Astronomy.* New York: Crescent Books, 1962.

Hughes, David W. "Six Stages in the History of the Astronomical Unit." *Journal of Astronomical History and Heritage* 4:1 (2001): 15–28.

International Conference Held at Washington for the Purpose of Fixing a Prime Meridian and a Universal Day, October, 1884: Protocols of the Proceedings. Washington: Gibson Bros., 1884.

Janiczek, P. M. "Remarks on the Transit of Venus Expedition of 1874." In *Sky with Ocean Joined,* Steven J. Dick and LeRoy E. Doggett, eds., 53–72. Washington: U.S. Naval Observatory, 1983.

Johns, Adrian. *The Nature of the Book: Print and Knowledge in the Making.* Chicago: University of Chicago Press, 1998.

Johnson, Francis R. "Gresham College: Precursor of the Royal Society." *Journal of the History of Ideas* 1:4 (October 1940): 413–438.

Johnson, Rubellite Kawena, and John Kaipo Mahelona. *Na Inoa Hoku: A Catalogue of Hawaiian and Pacific Star Names.* Honolulu: Topgallant Publishing, 1975.

Judd, Gerrit P. *Hawaii: An Informal History.* New York: Collier Books, 1961.

Kent, Harold Winfield. *Charles Reed Bishop, Man of Hawaii.* Palo Alto, CA: Pacific Books, 1965.

Keynes, Margaret. *Leonard Darwin, 1850–1943.* Cambridge: Privately published at the University Press, 1943.

King, Henry C. *The History of the Telescope*. London: Charles Griffin, 1955.

"King Kalakaua's Tour Round the World." Honolulu: P. C. Advertiser, October 1881.

Koestler, Arthur. *The Sleepwalkers: A History of Man's Changing Vision of the Universe*. New York: Grosset and Dunlap, 1963.

Krisciunas, Kevin. *Astronomical Centers of the World*. Cambridge: Cambridge University Press, 1988.

Kyselka, Will. "On the Rising of the Pleiades." *Hawaiian Journal of History* 27 (1993): 173–183.

Lankford, John. "Photography and the Nineteenth-Century Transits of Venus." *Technology and Culture* 28:3 (July 1987): 648–657.

Leader, Damian Riehl. *A History of the University of Cambridge*. Vol. 1. Cambridge: Cambridge University Press, 1988.

Leedham-Green, Elisabeth. *A Concise History of the University of Cambridge*. Cambridge: Cambridge University Press, 1996.

Lili'uokalani. "Diaries" (1887). Transcribed by Carol Kawananakoa. M 93, folder 117, Hawai'i State Archives.

———. *Hawaii's Story by Hawaii's Queen*. Rutland, VT: Charles E. Tuttle, 1964. First published by Lothrop, Lee and Shepard, Boston, 1898.

Lockyer, T. Mary, and Winifred L. Lockyer. *Life and Work of Sir Norman Lockyer*. London: Macmillan, 1928.

Lownes, Albert E. "The 1769 Transit of Venus and its Relation to Early American Astronomy." *Sky & Telescope* (April 1943): 3–5.

Lyman, Chester S. "The Hawaiian Journals of Chester Smith Lyman, 15 May 1846 to 3 July 1847." HMCS, Honolulu.

———. "On Venus as a Luminous Ring." *The American Journal of Science* 9:49 (1875, 3rd series): 47–48.

———. *Around the Horn to the Sandwich Islands and California, 1845–1850*. Frederick J. Teggart, ed. New Haven, CT: Yale University Press, 1924.

Macdonald, Gordon A., Agatin T. Abbott, and Frank L. Peterson. *Volcanoes in the Sea: The Geology of Hawaii*. 2nd ed. Honolulu: University of Hawai'i Press, 1983.

Maor, Eli. *June 8, 2004: Venus in Transit*. Princeton, NJ: Princeton University Press, 2000.

Maskelyne, Nevil. "Instructions Relative to the Observation of the Ensuing Transit of the Planet Venus over the Sun's Disk, on the 3d of June 1769." In *The Nautical Almanac and Astronomical Ephemeris for the Year 1769*. London: 1768.

Mason, Stephen F. *A History of the Sciences*. New York: Collier, 1962.

McCabe, James O. *The San Juan Water Boundary Question*. Toronto: University of Toronto Press, 1964.

McConnell, Anita. *Instrument Makers to the World: A History of Cooke, Troughton and Simms.* York: William Sessions, 1992.

Meadows, A. J. *Greenwich Observatory.* Vol. 2. London: Taylor and Francis, 1975.

———. "Airy and After." *Nature* 255 (June 19, 1975): 592–595.

Medcalf, Gordon. *Hawaiian Royal Orders: Insignia, Classes, Regulations, and Members.* Honolulu: Oceania Coin, 1963.

Meeus, Jean. "The Transits of Venus, 3000 B.C. to A.D. 3000." *Journal of the British Astronomical Association* 68:3 (1958): 98–108.

Menton, Linda. "'Everything That is Lovely and of Good Report:' The Hawaiian Chiefs' Children's School, 1839–1850." Ph.D. dissertation, University of Hawai'i, 1982.

Menton, Linda K. and Eileen H. Tamura. *A History of Hawaii.* 2nd ed. Honolulu: University of Hawai'i Curriculum Research and Development Group, 1999.

Mitchell, Donald D. *Resource Units in Hawaiian Culture.* Honolulu: Kamehameha Schools Press, 1969; revised 1972.

Mookini, Esther T. "The Hawaiian Newspapers." Working Papers in Hawaiian Studies, vol. 1, no. 1, 1973.

Motteler, Lee S. "Hawai'i's First Chart? A Recent Rediscovery." Bernice P. Bishop Museum Occasional Papers 24 (17), August 1980.

Murdin, Lesley. *Under Newton's Shadow: Astronomical Practices in the Seventeenth Century.* Bristol: Adam Hilger, 1985.

Murray, Keith A. *The Pig War.* Tacoma: Washington State Historical Society, 1968.

Newcomb, Simon. *Popular Astronomy.* London: Macmillan, 1878.

———. *Side-Lights on Astronomy.* New York: Harper and Brothers, 1906.

———. ed. *Observations of the Transit of Venus, December 8–9, 1874, Made and Reduced under the Direction of the Commission Created by Congress.* Part 1. Washington, D.C.: Government Printing Office, 1880.

———. *Observations of the Transit of Venus, December 8–9, 1874.* Part 2. Washington, D.C., 1881.

Newton, Isaac. *Mathematical Principles of Natural Philosophy.* Translated by Andrew Motte, revised by Florian Cajori. Great Books of the Western World, vol. 34. Chicago: Encyclopedia Britannica, 1952. Copyright 1934 by the regents of the University of California and reprinted by arrangement with the University of California Press.

Norman, Daniel. "The Development of Astronomical Photography." *Osiris* 5 (1938): 560–594.

Osterbrock, Donald E., John R. Gustafson, and W. J. Shiloh Unruh. *Eye on the Sky: Lick Observatory's First Century.* Berkeley and Los Angeles: University of California Press, 1988.

Ovason, David. *The Secret Architecture of Our Nation's Capital.* New York: Harper Collins, 2000.

Perry, S. J. "The Methods Employed and the Results Obtained in the Late Transit of Venus Expedition." In *South Kensington Museum: Free Evening Lectures, Delivered in Connection with the Special Loan Collection of Scientific Apparatus, 1876,* 39–66. London: Chapman and Hall.

Plews, John H. R. "Charles Darwin and Hawaiian Sex Ratios, or, Genius is a Capacity for Making Compensating Errors." *The Hawaiian Journal of History* 14 (1980): 26–49.

Price, A. Grenfell, ed. *The Explorations of Captain James Cook in the Pacific as Told by Selections of His Own Journals, 1768–1779.* New York: Dover, 1971.

Proctor, Richard A. *Transits of Venus: A Popular Account of Past and Coming Transits from the First Observed by Horrocks A.D. 1639 to the Transit of A.D. 2012.* London: Longmans, Green, and Co., 1874; 2nd ed., 1875; 3rd ed., 1878; 4th ed., 1882.

———. *Studies of Venus Transits.* London: Longmans, Green, and Co., 1882.

Prodger, Phillip. "Photography and *The Expression of the Emotions.*" In Charles Darwin, *The Expression of the Emotions in Man and Animals,* 399–410. 3rd ed., introduction by Paul Ekman. Oxford: Oxford University Press, 1998.

Pukui, Mary Kawena, Samuel H. Elbert, and Esther T. Mookini. *Place Names of Hawaii.* 2nd ed. Honolulu: University of Hawai'i Press, 1974.

Raverat, Gwen. *Period Piece: A Cambridge Childhood.* London: Faber and Faber, 1952.

Rehbock, Philip F. "The History of Photographic Invention." *Humanities News* 2:3 (summer 1981): 3ff.

Report of the Electrical Conference at Philadelphia in September, 1884. Washington, D.C.: Government Printing Office, 1886.

Restarick, Henry Bond. *Hawaii 1778–1920 from the Viewpoint of a Bishop.* Honolulu: Paradise of the Pacific, 1924.

Ronan, Colin A. *Their Majesties' Astronomers: A Survey of Astronomy in Britain between the two Elizabeths.* London: Bodley Head, 1967.

———. *Astronomers Royal.* Garden City, NY: Doubleday, 1969.

Rothermel, Holly. "Images of the Sun: Warren De la Rue, George Biddell Airy and Celestial Photography." *British Journal for the History of Science* 26 (1993): 137–169.

Russell, John L. "English Astronomy before 1675." *Nature* 255 (June 19, 1975): 583–587.

Sagan, Carl. *Pale Blue Dot.* New York: Random House, 1994.

Sarton, George. "Vindication of Father Hell." *Isis* 35:100 (Spring 1944): 97–105.

Satterthwaite, Gilbert E. "Airy's Transit Circle." *Journal of Astronomical History and Heritage* 4:8 (2001): 115–141.

Schaefer, Bradley E. "The Transit of Venus and the Notorious Black Drop Effect." *Journal for the History of Astronomy* 32 (2001): 325–336.

Sellers, David. *The Transit of Venus.* Leeds: Maga Velda Press, 2001.

Short, James. "The Observations of the Internal Contact of Venus with the Sun's Limb in the Late Transit, Made in different Places of Europe, Compared with the Time of the Same Contact Observed at the Cape of Good Hope, and the Parallax of the Sun from Thence Determined." *Philosophical Transactions* 52:2 (1762): 611–628.

Sprat, Thomas. *The History of the Royal Society of London, for the Improving of Natural Knowledge.* Edited by Jackson I. Cope and Harold Whitmore Jones. St. Louis: Washington University Press, 1958. Originally published in London, 1667.

Stone, E. J. "A Rediscussion of the Observations of the Transit of Venus, 1769." MNRAS 28:9, Supplementary Notice (1868?): 255–266.

————. "On the Telescopic Observations of the Transit of Venus 1874, Made in the Expedition of the British Government, and on the Conclusions to be Deduced from Those Observations." MNRAS 38:5 (March 1878): 279–295.

Tanner, J. R., ed. *The Historical Register of the University of Cambridge . . . to the Year 1910.* Cambridge: Cambridge University Press, 1917.

Taylor, E. G. R. *The Haven-Finding Art: A History of Navigation from Odysseus to Captain Cook.* London: Hollis and Carter, 1958.

Tiles, Mary, and Jim Tiles. *An Introduction to Historical Epistemology.* Cambridge (USA) and Oxford (UK): Blackwell Publishers, 1993.

Todd, D. P. "The Solar Parallax as Derived from the American Photographs of the Transit of Venus, 1874, December 8–9." *American Journal of Science* 21:126 (3rd series, 1881): 491–493.

Tupman, G. L. "Note on the Mean Solar Parallax as Derived from the Observations of the Recent Transit of Venus." MNRAS 38:5 (March 1878): 334.

————. "On the Mean Solar Parallax as Derived from the Observations of the Transit of Venus, 1874." MNRAS 38:8 (June 1878): 429–457.

————. "On the Photographs of the Transit of Venus." MNRAS 38:9, Supplementary Notice (1878): 508–513.

Van Helden, Albert. *Measuring the Universe: Cosmic Dimensions from Aristarchus to Halley.* Chicago: University of Chicago Press, 1985.

Vaucouleurs, G. de. *The Astronomical Unit of Distance: Solar Parallax and Related Constants.* Memorandum RM-2944-NASA, December 1961, the RAND Corporation.

Vouri, Michael. *The Pig War: Standoff at Griffin Bay.* Friday Harbor, WA: Griffin Bay Bookstore, 1999.

Warner, Deborah Jean. *Alvan Clark & Sons: Artists in Optics.* Washington: Smithsonian Institution Press, 1968.

Warren, Mashuri L. *Introductory Physics.* San Francisco: W. H. Freeman, 1979.

Weld, Charles Richard. *A History of the Royal Society*. Vol. 2. London: John W. Parker, 1848.

Whatton, Arundell Blount. *Memoir of the Life and Labors of the Rev. Jeremiah Horrox, Curate of Hoole, near Preston; to which is Appended a Translation of his Celebrated Discourse upon the Transit of Venus across the Sun*. London, 1859.

Wilkins, G. A. "The System of Astronomical Constants—Part 1." *Quarterly Journal of the Royal Astronomical Society* 5:1 (March 1964): 23–31.

Wilson, James Grant, and John Fiske, eds. *Appletons' Cyclopedia of American Biography*. Vol. 5. New York: D. Appleton, 1888.

Winkler, Mary G., and Albert Van Helden. "Representing the Heavens: Galileo and Visual Astronomy." *Isis* 83:2 (June 1992): 195–217.

———. "Johannes Hevelius and the Visual Language of Astronomy." In *Renaissance and Revolution: Humanists, Scholars, Craftsmen, and Natural Philosophers in Early Modern Europe*, ed. by J. V. Field and Frank A. J. L. James, 97–116. Cambridge: Cambridge University Press, 1994.

Woolf, Harry. *The Transits of Venus: A Study of Eighteenth-Century Science*. Princeton, NJ: Princeton University Press, 1959.

Wright, Helen. *James Lick's Monument*. Cambridge: Cambridge University Press, 1987.